THROUGH SECRET CHANNELS

Mahmoud Abbas
(Abu Mazen)

GARNET PUBLISHING

Paperback ISBN 1 85964 047 8
Hardback ISBN 1 85964 063 X

First English edition

British Library Cataloguing-in-Publication Data
A catalogue record for this book is available from the British Library

Cover design: Dave Rose & Mark Slader
Printed in Lebanon

Typeset in Baskerville MT 11/12 point

Published by Garnet Publishing Ltd
8 Southern Court, South Street
Reading, RG1 4QS, UK

CONTENTS

1

Flying to Washington – Reminiscences

On Sunday, 12 September 1993, our delegation left Tunis on board the private jet of His Majesty King Hassan II of Morocco which he had put at the disposal of the Palestinian leadership. I kept to myself for most of the ten-and-a-half-hour flight, reviewing what we had accomplished over thirty years of struggle and nearly half a century of estrangement and refuge-in-exile. Was this the trip back home? Or was it the journey towards signing the surrender of a major part of our homeland? Why was I heading for a place where I would be signing an agreement which might not offer me a home or a place of residence? Would what we were about to do open the gates of a future for us or shut them? Had we forfeited the people's rights or preserved them?

It was a heavy burden and a great responsibility. The risks could well outweigh the benefits. How would our people react at home and in the diaspora? Who would be in favour and who would oppose? And what would history say about us? Can the ten hours of flying time from Tunis to Washington summarize the journey of homelessness that has lasted decades? Can we forget those whose blood has nourished the soil of the homeland? Can we, at the gates of an historic accomplishment, forget the generations of martyrs who have made this achievement possible? The recent history of Palestine was like a train that has travelled through all weathers and across all terrains, its passengers boarding and alighting, but pressing ahead to its destination. It was like a ship tossing on a dark and raging sea, hoping to come at last to a safe harbour.

There have been four revolutions and five wars. There has been no respite from the struggle, no relief, no rest for the fighters. Our grand-fathers did not have a tranquil and stable life, nor have their grand-children been allowed a human existence. They have fought for a hope, which at the beginning was like a mirage. But they did not despair, and they did not quit. One generation passed the flag to the next and put their trust in them. They did not surrender the flag, nor did they betray the trust.

While we pay homage to the Mufti of Palestine, to Ahmad Hilmi

Abdel-Baqi, Ahmad al-Shuqairi and Yahya Hammouda, as symbols of our people, we do not and will not forget the martyrs and leaders of the revolutions, beginning with Izz-eddin al-Qassam, Sheikh Farhan al-Saadi, Sheikh Hassan Salama, Abdel-Qader al-Husseini and Abdel-Raheem Mahmoud. To the martyrs of our contemporary revolution we owe much, for it was their sacrifice that paved the way, unlocked the doors and revived hopes. Ahmad al-Musa was the first martyr, followed by Abdel-Fattah al-Hammud, Abu Sabri, Abu Ali Iyad, Kamal Udwan, Muhammad al-Najjar, Kamal Nasser, Ghassan Kanafani, Saad Sayel and Majed Abu Sharar, and tens of thousands of troops, the officers and fighting men, the women, the children and the elderly. Perhaps their souls will find rest now that some of the hope is becoming a reality. Now too, some of the dreams are starting to come true, and the people feel a sense of belonging and carry an identity, so that the young Palestinian can say to his father, 'I was without an identity; your blood has granted it to me.'

There were many questions on my mind during the flight to Washington. I examined the faces around me, and saw others in my mind's eye, but I always came back to myself, for while everyone else, present or absent, could declare themselves innocent, it was I who would stand before the world to sign an agreement with the Israelis and take the responsibility.

In the end I concluded two things: first that I was engaged in an historic undertaking and was presenting our people with a great achievement, and second, that reckless actions and a backward-looking mentality on either side would wreck this achievement. Thus, I was prey to two contradictory feelings: on the one hand there was a sense of achievement, on the other there was fear about its realization in the future.

On arrival at Andrews Air Force Base in Washington DC, that special airport where state guests and officials arriving in the United States land, we were met by Edward Djerejian, US Assistant Secretary of State for Near East and South Asian Affairs, the protocol chief at the State Department, and by various Arab ambassadors. A number of well-known Palestinian figures were also there. We were whisked off to the hotel where we were caught up in a big reception for American, Arab and Palestinian personalities. For the first time we met former Presidents Jimmy Carter and George Bush and other individuals who had arrived to greet the Palestinian delegation. For me, Carter was a particularly sympathetic character, whose obvious sincerity made those meeting him like him from the first moment. As for Bush, who had dealt with some momentous issues in American history, he appeared to be a modest and decent man.

The Palestine Liberation Organization and its leadership had moved very swiftly from being a terrorist organization (according to the American Administration) to one worthy of the White House's interest. I was reminded of the moment at which the United States had begun a dialogue with the PLO after the Palestine National Council (PNC) had decided to set in motion the peace drive, and the PLO Chairman's address to the UN General Assembly specially convened in Geneva in December 1988. That dialogue did not make much progress, and being confined to closed circles, eventually ceased. The more important dialogue was in fact taking place outside the official meetings, behind closed doors in Tunis where the American Ambassador to Tunisia, Robert Pelletreau, his assistant Edmund Hull and I discussed in depth the substantive issues of the Arab–Israeli conflict. At the centre of these discussions was the target we had set for ourselves: the beginning of a Palestinian–Israeli dialogue that would be the key to peace. The American Ambassador was convinced that only the Labour party was capable of initiating such dialogue, and he was anxious about the obstinacy of Likud and its assumption of power in Israel.

I reviewed those days as I stood on a podium at the White House, to the left of the Secretary of State, Warren Christopher. President Bill Clinton stood one step away. The President congratulated us, as did his wife, Vice-President Al Gore and his wife, then former Presidents Jimmy Carter and George Bush, some senior State Department officials and the guest of honour, the Norwegian Foreign Minister, Johan Joergen Holst, the man who had overseen the secret Oslo negotiations so superbly. We stood under the blazing sun for an hour and a half. The heat of the moment quite outweighed the heat of the sun. As I stood on the White House lawn in the bright light, I felt that our people too had assumed their place in the sun, a people whose right of existence had been ignored. Thousands of eyes, hundreds of cameras and millions of people were anxiously watching these scenes and this small podium on which a new page in the history of the region and maybe of the world was being made.

After finishing my speech, and in the absence of pre-planned protocol arrangements, I had to shake President Clinton's hand, but I also went and shook hands with Yitzhak Rabin, Andrei Kozyrev, the Russian Foreign Minister, and Shimon Peres. This gesture was welcomed by the audience who applauded vigorously, though handshaking is contrary to protocol. People told me afterwards about many things that I did not notice myself then; they said, for example, that President Clinton had positioned my chair as I sat down to sign. Perhaps the emotion and the heat of the moment were to blame for my blankness.

A few days before, no Israeli official would have dared to come face to face with members of the PLO, and some months before that Israeli citizens had been banned from mentioning the PLO let alone having contact with its officials. Many of them who had met secretly with us had asked that we keep the meetings secret so that they would not be tried and imprisoned. We kept their secrets. The hub of our discussions had concerned one point: how do we achieve peace? We knew that the ones talking to us were not decision makers, but we hoped they would pass on our message to those who were. We knew also that the way to the heart of the Israeli people was long, since they did not understand us, did not want to understand us and were not permitted to understand us. However, we considered these contacts to be positive because they were taking place in the shadow of an ongoing war between us and the Israelis and in the face of an Israeli law which officially banned such meetings. From my perspective these meetings were another kind of offensive: fighting the proponents of war.

Israeli anxiety was always revealed in specific questions. We knew these were not just personal questions, but questions that the Israeli Government would also pose to know our real views on certain issues. Not only Israelis asked them, but also American personalities like Harold Sanders, William Quandt,[1] Owen Owen and Dan Abraham and others. The kind of questions were typically as follows:

- Did we really want an independent Palestinian state?
- Would such a state enter into a confederation with Jordan?
- Would it have relations with the Soviets, and to what extent?
- Would it have an army, and what kind of army?
- How did we perceive coexistence and cooperation with Israel if there was peace?
- What kind of borders would connect Palestine and Israel?
- What solution did we envisage for the problem of the refugees?
- How did we see the future of Jerusalem?

My responses to these questions were that we wanted an independent state like other peoples seeking national independence, but that we wanted confederation with Jordan and that we were prepared to give serious consideration to an application from Israel for membership in

---

[1] At a meeting with the Americans in Tunis on 15 February 1989. This meeting also included Herman Eilts, Thomas Freedman, Karen Dawisha and Helena Cobban from the Brookings Institute.

this confederation. As for the relationship with the Soviets, we were not communists and would not build a communist state, and it was not in our interest to serve as a communist base in the Middle East.

Whenever these Americans and Israelis expressed fears of a Palestinian state army, we would reply that the army was not an end in itself but a means of defence, and once there was security it would become redundant. Would the Americans be prepared to send an army to act as a buffer between us and the Israelis? Or would they accept United Nations forces for the task? Everyone who visited us asked us to recognize Resolutions 242 and 338, insisting that recognition of these resolutions would clear the road to peace and would definitely persuade the Israeli Government to enter into negotiations with the PLO. Ironically, the most contentious point in the Washington and Oslo negotiations related to the implementation of Resolutions 242 and 338. Until the last moment, Israeli delegations, especially in Oslo, would offer proposals and counter-proposals to avoid the word 'implementation' of the two resolutions.

What uniformly embarrassed both the Israelis and Americans was my statement expressing our desire for full coexistence and open borders to facilitate work, residence, exchange of goods and finance. When they rejected the idea, I would counter with a proposal for totally closed borders, which they would also reject. I would then request their proposal for a suitable formula for coexistence and indicate our readiness to accept it!

The most complex issue faced by Israeli moderates was that of the refugees. They refused to discuss the refugee issue or to refer it to international arbitration. Negotiations with the RATS party had stalled on the refugee issue because their negotiator, Didi Tsoker, adamantly refused to mention international arbitration for this problem at the end of many negotiation rounds, the last of which was held in Prague in former Czechoslovakia on 31 January 1989.

Everyone avoided discussing Jerusalem, regarded it as a complex problem and suggested postponing discussion of it. Many others consider it a 'red line' not to be crossed.

All these images were rushing through my mind on board the plane to Washington. It was as though I was trying to condense the long period of hardship and struggle into the brief hours before we were due to arrive in Washington to begin a new chapter in this long and still unfinished saga. I did not think that signing would end everything, but saw it rather as a beginning for many things particularly since the accord did not settle many issues and did not clarify many points that still required continuous hard work.

My memory sailed far back in time, to the days when I had devoted my time to following up developments in Israeli society and had been keen to meet any Israelis willing to meet me. I suffered much criticism from the people closest to me in Fatah. They were often sarcastic, asking, 'Can you change Israeli society through these simpletons you are meeting? What effect does this handful of people from the lowliest echelons of Israeli society have?'

In 1968 some of the Fatah leaders launched the slogan Democratic Palestinian State. The slogan kept its special lustre for a long time until it was killed off by the Israeli media. The Israelis handled it with an obvious lack of interest. However, in it I found rich material for potential implementation, and this would require real coexistence with an Israeli society we did not know. This was the starting point. We had to attain peace. But how?

I recalled that on 11 March 1983, following the sixteenth session of the Palestine National Council in which the Council had reiterated the PLO's position on contacting progressive and democratic Israeli factions, the martyr Abu Iyad, the prominent Fatah leader, visited Hungary where he discussed the PNC resolutions with state and party officials. He elaborated on the resolution regarding meetings with Jewish factions and was informed by the Hungarians that since the Peace Now delegation was in Hungary, they considered it a good opportunity to arrange a meeting between the two sides, provided Abu Iyad and the Israelis did not object. Abu Iyad was taken by surprise because he had never met Israelis before, and was quite unprepared for meetings of this type, which he had only talked about but had never had any desire to conduct. But he could not refuse, and the meeting took place. It lasted for four hours and was attended on the Israeli side by the famous Israeli journalist Hana Zimmer and a number of Labour Party members.

Whenever I review the proceedings of that meeting I remember all the stages of the Palestinian–Israeli conflict because that encounter summarized seventy years of strife. It began aggressively with both sides exchanging accusations and trading fiery, offensive remarks and ended with both parties totally convinced of the need for peace that would be in the interest of both peoples, and of their right to self-determination. They agreed to keep the meeting a secret, but Hana Zimmer published it in full in her newspaper *Haaretz*.

Later came the meeting held between 3 and 5 July 1989, when two delegations, one Palestinian and the other Isreali, headed to Toledo, the city that had been the model for Islamic–Jewish coexistence during the Andalusian era. In fact the Iraeli delegation did not consist entirely of

Israelis but included naturalized or expatriate Hasidic Jews living in countries such as France, Canada, the United States and Morocco. Thus we had the irony of forty-five individuals whose ancestors had coexisted five hundred years previously, confronting each other with anger, bitterness and hostility which had arisen relatively recently.

That meeting began with difficult negotiations over protocol, seating arrangements, the order of speeches and who would greet the other first. We were two sides who hailed from opposing camps who were embroiled in a raging and bloody war. But after two hours of tension, the lines became blurred and during the seventy remaining hours one could no longer distinguish one side from the other. The delegations shared their experiences, memories and troubles. The Jews liked to remind the Palestinians of their and their parents' memories of the Arab world. They did not shy away from pointing out similarities and differences. They used this opportunity to express individually and directly their support for the Palestinian people's right to self-determination and an independent state. The seventy hours came to an end with everybody wanting more time.

Israeli society has progressed. These contacts were not the only reason behind this progress. There were many other reasons, particularly the continued struggle of the Palestinian people and the intifada, the uprising, of the 'children of the stones'. But through these contacts the message of this struggle was delivered to the Israelis: Your obstinacy is to no avail, we must sit round the table. Here is our voice calling out to you; listen to the voice of reason, look to the future of your children.

Years later, that handful of people had grown to encompass decision makers, members of the Knesset and people of all leanings and parties, especially from the Labour Party which had become a partner in the administration of the State. On 22 September 1991 the French news agency received a statement, signed by 24 Knesset members from the Labour, RATS,[1] Mapam and Shinui[2] parties, calling on the PNC members to soften their position and agree to the holding of a peace conference. It reminded the Palestinian leadership that only in the context of peace with Israel could the Palestinian national problems be solved and that only in that context could Israel achieve security *vis-à-vis* the Arab peoples. Among the signatories were Ezer Weizmann (the current President, 1995), ministers Haim Ramon, Yossi Sarid, Amnon

[1] Movement for Peace and Citizens' Rights.
[2] Movement for Change.

Rubinstein and Shulamit Aloni and the Deputy Foreign Minister Yossi Beilin. The latter was one of those who was responsible for initiating the Oslo negotiations and following them up until the end.

The press and news agencies have often reported me as having met Ezer Weizmann, who had on more than one occasion declared his willingness to meet a PLO official. He was unable to do so because of intense pressure exerted by the Labour leadership; indeed he almost lost his portfolio when Shamir, the then Prime Minister, waged a campaign against him after he had met the PLO representative, Nabil Ramlawi, in Geneva. However, indirect contacts with him were made. On one occasion he had expressed his desire to visit the Soviet Union, but the USSR was hesitant to invite him because there were no diplomatic relations between the two countries and was afraid of Arab criticism. When I visited the Soviet Foreign Ministry I brought this subject up. The Soviets were amazed when I told them I welcomed such an invitation, but I explained that Weizmann was a party dove and that indeed such a meeting would be beneficial. It so happened that after the meeting had taken place, the Soviets recognized the State of Palestine and upgraded the PLO office in Moscow to an embassy. Strangely, there were people in Israel who accused Weizmann of having requested the Soviets to upgrade the PLO's representational status.

And thus we are back to the present. Hours after the signing in Washington DC, I met Shimon Peres at his quarters. I had not requested such a meeting, but our delegation had telephoned, wanting to discuss amending the names of the two signatories to the agreement, and his secretary thought I wanted to meet Peres. I had no objection to a meeting with Peres now that the accord had been concluded. Indeed I had had no qualms about meeting him previously, especially since the media had reported that we had met more than once, and he had never tried to deny any of these reports.

But today, after the signing, we were meeting in public in front of the media for forty minutes. His delegation which had run the Oslo negotiations and our delegation, as well as Yasser Abd Rabbo, the chief Palestinian interlocutor with the US, were in attendance. Observing that the two teams were having a warm exchange, a sign of a friendly relationship and shared memories, Peres turned to me and said: 'It seems that we two are the only strangers in this session.' Peres tried to be objective and practical when speaking about the future. He expressed a desire for the economic development of the occupied territories, and told me that he had asked the Europeans to prepare an economic development programme for the territories during his previous European tour. I tried to study this personality whom I knew only through the press, messengers, the Oslo negotiations and dozens of special reports to which I had access. I was comparing my image of him with the real man in front of me.

The real picture was no different from the one that I had sketched in my imagination. I noticed that he was a diplomat with a clear vision of the future and a desire for peace. From a passing remark he made I deduced he was at odds with Yitzhak Rabin on many issues; when a member of our delegation expressed dissatisfaction with Rabin's speech during the ceremony, Peres made a gesture that seemed to say: 'Don't pay too much attention.' He followed this up by saying, 'You know he is here and four of his soldiers have been killed today, so we hope you can appreciate the circumstances.' He added, 'We can argue over a word for a year, but if we agree to it, rest assured that we will be wholly committed to it.'

Peres's deputy, Yossi Beilin, took part in the meeting. We talked in a relaxed manner, dropping all reserve and ignoring protocol. The other thing that drew my attention was that he looked like a young man in his twenties although he was really in his forties. He has a presence in the Labour Party and was one of a few who had maintained a good relationship with Peres and did not side with Rabin as many others did. I tried quickly to sum up Joel Singer, who had been an extreme hawk in Oslo. His hawkishness, it seemed to me, was like the hawkishness of Abu Ala, our chief negotiator in Oslo.[1] He told me with a laugh, 'Please lend us Abu Ala if we enter into difficult negotiations with any party.'

In Washington DC, it was as though there had been an instant transformation. Everything had moved from one extreme to the other, with various American figures coming in droves to meet us, and with the media hailing the PLO's constructive attitude and its fine efforts to achieve peace. Jews and Arabs, enemies before that day, 13 September 1993, suddenly were organizing joint receptions, receiving congratulations and good wishes, poised to erase decades of enmity.

Between the signing of the Declaration of Principles and our departure, everywhere we went we were met with welcoming smiles and requests for autographs until we felt like film stars. But as we were leaving Washington DC, the joy of the occasion began to fade and to be replaced by the anxieties about the future.

---

[1] Ahmad Qurei, or Abu Ala as he is commonly known, was at the time of the Oslo talks the Director-General of the Economics Department of the PLO. He is now Minister of the Economy of the Palestinian Authority.

2

The Beginnings

After prolonged attempts, both in the diaspora and in the Palestinian homeland, the Palestine Liberation Organization was set up in 1964. The PLO was effectively the offspring of the Arab regimes. It did not meet the aspirations of the masses and although the masses knew that anything emanating from these regimes would simply inherit all their qualities and weaknesses, they nevertheless embraced it as the banner they had lacked since the catastrophe, the standard under which they could muster, and a symbolic homeland that replaced the reality of the lost homeland.

In the same year the Fatah movement completed preparations for the launching of a military revolution in the occupied land. These two bodies, Fatah and the PLO, complemented one another in the context of the Palestinian struggle. While the PLO undertook an official and public role in an attempt to consolidate the position of the Palestinian people on the international political stage, the Fatah movement was the popular expression of this people's desire to liberate the homeland and to return to it.

Four years later, it became obvious that Fatah, the Revolution, was more capable of expressing the people's wishes and speaking on their behalf, since the PLO remained constricted in its dealings by the attitudes of the Arab regimes. The Revolution could engage more freely in various kinds of military and non-military struggle. Any revolution that has a measure of freedom in military action can also launch political initiatives that seem necessary for the survival of its struggle. Any initiative that our Revolution took, stemmed from its experiences on the ground and the difficult realities it had to face. This was why we periodically reviewed what had passed and attempted to predict what would happen next.

Among certain Palestinian leaders an idea began to germinate, which proposed the establishment of a Democratic Palestinian State in which Jews, Christians and Muslims would be equal in rights and in duties.[1] This was the beginning of political initiatives launched by the Palestinian Revolution that called for political solutions to the Palestinian issue on the basis of realities: the prevailing international circumstances and the general Arab situation. This idea meant a tremendous concession on the part of the Palestinian people because it granted the Jews the right to live in Palestine and recognized the legality of their existence there. The idea emanated basically from Arab impotence and the inability of Palestinians to liberate their homeland single-handedly. It was, however, an honest and courageous view, which recognized the international climate, the limitations of the Arabs on the one hand and Israel's strength on the other.

In 1948 Israel occupied part of our land and displaced part of our people. Then in 1967 it occupied the remainder of this land and displaced another part of our people. All the Palestinian people had become either displaced or under occupation. Israel also occupied a part of Syria's Golan Heights and all of Egypt's Sinai. Thus all we knew of Israel were the manifestations of its power and omnipotence. Beyond that we were kept in the dark about the Israeli people. The slogan 'Know Thine Enemy' was reiterated everywhere, but was not acted upon. The Arab masses therefore lived in a state of ignorance, deliberately barred from knowing their enemy. At times we feared and dreaded him, sometimes to the point of terror, at other times we underestimated him to the point of apathy. It was considered reprehensible for a Palestinian or an Arab to be caught following the news of Israeli society or reading a book about Israel. To acquaint oneself with this society's secrets, its lifestyle, the way it thinks and behaves, was the only way of discovering its weaknesses and its strengths, but this was denied us.

The first principle of a successful military campaign requires the commander to reconnoitre the ground and understand the enemy before an attack is mounted. In political terms, governments send out envoys, spies and intelligence officers to foreign countries to observe at close quarters the nature of the people and the composition of the society in order to take the appropriate action. As for us in the Arab world, the simple act of seeking knowledge about one's opponent used to provoke accusations of disloyalty and doubts about one's patriotism. We, the ordinary Arab people, believed that our superiors – the leaders, civil servants, intelligence officers and diplomats – were fully equipped with knowledge and information, but to our surprise we discovered that these

[1] The first proponent of this idea was Dr Nabil Shaath who became a member of Fatah's Central Committee in the 1980s and later headed the Palestinian delegation to the Washington and Taba (Egypt) negotiations.

people were quite ignorant about the enemy they were confronting with their fingers on the trigger. And they fought four wars against it.

In early 1970, after I had assumed responsibility for mobilization and organization within the Fatah movement, I found nothing with which to indoctrinate our cadres apart from a few books about revolutionary experiments that had preceded ours, such as those of Vietnam, China, Algeria and Guevara's Cuba. As for the Zionist experiment from Herzl to the establishment of the Jewish State and beyond we knew little more than a few simple headings devoid of any detail. One day I read an item in a local newspaper reporting that Jews from Arab countries now made up more than half of Israel's population. The report aroused my curiosity. How did the Arab States supply Israel with half its population? What was the relationship between them and the occidental Jews in Israel? There were other questions too that I could not answer, and thus a programme of reading and research into the intricacies and hidden aspects of Israeli society became necessary. Between 1970 and 1977 I published two books about Jewish emigration from the Arab States and the West, and about Israel's relations with the United States and the proponents of peace in its society. I also raised two slogans during this period. The first demanded that Arab States should seek to repatriate Jews who had emigrated or had been evicted; Egypt, Iraq, Libya, Tunisia, Morocco and Yemen responded by issuing either a statement or a governmental decision permitting the return of Jews. The second slogan called for contacts with Israeli factions so as to initiate a dialogue for the attainment of peace. The first slogan was opposed by certain Palestinian politicians and intellectuals, while the second was viciously attacked in official and popular Palestinian and Arab quarters. Among those who were convinced by this idea and paid the price for their conviction with their lives were the martyrs Saeed Hammawi, the PLO representative in Britain, Izz-eddin al-Qalaq, the PLO representative in France, Naeem Khodr, the PLO representative in Belgium, and Issam Sartawi to whom I had delegated the task of contacting pro-peace Israeli factions.

At the thirteenth session of the Palestine National Council which was held between 12 and 22 March 1977, Issam Sartawi was bitterly attacked for having met Israelis. All the factions in the PNC without exception joined in, including a number of leaders and cadres in the Fatah movement of which Sartawi was a member. I discovered that none of them knew what they were talking about, that their knowledge of Israel was limited to the simple fact that it was the enemy against whom continuous war should be waged. So, I set out to work on this weakness within our ranks, to let my views on how to deal with enemies infiltrate and to suggest ways of attaining our goal. I did not scorn the gun, which was one of the means to our end, but seven years of reading and writing had enabled me to delve into issues we had not considered before; so at the PNC meeting I got up and spoke confidently to my colleagues for forty-five minutes, touching on all the ideas that I wanted them to hear in an impromptu but organized fashion. Through the expression in their eyes and the silence in the hall I realized that they were hearing such words for the first time.

In defending Sartawi, I was defending my own ideas which I had expressed everywhere. If accusations are to be levelled at anyone, they must be levelled at me, because Sartawi did not act on his own initiative but upon my instructions. I would also like to point out that the decision to launch these contacts with the Israeli's was not only my own decision but was reached with the knowledge and agreement of a number of Fatah leaders who had begun to like such ideas. They, however, were not yet able to defend the desirability of such contacts because they lacked the necessary information and knowledge. Nor indeed did they have any great wish to take action in this respect because from their viewpoint at that time, the subject had not matured to the point where it could be seriously followed up.

After forty-eight hours the PNC arrived at a positive decision. It emphasized the importance of establishing relations with democratic and progressive Jewish factions which were struggling within and outside Israel against the letter and spirit of Zionism. This decision was reaffirmed at the fifteenth session, 9 to 11 April 1981, the sixteenth, 14 to 22 February 1983, the eighteenth, 20 to 25 April 1987, the nineteenth, 12 to 15 November 1988, as well as the fifth Fatah movement conference, 3 August 1989.

Thus making contact with Israel became legitimate and protected by the decision of the PNC. However, most Palestinians refused to believe in such a course, partly because of the age-old taboo against Israelis. In many instances, even Arabs with Israeli nationality were subject to the same boycott. At an international youth festival held in one of the East European countries the famous poet, Mahmoud Darwish, whose poems were recited at every official and popular function, arrived from Israel. Faisal al-Hourani, a Palestinian member of the Syrian Baath party, was also present. When the Baath leadership learned that Hourani had greeted Darwish, it expelled him from the party because he had shaken an Israeli hand. This mentality continued to dominate the minds of many people despite of the PNC's decision, and statements of condemnation continued to be made whenever Palestinians met people belonging to factions in Israel that had been approved of by the PNC. As already mentioned, many paid with their lives for their efforts to achieve understanding between the PLO and those factions in Israel wanting peace.

Our efforts pointed in two directions. First, all pro-peace Israeli factions grouped under the banner of the Peace Now movement. These factions have many different ideas and vary in their understanding of the peace process, but they are united by the general concept of 'peace' without defining the exact meaning of the word. Second, Oriental Jews of Andalusian descent who had previously lived in Arab countries as well as in Turkey and Bulgaria. They differ from Ashkenazi Jews in custom, tradition and belief, and form two-thirds of Israel's population. The circumstances of their arrival in Israel was often shrouded in mystery, and they lived, and many of them still do, at the bottom of the social ladder. Their status in the new society was largely due to their background, but possibly also to faulty planning by earlier Israeli settlers who were mostly Ashkenazi. The Oriental Jews were more violent and cruel towards the Arabs, because they wanted to integrate themselves with the ruling elite; to prove themselves more Zionist than the Ashkenazis they tended towards extremism. Consequently, they sided with the Herut movement which led the Israeli opposition against Labour in 1977. When the Likud coalition of Herut and its allies assumed power in Israel, the Oriental Jews believed they had realized their dreams and goals which they thought the Labour Party had obstructed for thirty years.

After 1977 we held dozens of meetings and attended dozens of conferences which grouped Israelis of all leanings, whether from Peace Now or Oriental Jews, with whom we tried to build bridges of peace linking Palestinians and Israelis. We were not dissuaded from our line by statements branding them enemies of the Arabs and the Palestinians, even though we knew they supported the extreme right. Through our meetings with them we got the feeling that they were prepared, as far as their influence and energies would allow, to act as a go-between for Palestinians and Israelis, Arabs and Jews. But the disinformation of the media and the propaganda of the Israeli Right often nullified the benefits of meetings that did take place, especially after the Knesset's decision of 6 August 1986 banning contacts with the PLO under penalty of imprisonment.

It is impossible for the Israelis to live forever in the Middle East without meeting their neighbours, and for Israel to remain an alien State in the heart of the Arab world. I do not believe that it is in the interest of Israelis to live by the words of Moshe Arens, the former Likud defence minister, who was born in America and emigrated to Israel to join Likud, where he proudly proclaimed, 'I know more about weeds in Alaska than I do about Arabs.' The Israelis used to complain to the world that the Palestinians in particular and the Arabs in general refused to accept the hand that was stretched to them in peace, because they wanted to destroy Israel and throw the Jews into the sea. At the same time, the Israelis never tired of declaring their acceptance of international legality as a basis for a political solution, convinced that the Arabs were not prepared to do the same. Thus our initiatives after 1977 embarrassed the Israelis and prompted them to invent reasons for not responding to us. They would not talk with terrorists, saboteurs and murderers, they would say.

The Knesset's decision of 1986 banning contact with the PLO did not prevent a number of individual Israelis from trying to bypass it for the noble cause of peace, even though they knew that they would be liable to imprisonment. Here we must mention Abi Nathan, the owner of Radio Peace, which went on the air in the early 1960s. A Jew of Iranian descent, he served as an air force pilot in 1948. He was ordered to bomb some villages in Galilee, and told to repeat the bombing the following day. He was never able to forget what he saw that day from his plane; the sight of women, children and the elderly roaming blindly the mountains and valleys, completely aimless, homeless, their lives shattered. Unable to inflict further misery, Nathan flew on to the bay of Acre, dropped his bombs into the sea and returned to base. He then resigned from the air force and dedicated his life to peace, setting up a radio station in the middle of the Mediterranean. On one occasion, during President Nasser's time, he sailed in his radio-ship to Port Said to talk about peace with the Egyptians. He was promptly arrested by the Egyptian authorities and deported, but he remained undaunted. Abi Nathan continued to keep in touch with us despite the Knesset's proscription. He challenged it and seemed to be tempting punishment, but he believed that if he was tried and imprisoned, the Israeli people's conscience would be stirred. He was in fact imprisoned twice, each time for a year, but prison failed to change his convictions. Rather, it strengthened his resolve to push ahead with his call for peace. This very wealthy man always dressed in black, saying, 'I will not change my black clothes until I see the end of the Israeli occupation of the West Bank and the Gaza Strip.'

I must also mention another important proponent of peace, General Metitiahu Peled, who played a vital role in the June 1967 war. When the war ended he resigned from the army, took Arabic lessons and became a professor of Arabic at Tel Aviv University. Peled then met Uri Avniri, Arieh Eliav and others who had opened a channel with the PLO through the martyr Issam Sartawi. These contacts and meetings went on for a long time. Peled ran successfully for a Knesset seat under the progressive roster that grouped him with Muhammad Miari, leader of the (Arab) Progressive List, but when he failed to win re-election in the twelfth election he began to speak about the necessity for peace in the Middle East at seminars held in the United States. In spite of the frustrations this man experienced at the hands of his Arab allies in Israel, his determination did not flag nor did his calls for peace diminish. We can only mention him and others with the utmost respect and appreciation. When peace reigns in the region, the proponents of peace both in Israel and in the State of Palestine must remember and acknowledge them.

As already indicated, we hoped that our meetings with the Peace Now movement and other Oriental Jews as a group could form a bridge between Arabs and Israelis. We held three major meetings with these people. The first was in Romania on 6 November 1986, the second in Hungary on 12 June 1987, and the third, and most important one, in Toledo, Spain, on 5 July 1989. This meeting was arranged by Mrs Simone Bitton, a Moroccan Jew who lived in Israel during her childhood and youth, and then emigrated permanently to France. She did not, however, sever her links with Israel, nor did she forget her main task which was to arrange meetings and to provide information. To her fell the responsibility of arranging this meeting in Toledo. The participants included Shlomo Elbaz, a university professor and a senior Jewish Agency employee, Serge Bordogo, the leader of the Moroccan Jews (who became Morocco's Minister of Tourism), Naeem Jalaadi the leader of Oriental Jews in America, and André Azoulay, the president of the Dialogue and Identity Society which is based in France (he became adviser to King Hassan II). There were forty other Oriental Jews from Israel and elsewhere, all of them enjoying influence and high repute among their peers. I left Toledo before the three-day session ended. I did not ask the Jews to issue a statement nor to speak to the press so as not to embarrass them. The outcome of the dialogue was sufficient for me. However, they insisted on issuing a statement in which they commended the PLO's recognition of international resolutions and its renunciation of terrorism; they also demanded the setting up of a Palestinian State along-side the State of Israel.

Thus the peace accord we signed at the White House in Washington DC on 13 September 1993 did not just happen by chance, nor did it happen as a result of negotiations in the United States or Oslo. Rather, it resulted from a cumulative build-up to which the media and the political and military activities of the Palestinian Revolution had contributed.

Moreover, there was the immense contribution of the six years of uprising, the intifada, which had claimed and maimed thousands of children, women and men as its victims. The end of the Cold War and its consequences, the breakup of the socialist camp and the trauma caused by the Gulf war also played their part in the political windmill. The extensive networks of contacts which the PLO had set up with local Israeli and international Jewish factions, which were (or became) champions of peace, played an important role in the transformation and convergence of Israeli public opinion; they did so by emphasizing that coexistence was possible and the achievement of peace was no longer impossible. As we honour our fallen heroes, we honour the heroes of peace.

The PLO must be given credit too, for it paved the way to peace in the Middle East. Prompted by the strength and momentum of the Palestinian uprising, it decided at the nineteenth session of the PNC in 1988 to accept Security Council Resolutions 242 and 338 which the world had designated the basis for settling the region's conflict.

In the coming chapters we will examine the role of certain countries in the Middle East peace process and also look at the trials that the PLO and many individuals had to endure to end the conflict that had gripped the world for more than half a century.

3

PLO's Démarche

After the 1967 war the United Nations passed Resolution 242 on 22 November 1967. This called on Israel to withdraw from the territories it had occupied in the conflict and affirmed the necessity for a just settlement of the refugee problem and for guaranteeing the right of all States in the area to live in peace within secure and recognized borders. The preamble emphasized the inadmissibility of the acquisition of territory by force. After the war of October 1973, Security Council Resolution 338 of 22 October 1973 called on all the parties to the fighting to start negotiation under appropriate auspices aimed at establishing just and durable peace. Subsequently, the two superpowers convened the Geneva conference. Egypt and Jordan attended while Syria abstained. We were not invited, but Egypt tried to guarantee us some sort of representation, although at the time this was to no avail because of the efforts exerted by the American Secretary of State Henry Kissinger on his shuttle missions to the Middle East. In 1977 Cyrus Vance suggested to the Egyptians and Saudis that the PLO should deal positively with Resolution 242 and announce whatever reservations it might have, in which event he would be willing to initiate an American dialogue with the organization.

The resolutions of the twelfth session of the PNC held in June 1974 stated that we rejected Resolution 242 because it dealt with the issue of Palestine as an issue of refugees. What the PLO should have said was that if Resolution 242 had not dealt with the issue of Palestine as a refugee problem and had instead dealt with it as an issue of a people with legitimate rights, we would have accepted it. This formula was suggested by the former Egyptian Foreign Minister Ismail Fahmi and the Saudi Foreign Minister Saud al-Faisal. This would not have changed the substance of our position and we could have announced it without fear of losing ground. On the contrary, we could have won American recognition.

Time passed. On every visit by an official Palestinian delegation to Moscow, Andrei Gromyko would say to its members: 'You have no solution if you do not accept Resolutions 242 and 338. You are holding a card in your hand that is like a valuable cheque, but you have to play it at the right time. If you leave it too late it will lose its value. Please let us handle this cheque for you and we will talk it through with the Americans, Europeans and Israelis, and maybe we can find a solution for you.' The answer was always: 'We cannot accept the resolutions.'

Certain Palestinian factions used to boast of the relationship with the Soviets, who they regarded as the symbols of progress and socialism, the supporters of oppressed peoples and the backbone of international libera-tion movements. Many, if not most, of these factions adopted Marxism in order to identify with the Soviets and they used to invent a kind of alliance with them about which they boasted on every occasion. The Soviets were the last to know of such a relationship because the only point of contact between us was the issue of the Middle East, and even on this subject there was no common ground because they approached the problem through Resolution 242 which we had rejected.

During the three-month long siege of Beirut in 1982, certain Palestinian political figures in Amman sent a letter to the leadership, signed by two lawyers, Ibrahim Bakr and Yasser Amr (at the time of writing a member of the PLO Executive Committee) suggesting that acceptance of Resolutions 242 and 338 should be declared immediately because this would help to break the siege, to preserve the PLO and change the hostile international atmosphere. When the siege of Beirut ended and following the second Fez summit, which was held in 1982, a number of resolutions were adopted which were based on the principles of international legality, on the plan formulated by President Bourguiba and King Fahd and on the comments of other Arab leaders. These resolutions included:

1. Israeli withdrawal from all Arab lands occupied in 1967, including Arab Jerusalem.
2. Removal of [Jewish] settlements established after 1967 in occupied Arab lands.
3. Guaranteeing freedom of worship in the holy places.
4. Confirmation of the right of Palestinian people to self-determination and to the exercise of their inalienable right under the leadership of the PLO, the sole and legitimate representative of the Palestinian people. Compensation would be due to any Palestinian not willing to return.
5. There would be a transitional period for the West Bank and the Gaza Strip, under the auspices of the United Nations, for a period not exceeding a few months.

6. Establishment of the independent Palestinian State with Jerusalem as its capital.
7. The Security Council would guarantee peace among all States in the region, including the independent Palestinian State.
8. Implementation of these principles would be guaranteed by the Security Council.

The intifada, or uprising, erupted on 7 December 1987 to resist the occupation. Basic rules were needed to direct its activities and to prevent it from becoming a stampede or a bubble that would quickly burst and vanish. Discussion of the political aims of the uprising required a mind uncluttered by sterile slogans and rhetoric, a mind that would deal sensitively with the interests and needs of the people. Our people were living in harsh conditions, and rather than boast about the achievements of the uprising, it was important to remember the victims, the uncertain future of the intrepid 'children of the stones', who were fighting the army of occupation day and night, their parents and their relatives, all needing food, decent shelter, education, health care and hope for a better future.

A few months after the outbreak of the intifada I sat with Naim al-Ashqar, a politbureau member of the Palestinian Communist Party and a man whom I respected for his wisdom. I put a very specific question to him: 'Are you prepared to think with me without being restricted by 'red lines' and worrying about what we regard as forbidden?' 'Yes,' he said. 'Do you agree with me that the intifada erupted as a way of bringing about the withdrawal of Israeli forces from Gaza and the West Bank?' I asked. 'Yes,' he responded. 'Do you think our people in Gaza and the West Bank would agree if we were to ask them to continue throwing stones for as long as it takes to drive the Israelis out of Haifa, Jaffa and Acre?' I asked. 'No,' he retorted. I asked 'What would be their response?' 'They would throw the stones at us,' he replied. So I said, 'Then let us discuss what we can offer them.'

This is how we began to consider the acceptance of Resolutions 242 and 338 as a basis for a political process, which later became known as the Palestinian political initiative. We made sure that the details of the idea remained secret. We would speak of it in general terms to the Palestinian leadership, to certain leaderships in the Arab world and to the Soviet Union. We visited Egypt and presented the idea to Foreign Minister Ismat Abdel-Mageed,[1] who welcomed it enthusiastically, remarking that such action would represent a historic breakthrough in the struggle of the Palestinian people, adding that it would have a significant impact on the

---

[1] Dr Abdel-Mageed is now Secretary-General of the Arab League.

West and also on Israel which would not be able to reject it. We also visited Moscow and met Alexander Bessmertnikh, who later became Foreign Minister. The meeting was also attended by Central Committee *apparatchiks* who warmly welcomed the new thinking of the PLO and assured us that this would clear the way for a satisfactory solution of the Palestinian issue. The Soviets added that the United States could not oppose this stance and felt sure that it would open a dialogue with the PLO once the PNC passed resolutions in this regard.

But such resolutions could not be passed by the PNC without there being other resolutions of a morale-boosting nature to mitigate their effect. There was talk of the need for a Palestinian declaration of independence, but there was the fear that such a declaration might defeat the purpose of the Palestinian political initiative, rendering the acceptance of Resolution 242 by the PNC an empty gesture. But there was no other convincing alternative. Certain Palestinian jurists set out to prepare a draft declaration of independence, but this proved too unsubtle and had to be redrafted. So we assigned the task to Mahmoud Darwish who employed all his intellectual and linguistic powers to present a refined version, which harmonized with the Palestinian political initiative while pleasing the hawks in our ranks.

At its meeting in Algiers on 15 November 1988 the PNC, the highest legislative authority, adopted the political initiative by an absolute majority and the Declaration of Independence unanimously. The PNC defined Palestinian rights and committed itself to the realization of these rights as the minimum acceptable condition for a political settlement of the Palestinian issue. The uprising and its multifarious influence on events in Israel were the solid building blocks on which the PNC was able to formulate the Palestinian position. Over one hundred countries including all the Arab countries recognized the new Palestinian State. Some people took that recognition at its face value, not realizing that it was the rational thinking behind the Palestinian peace initiative that had made this recognition inevitable. In the same vein, it may be said that recognition of the State of Palestine represented a worldwide encouragement of the course that the PLO had taken.

At that PNC session, the Fatah leadership, the Communist Party and a number of independents adopted the political initiative. Nayef Hawatmeh, leader of the Democratic Front for the Liberation of Palestine (DFLP), was forced to concur at the last moment when members of his politbureau threatened to break away. History must record that the martyr Abu Iyad played a crucial role at that session in convincing the PNC to accept the initiative. He delivered a powerful speech in which he explained the advantages of the initiative and urged the PNC to ratify it. The most important aspect of the initiative was that it brought international legality to the PLO position which the international community considered to be a necessary basis for the resolution of the Palestinian problem and the wider conflict in the Middle East.

The PNC adjourned, and we felt that the United States would be pleased with the Council's resolutions. In the event, however, the United States was not happy enough to engage the PLO in a dialogue because renunciation of terrorism by the PLO still needed to be clearly spelt out. On the other hand, the PNC's resolutions did make a noticeable impact on the American Jewish community which set out to initiate a dialogue with the PLO. This was facilitated by the Swedish Government, which enthusiastically offered to host such a dialogue. With a keen eye to the future, the Swedes were thus able to establish for themselves an international role in Middle Eastern politics.

The principal aim of the PNC resolutions (including acceptance of UN Resolution 242) was to stifle the pretexts that Europe, America and Israel had been employing to justify their position *vis-à-vis* the PLO and the Palestinian issue. We began to notice the sense of isolation and confusion that the United States and Israel were experiencing as a result of the PNC resolutions and their worldwide repercussions. All the Western European countries, whether they recognized the new Palestinian State or not, reacted favourably to the resolutions, arguing that the Council's action was positive and that it therefore should be reciprocated by the United States and Israel.

Affairs in the United States were in abeyance during the transition between presidencies: the outgoing president was not interested in making momentous decisions, while the new president was not yet empowered to make any decisions. We supposed the American Administration would understand that the message we broadcast through the PNC defined our future policy, one that was welcomed by most countries of the world. However, this supposition was misplaced. The US Administration remained impassive and publicly insisted that unless there was further clarification using specific expressions, it would not change its position towards the PLO. Privately, I felt that this attitude was untenable and could not for long ignore the changes on the ground and the new stance of the PLO which stemmed from the experience of a quarter of a century of struggle. The US Administration soon arrived at a compromise which allowed it to maintain its official position of banning contact with the PLO, while opening unofficial channels with the PLO bureau chiefs in Ankara, Algiers and Tunis through the US ambassadors and senior diplomatic staff in these capitals. These meetings remained a closely guarded secret at America's request.

The Administration soon realized, however, that these secret and unofficial channels were not bearing fruit. It then suggested that American Jewish community leaders should contact the PLO to sound it out, and that the outcome would determine its future moves. Meanwhile the American Jewish community organized a series of visits to Israel to protest about the government's policy and to express concern at the harm being done to America's Jews and to Israel's own image as a model Western state in the Middle East.

On 21 November 1988 our representative in Stockholm informed us that a number of notable Republican and Democrat American Jews had expressed their desire to meet PLO members and to become acquainted with the PNC resolutions so that a mutual agreement or statement on a number of issues could be arrived at. We did not give this matter much thought in the beginning. We had already on a number of occasions met with Jewish American personalities who had had no impact at all on the American Administration or Israel. Even so, we sent a delegation to meet them, headed by Khaled al-Hassan, Chairman of the PNC Foreign Relations Committee,[1] and including Hisham Mustapha, Director in the PLO International Department,[2] Afif Safieh, London representative of the PLO, and Eugene Makhlouf, our Stockholm representative. Later we realized that the dialogue had been sponsored by the Swedish Foreign Ministry, and that the Swedish Government had expressed deep interest in a meeting of the two delegations. In the end, the leaders of the two delegations prepared a statement which was not released then and which has remained under wraps until now. This is the text:

Strictly Confidential

The Swedish Foreign Minister Mr Sten Andersson invited to Stockholm the following representatives of the PLO as well as the following American Jewish personalities, who met together on 21 November, 1988:

Mr Khaled Al Hassan	Mrs Rita E Hauser
Mr Hisham Mustapha	Mr Stanley K. Sheinbaum
Mr Afif Safieh	Ms Drora Kass
Mr Eugene Makhlouf	

[1] Deceased in Morocco in October 1994.
[2] A close assistant of mine.

The first meeting was opened by Mr Sten Andersson and all meetings were attended by Swedish Foreign Ministry officials.

The Palestine National Council met in Algiers from 12 to 15 November, 1988, and announced the Declaration of Independence which proclaimed the State of Palestine and issued a Political Statement.

The following explanation was given by the representatives of the PLO of certain important points in the Palestinian Declaration of Independence and the Political Statement adopted by the PNC in Algiers.

The PNC:

1. agreed to enter into peace negotiations at an international conference under the auspices of the UN and with the participation of the permanent members of the Security Council and the PLO as the sole legitimate representative of the Palestinian people, on an equal footing with the other parties to the conflict; such an international conference is to be held on the basis of UN Resolutions 242 and 338 and the right of the Palestinian people to self-determination, without external interference, as provided in the UN Charter, including the right to an independent state, which conference should resolve the Palestinian problem in all its aspects;
2. accepted the existence of Israel as a state in the region;
3. declared its rejection and condemnation of terrorism in all its forms, including state terrorism;
4. called for a solution to the Palestinian refugee problem in accordance with international law and practices and relevant UN resolutions (including the right of return or compensation).

The American personalities strongly supported and applauded the Palestinian Declaration of Independence and the Political Statement adopted in Algiers and felt there was no further impediment to a direct dialogue between the United States Government and the PLO.

Several statements were issued at that time by Israeli leaders, intellectuals and journalists declaring that America must save them from themselves, that no peace could be achieved so long as the mentality of their leaders remained as it was, that they were heading for suicide, and that the Middle East needed an imposed solution.

Sensible Israelis were looking for a solution dictated by the US, but America itself was not convinced of the need for a solution and considered the circumstances inopportune anyway. For forty years America was content with the status quo which, I suspect, it considered the perfect solution. The status quo was a state of no-war and allowed America to bleed the wealth of the region and so dominate it and keep it in its sphere of influence.

There is no doubt that many important and serious developments in the region and in the world forced America to reconsider its policy towards the Palestinian issue. Although outwardly it continued to cling to its position *vis-à-vis* the PLO it began to recognize that a change was necessary. We can thus review the reasons that led America to adopt a new stance:

1. International *détente*: Ever since the two superpowers arrived at an agreement on medium-range nuclear weapons, and after it had become common practice to solve international disputes by negotiation, there was an urgent need to bring the most explosive issue of the Middle East up for discussion.
2. The intifada (uprising) which reflected the explosiveness of the Palestine question and proved to the world in general, and to America in particular, that the Palestinians had not melted away in the desert as former US Secretary of State John Foster Dulles had predicted in the 1950s.
3. The situation arising from the Israeli elections which consolidated a form of radicalism and fundamentalism in Israeli politics: this harmed in one way or another the reputation of Israel and caused a chasm between Israel's Jews and world Jewry.
4. The American desire to guarantee the flow of reasonably priced oil from the Gulf to the international, and especially American, markets, and to regain the Arab armaments markets which had turned to Europe for arms purchases.
5. The growing European role in dealing with the Middle East, and America's fear of Europe becoming a future partner in the region, a circumstance which is unacceptable to America.
6. King Hussein's abandonment of the West Bank by severing its links with it and withdrawing from the scene thus putting an end to the concept of the Jordanian option.
7. Signs of increasing criticism of the behaviour of American Jews in the US media. Such criticism worries the American Administration because it might evolve into a form of hostility between American citizens in general and American Jews. This is unacceptable to the Administration which wants to preserve the image of the 'Zionist

lobby', especially in the Arab world, while preventing such an image from taking root in the minds of American citizens. In other words, a steady magnification of that image could have dire consequences. The ordinary American citizen is beginning to truly tire of this 'Zionist lobby' and is already speaking with conviction of the hegemony and dominance of the Jews over the American leadership.

8. This image in particular has given rise to an illusion among Zionist organizations in America that they have the ability to dominate American decision making, a fact which encouraged them to step up their activities; this in turn prompted the Administration to take measures to restrict their activities to those which were officially sanctioned. The American–Israeli Public Affairs Committee was a case in point.

The contacts between the PLO and the American Jews at Stockholm would have ended as soon as they had begun had not the Swedish Government invited Yasser Arafat for a quick visit insisting it took place as soon as possible. Arafat accepted the invitation and travelled to Sweden on 6 December 1988 with Yasser Abd Rabbo and Mahmoud Darwish. As the talks got under way, the Swedish Foreign Minister Andersson produced a letter he had received from George Shultz containing a proposal aimed at paving the way for a dialogue between the US and the PLO and eventually to a peaceful settlement of the conflict. The proposal was that the PLO would issue a conciliatory statement to which the US would reply. Shultz had fixed both these statements in advance. However, our delegation began to amend an item here and an item there, passing each amendment on to the Swedish Foreign Minister, who would then come back with America's reply. Arafat, while assuring the Swedes of his personal acceptance of the proposal, requested a chance to present it to the PLO Executive Committee. In the meantime, he held a press conference in which he spoke about Khaled al-Hassan's agreement with the American Jews saying that the agreement was a good reading of the PNC resolutions. He referred to the PLO position with regard to Resolution 242 and the use of violence and so forth.

It is ironic that the exchange between the American Government and the PLO via Sweden remained secret, while the unofficial dialogue between private American citizens and the PLO was widely publicized, especially if one assumes that the American Jews were used as cover for the secret dialogue. Reactions to Arafat's statements at the press conference were mixed. Shultz commented that these were not encouraging enough to form the basis of bilateral talks between the PLO and the United States. On the same day, 7 December 1988, Senator Richard Murphy said that the United States hoped that Arafat would recognize Israel in the speech which the PLO leader was due to deliver at the UN General Assembly in Geneva. On that day too, Shimon Peres said Arafat's statement gave additional clarification to the evasive position that had been announced in Algiers, and added, 'Only a clear declaration by the PLO announcing an end to terrorism and agitation, accepting unequivocally Security Council Resolution 242 and openly recognizing Israel's right to live in peace can make us take this organization seriously.' When Yitzhak Shamir was asked what he thought of Arafat's statements he said, 'I do not see, nor do I expect, any fundamental change. They set up their organization to destroy Israel and when they conclude that this goal will not be achieved, they will disband.' In contrast, the head of the Jewish American delegation, Rita Hauser, also speaking that day, said Arafat's statements in Sweden had clarified the Algiers resolutions and had clearly proclaimed his recognition of the State of Israel. These clarifications, she stated, paved the way for direct talks between the United States and the PLO. The State Department's spokesman commented on the reports from Stockholm, saying: 'If press reports from the Swedish capital are confirmed then these are nothing but an explanation of the PLO's dual position. The PLO has attempted, through Sweden, to give credibility to the Algiers resolutions but this remains nothing more than an attempt.'

To go back to Shultz's proposal forwarded to the PLO delegation in Stockholm by the Swedish Foreign Minister, our delegation did not wholly agree to the text drafted by the Americans for the PLO nor to that for the United States, and suggested a number of amendments. In the end the texts emerged looking something like this:[1]

Proposed statement by the PLO
In contributing to the search for a just and lasting peace in the Middle East, the Executive Committee of the Palestine Liberation Organization, undertaking the role of the Interim Government of the State of Palestine, wishes to make the following official statement:
1. It is prepared to enter into negotiation with Israel in order to reach a comprehensive settlement of the Arab–Israeli conflict within the framework of an international conference and on the basis of Security Council Resolutions 242 and 338.

---

[1] Both texts are translated from Arabic.

2. It affirms its desire for peaceful coexistence with Israel and other neighbouring states and its respect for their right to exist in peace within secure and internationally recognized borders. The democratic Palestinian State which is to be set up on the Palestinian territories occupied in 1967 pledges the same.
3. It renounces and condemns to all forms of individual, collective and state terrorism.
4. It is prepared to arrive at a ban, on a mutual basis, on all forms of violence once negotiations begin.

The American text

The PLO has issued a statement accepting Security Council Resolutions 242 and 338, recognizing Israel's right to exist and renouncing violence. As a result, the United States of America is prepared to begin a substantive dialogue with the PLO representatives. The United States believes that negotiations for a peaceful resolution of the Arab–Israeli conflict must be based on Resolutions 242 and 338. It calls upon all parties to renew without delay their efforts in the search for peace. The United States recognizes that the Palestinian people's representatives have the right to raise all the issues they want in the negotiations.

This statement was to be followed by a number of prearranged questions which were to be put by journalists to George Shultz.[1]

First question: Does your statement mean that the Palestinians can bring their position on a Palestinian State to the negotiating table?

Answer: Yes. The Palestinians, from our viewpoint, have the right to follow up their desire to establish an independent state through negotiations. Results can always be attained through the negotiating process and direct exchanges between the parties concerned.

Second question: Do you agree that the negotiations should take place within the framework of the international conference?

Answer: The United States has for some time supported direct negotiations. However, we are prepared to consider any suggestion that would lead to direct negotiations for a comprehensive peace. The initiative I floated early this year calls for an international conference that would launch direct negotiations. Such a conference should be organized in such a way that it does not become a substitute for direct negotiations.

[1] Translated from Arabic.

Our delegation took these two texts back to Tunis to present them to the Executive Committee which convened a three-day special meeting for this purpose. A long debate ensued over every single point. Some tried to portray these texts as overelaborated versions of the PNC's resolutions, but the majority did not share this view. Consequently, the discussions turned to the guarantees that we might get from the United States and the results we might achieve; eventually the Executive Committee approved the texts.

Meanwhile, intensive consultations were taking place with the Soviet Union. We summoned the Soviet Chargé d'Affaires in Tunis and informed him of the details of the American initiative. In fact, before returning to Tunis our delegation had already met the Soviet Ambassador in Sweden, had put him in the picture and had requested a quick response from the Soviet Foreign Ministry. But because many of the members of the Soviet Cabinet were travelling with President Gorbachev to attend the United Nations sessions and also to meet the outgoing President (Reagan) and the President-elect (Bush) as well as to visit Cuba and Britain, their response was delayed. We warned them that the Americans were very anxious to meet us and would therefore try to influence the Soviets to back them, hoping that Gorbachev might endorse their position in the speech he was due to give in New York. We also told them that they might intimate that the Soviets were now out of the game and that we, the Palestinians, had greatly contributed to their exclusion. As we wanted to clear the air with the Soviets, we said we would wait for their response before conveying our final position to the Swedes. I then went to Moscow while Mahmoud Darwish stood by to go to Stockholm to inform the Swedish Foreign Minister of our position.

The situation was reviewed in Moscow with the Soviet Foreign Minister. The Soviet opinion was that whether the American reaction was one of commitment to the agreement or not, this step would have significant repercussions worldwide. In the future, the exchange of views should be intensified. The present American Administration might try to open the way for the incoming Administration and repeat the mistake of not granting Arafat an entry visa to the United States to speak before the United Nations General Assembly in New York. It was also possible that the present Administration might try to influence the Israeli position in one way or another, and that the American reaction might energize the Palestinian down-to-earth approach as well as Soviet policy in the Middle East. It was therefore necessary that the PLO and the Soviet Union should continue to exchange information and views in detail, if effective results were to be achieved.

We discussed what the Israeli reaction would be. We predicted that there would be senseless killings and a general stepping up of acts of aggression and that Israel would become increasingly isolated, with our common policy contributing greatly to that. We also reviewed the complex situation within Israel that would result from the formation of the new cabinet. The Israelis trusted James Baker in spite of his wide-ranging relations with the Arabs. Israeli intransigence had always depended on American support, but the feeling was now that no matter how things were in Israel, the Palestinians would win.

It will be recalled that when the United States refused Arafat an entry visa to address the United Nations in New York, we appealed to the General Assembly which voted 154 to 2 (America and Israel) to relocate the General Assembly meeting to Geneva, the UN's second headquarters. On 14 December 1988 in Geneva, Arafat delivered his speech which was well received internationally, but America still refused to accept the PLO position at face value on the grounds that it did not meet America's conditions which would allow a dialogue with the PLO to commence.

However, the Swedish Foreign Minister, who was the official go-between in this matter and who knew the whole truth, and that Arafat had not delivered the text required of him verbatim, insisted on going up to the podium to address the Assembly. He said that he could confirm that Mr Arafat's speech had fully met Washington's conditions for the initiation of an American–Palestinian dialogue. If any amongst us in the PLO had any doubts about his loyalty this speech expelled them completely. In his speech Arafat had clearly confirmed his readiness to negotiate with Israel on the basis of Security Council Resolutions 242 and 338. He had also underscored his recognition of Israel's right to exist within secure and recognized borders and condemned all forms of terrorism including state terrorism. These had been Washington's demands of Arafat.

There were sharp and intense exchanges in the corridors of the UN over the American position. Arab Foreign Ministers in Geneva tried to calm Arafat and asked him not to let himself be provoked. They assured him that America's approval was on its way. A number of Arab leaders, such as King Hussein of Jordan and President Mubarak of Egypt, also contacted him for the same purpose. Meanwhile, intensive contacts were taking place with America to urge it to accept the PLO position. But the Americans did not respond to these calls and limited themselves to saying that Arafat had not met all their conditions. At this point our delegation as well as our friends split into two camps. One was of the opinion that Arafat should clarify matters by using the words required of him in order to deprive America of its pretexts and excuses, while the other considered that the PLO had given enough away.

I was at that time in Moscow following up various matters. My own view was that if further clarification was needed then so be it, provided we adhered to the framework of the PNC resolutions. America's insistence that certain words should be used was nothing but wrangling and provided a pretext not to have a dialogue with the PLO. Like others, I believed that a dialogue with America would not merely be a sideshow but a watershed. The whole purpose of our new approach as expressed in the PNC resolutions was to win over adversaries and embarrass our enemies or make them change their position. Arafat knew this and sought a way out that would put the Americans in a tight corner and force them to initiate a dialogue. To Geneva therefore came Haseeb Sabbagh and Basil Aql, two prominent Palestinian businessmen and members of the PLO Central Committee. They had followed developments intently, and when they found that the situation had reached an impasse, Sabbagh telephoned Richard Murphy in the American Administration and discussed with him in exhaustive detail the means by which a formula acceptable to both sides could be agreed so as to save the peace process. This depended on one expression: 'Renunciation of terrorism'. Finally, Arafat was prevailed upon to employ this expression at the press conference he was to convene an hour later. This is what he said:

> Let me clarify my viewpoint in front of you. Our desire for peace is a strategy and not a temporary tactic. We are working for peace no matter what happens, no matter what happens. Our State offers salvation to the Palestinians and peace for both Palestinians and Israelis. The right to self-determination means the survival of the Palestinians; our survival does not destroy the survival of the Israelis as their leaders claim. Yesterday in my speech I pointed to UN Resolution 141 as a basis for Palestinian independence. I also indicated our acceptance of Resolutions 242 and 338 as a basis for negotiations with Israel within the framework of an international conference. The Palestine National Council accepted all three Resolutions at the Algiers session.
>
> In my speech yesterday it was clear that we meant that our people had a right to freedom and national independence in accordance with Resolution 181 and the right of all parties in the Middle East to a peaceful and secure existence, including, as I said, the State of Palestine and Israel and the other neighbours in accordance with Resolutions 242 and 338.

As for terrorism, I declared unequivocally yesterday, and repeat now, that we totally and categorically renounce all forms of individual, collective and state-sponsored terrorism.

In Geneva and Algiers, we clarified our position. Any talk to the effect that 'Palestinians should offer more' (do you remember this catchphrase?) or that 'it is not enough' or 'the Palestinians are playing at propaganda' or 'exercising public relations manoeuvres' would be harmful and unfruitful. Enough. All remaining matters must be discussed at the [negotiating] table at the international conference.

Let it be clear that neither Arafat nor anyone else can halt the uprising. The uprising will end only when tangible and practical steps are taken towards the realization of our national goals and the establishment of the Palestine State. In this context I expect the European Community countries to play a more active role in consolidating peace in our region. They have a political and moral responsibility and can handle it.

Finally, I declare before you, and request that you quote me as saying, that we want peace, that we are committed to peace, and that we want to live in our Palestinian State and let others live. Thank you.[1]

A few hours after the press conference, Arafat left Geneva for Berlin. While en route, the news reached us that the American Administration would be releasing a statement within the hour announcing that the US would begin a dialogue with the PLO. In less than an hour two statements were released, one by Secretary of State George Shultz and the other by President Ronald Reagan, proclaiming the beginning of a dialogue with the PLO and appointing the American Ambassador in Tunisia to represent the United States in this endeavour.

Thus an important victory was won. We had surmounted an obstacle that had been placed in our path by Henry Kissinger fourteen years previously, when he officially promised Israel that the United States would not talk to the PLO unless it accepted Resolutions 242 and 338 and Israel's right to exist. Later, he had added a third condition, namely renunciation of violence. Not only had he given such an undertaking as the Secretary of State of the United States, but he had also secured a ruling from the American Congress on the matter.

What did an American dialogue with us mean? It meant that we, the PLO, had definitely become an official and integral part of any dialogue

---

[1] Translated from Arabic.

on the Middle East conflict. If America was serious about achieving a comprehensive peace settlement then Israel would recognize our existence, one way or another. Without American support Israel would be unable to stand alone in the face of world opinion. The seriousness of America's intentions was something we would discover in the near future.

This development had a mixed reception. George Habash welcomed the US Administration's decision and considered it yet another victory for the Palestinian Revolution. The Palestinians received it positively, concluding instinctively that a dialogue with America was not a peripheral matter of legality, but one of tremendous practical importance because it pitted Israel against the world and even against the US in a confrontation that it could not win. In the Arab world, reactions were mostly positive with the Arab media reporting the statements of support from Arab leaders.

Reactions in Israel ranged from condemnation to friendly reception, although fear of America's move predominated. Some saw it as the straw that broke the camel's back. Israel had been used to hiding behind American implacability; now it was exposed and isolated. A statement released by the Israeli Prime Minister's office on 15 December 1988 expressed regret at the American Administration's decision and predicted that the new American position would not lead to peace. It stressed that Israel would not change its position regarding the PLO and would not negotiate with it. It further said the US decision gave cause for concern in Israel, and that the PLO would demand US recognition of the Palestinian State which it had declared. Such a demand would pose a threat to Israel's security and could not be ignored.

Statements by Rabin and Peres highlighted the need to review the fundamental changes in the region and called for an Israeli political initiative that would adequately deal with the developments that would result from the American decision. It seemed that now there was a possibility that Israel would agree to negotiate with the Palestinians who had not only accepted the UN resolutions but had also condemned terrorism. Certain statements issued by the Israeli Left stressed the need for direct negotiations with the PLO.

There were diverse reactions in the US and elsewhere. Some praised the American step which they considered a service to peace and a commitment to Israel's safety and security, and one that would test Arafat's propensity to match actions with words. Some of these statements insisted that the continuation of the American–Palestinian dialogue hinged upon Arafat and the PLO keeping their word, ensuring that no acts of terrorism were perpetrated. However, a statement made by Richard Murphy in a television programme on 18 December 1988 showed that America understood Arafat's situation and the limits to which he could control opposing Palestinian factions. He said that the United States was willing to consider each act of terrorism on its own and determine who was involved in each incident. America, he added, was concerned that the PLO should not be involved in any such incident and that it expected the PLO to expel anyone involved in any terrorist operation from its ranks. Some in the US Administration demanded that Israel should now take the political initiative and, if it really wanted security, that it should recognize that Palestinians had legitimate political rights.

Perhaps the most noteworthy statement came from the French Foreign Minister, Roland Dumas, on Radio Monte Carlo on 16 December 1988. He expressed satisfaction with the American decision which his country considered a step forward on the road to peace. He hoped the five permanent members of the Security Council would quickly convene a meeting to discuss ways of stimulating the peace process.

Although the Palestinian–American talks continued via the US Embassy in Tunis, they did not advance beyond general discussions and did not lead to practical steps that would energize the peace process. In fact the dialogue was suspended when a group linked to Abul Abbas[1] carried out a raid on a beach in Tel Aviv in May 1989. The United States used this incident as an excuse to break off the talks on the grounds that the raid had violated the conditions on which they were founded.

[1] Leader of the Palestine Liberation Front (PLF).

4

Unofficial Channels to Likud

Following the invasion of Lebanon in 1982, I had a meeting in Moscow with the Israeli Communist Party Secretary-General, Meir Vilner, in the course of which he related an incident involving Ariel Sharon at the Knesset. Vilner was leaving as Sharon was going in. Their eyes met, but no words were exchanged. Sharon grabbed Vilner's shoulder and demanded, 'Why do you not greet me? Why do you turn away from me?' Vilner replied, 'I do not greet a bloodletter.' 'Are you talking about the Palestinians?' Sharon asked. 'Yes', said Vilner, 'I mean the blood of Palestinians, I mean the siege of Beirut. I mean your lust for killing. Don't you think they are human beings like us who also have rights?' As Vilner walked out of the door Sharon said, 'One day you will realize that it is I who will establish the Palestinian State.' So I asked Vilner, 'Do you believe that he is truthful about what he said or did he mean Jordan when he referred to the Palestinian State, as is his custom?' Vilner replied, 'I don't know exactly, but there was an edge to his voice that I had not heard before. He may mean what I have just told you, maybe not. I am simply relating this incident for you to examine. In politics there are no constants or certainties. With politicians everything is open to discussion.'

I found it strange to hear such talk from an extremist Likud leader such as Sharon whose policy towards the Palestinians was to deport them! The Herut slogan, which still prevails, considered the land at either bank of the Jordan to be the national homeland of the Jews. The caption under the map of the area read: 'This is ours. So is this. And only through this.' The word 'this' pointed to a gun. Vladimir Jabotinsky, founder of Revisionism, left the World Zionist Organization because it did not wholeheartedly pursue the goals of the Zionist movement and had instead accepted only the territory of Palestine as the national homeland of the Jews.

The Vilner–Sharon exchange stuck in my mind. Why, I wondered, can't it be true? Why do we not try to contact this man or others of his party? Dialogue takes place between enemies, not friends. The PNC had passed a resolution permitting us to contact Israeli factions that recognize our rights. I wanted the PNC to widen the scope – to include rejectionist and even hostile factions because contacts with them were likely to lead to agreements with a range of forces in Israel.

When Likud assumed power in 1977, the Labour Party had become marginalized and weak, especially when Yigal Yadin had split from its ranks taking a number of its leaders with him. In subsequent elections it failed to regain its position, while Likud and its allies from the Labour hawks and religious parties retained dominance. When votes were tied, Likud had a better chance of forming a government than Labour because, after thirty years in opposition, Likud had become a solid party with a lust for power. During that period Labour had declined and become divided as a result of the personal and the political rivalry between Rabin and Peres. We therefore had no option but to search within Likud's ranks for someone willing to meet and talk with us. It was then that the Amirav–Nusseiba meeting took place.

This meeting was accompanied by other activities and meetings in various places that produced a form of political debate among both Israelis and Palestinians. Although these meetings did not bear fruit at the time, they did provide the groundwork for further dialogue, which over time furnished the cornerstones of the achievement of September 1993.

Throughout our armed struggle we were careful to send a signal to the Israelis inviting them to meet on common ground where we could discuss common concerns, hopes and dreams, and build a better future for the coming generations. When we reached the conclusion that the Israelis were here to stay we hoped that they too would reach the conclusion that dialogue with their neighbouring States was no substitute for dialogue with us, the owners and people of the land, a people who yearned for an identity and an address. The long and bitter years of exile had not tempered this yearning. Even those who lived a life of affluence abroad shared the same sense of deprivation; in fact their material success in the diaspora only increased their desire for what they lacked and needed.

The Palestinian–Israeli conflict stems from one people negating the existence of the other. It is the conflict of two peoples over one land each presenting proof of its ownership. However, the outcome of the conflict is not decided by the strength of the evidence presented, but by force, which is the ultimate arbiter in the real world. Our quarrel is with those who see the world from their own perspective and perceive history through their inherited dogmas. In the case of Israel, which enjoys technological, scientific and military superiority over us, as well as international backing, many of its citizens see no reason to change the status quo. This line of reasoning is shared by many members of Likud and the extremist religious and right-wing groups who remain impervious to the wind of change. This attitude has led Israel into an impasse in the Middle East from which it can extricate itself only through reason, by facing realities. First among these realities is the Palestinian people's right to their land. The Amirav–Nusseiba story shows that some people on the Right in Israel did face facts, albeit timidly. We shall see how it happened and where it ended.

The Amirav–Nusseiba Meeting

It began on 4 July 1987 at the home of Moshe Amirav, a member of Herut's central institutions, and a very close associate of Yitzhak Shamir. In attendance were Sari Nusseiba, a Palestinian academic from the University of Bir Zeit in the West Bank and Salah Zaheeqa, a Palestinian journalist in Israel. Discussions centred on the best solution to the Palestinian issue. Noted for his liberal views on this issue, Amirav is also renowned for opposing negotiations that do not include the PLO.

The go-between in this meeting was David Ish-Shalom, an Oriental Jew who had recently published a book in Hebrew titled *Horror and Hope* in 1987 in which he suggested the establishment of an unarmed Palestinian entity in 'Judaea and Samaria' and the Gaza Strip, to be headed by the PLO. He promoted his book amongst ministers as well as Knesset members, ranging from Labour to Herut. The Palestinians also listened to him. He discovered that beneath the surface there were currents in Herut which feared a continuation of the prevailing situation and which recognized that a solution to the Palestinian issue would be a means of preserving Israel's moral standing.

Moshe Amirav and many others in Herut believed that a Likud initiative towards the Palestinians would discomfit Maarakh (left-wing alignment) which would be unable to oppose it. As this would lead to a Likud victory in the 1988 elections, he saw a common interest for Likud and the Palestinians to establishing self-rule as an interim settlement acceptable to both sides. Such a settlement could only be concluded with the PLO since no Palestinian would agree to membership in an administrative body to run the territories without PLO approval.

Ish-Shalom and Amirav agreed to present these ideas to the Palestinians and to Herut respectively. When Amirav suggested these ideas to Shamir he neither rejected nor accepted them, although he did express fears that the Palestinians would use them to their own advantage within Herut. But Amirav later said that a group of leaders within Herut agreed with him that there was an urgent need to solve the Palestinian issue, although they placed obstacles in their own path. Among those were Minister Moshe Ktsaf and Knesset members Meir Shetreet, Dan Meridor, Ehud Olmert and Benyamin Begin, the son of the former Prime Minister.

Nusseiba and Zaheeqa presented these ideas to Faisal al-Husseini so that a second meeting could be arranged at Nusseiba's home in the village of Abu Dees on 13 July 1987. This was attended by the journalist Ish-Shalom, Amirav and Faisal Husseini. Both Amirav and Husseini agreed that neither Herut's dream of a Jewish state extending to both banks of the River Jordan, nor the Palestinian dream of Jaffa and Haifa would materialize. Discussion followed on various issues, initiated by Husseini and Amirav, to which Ish-Shalom contributed, and this was clearly an Israeli recognition of the legitimacy of the PLO's representation. They also talked about the future Palestinian State, international guarantees, cessation of violence and other issues. Husseini then left after agreeing that Amirav would prepare a working paper summarizing his ideas.

The third meeting took place at the Institute of Arab Studies on 30 July 1987 and was attended by Amirav, Ish-Shalom, Nusseiba and Husseini. Amirav said Knesset members Ehud Olmert and Dan Meridor and head of the Prime Minister's office would attend the meeting later but because news of the meeting had leaked to the *Alhamshar* newspaper they did not do so. Even so, Olmert met Nusseiba at his home, though without raising any topic of substance.

During the fourth meeting on 22 August 1987, we arrived at formulas for a memorandum of understanding that would form a basis for discussions. The possibility of Amirav travelling to Geneva to meet Arafat was also discussed. Other issues of detail were raised including the form of the Palestinian State's currency, embassies, passports or travel documents and others. It seemed that the participants were discussing a real peace accord.

The last meeting which also took place on 22 August 1987 was held at the Orient House in Jerusalem, an estate owned by the Husseini family and serves as centre for various Palestinian associations. Amirav said that he had delivered the working paper that he had prepared to important members of the delegation accompanying the Prime Minister to Romania. The paper included proposals for a phased settlement over three to five years and called for an unarmed Palestinian entity in the West Bank and Gaza, with East Jerusalem as its administrative capital. The entity would possess tangible and important characteristics such as a flag and a national anthem. There would be a confederate relationship with Jordan. During the interim period Israel would redeploy its forces outside Arab populated areas but would maintain control over strategic points, to be determined, along the River Jordan. There were three conditions for the initiation of negotiations. The first was mutual cessation of violence, the second a freeze on construction of Jewish settlements and the third a mutual recognition between Israel and the PLO. It was intended that the working paper would be presented to Arafat in Geneva. However, Husseini was arrested for eight days, and Amirav did not travel to Geneva because, he claimed, he had not received the green light from Shamir.

When these meetings became public knowledge Shamir admitted during an Israeli Cabinet meeting that he had known of the one that had taken place at Amirav's home but denied knowledge of the rest. But Amirav said that he had reported to Shamir on his meeting with Nusseiba, that he had received Amirav's paper and that therefore Shamir was fully in the picture. Ish-Shalom said that on 16 August 1987 Amirav had asked him to sign an undertaking that stated: 'Publication of statements or activities of the Prime Minister, his senior assistants and even Knesset members regarding contacts with the Palestinian national movement requires the advance written approval of Amirav.' This meant in effect that the Prime Minister and his assistants had been party to this initiative.

In an interview with *Haolam Hazeh* magazine on 6 October 1987 Sari Nusseiba said:

> David Ish-Shalom came to me and said he had friends in Likud who were interested in contacting the PLO, and that they were among those who had showed interest in the Israeli–Palestinian meetings in Bucharest and Budapest. At Amirav's home he mentioned the names of Dan Meridor and Ehud Olmert, the Knesset members, Dr Benyamin Zeiv Begin and Geola Cohen's son Hangby and others. Then he said he believed that the Palestinians were a people who had the same rights in Israel as the Jews, and that they had the right to self-determination, a state and the right to elect their own representatives; and if they believed the PLO to be their representative, so be it. However, he said that making these thoughts public would ruin him and asked that these meetings be kept secret. We did not bother to reveal the affair because revealing it would change nothing for us. The principles we spoke of are within the Palestinian position, but we respected his wishes and preserved the secrecy.[1]

When Ish-Shalom travelled to Geneva to ask Arafat if he was prepared to send a letter that included the items specified in the working paper,

---

[1] Translated from Arabic.

Arafat inquired whether he was a representative of the Israeli Government. When Ish-Shalom replied in the negative Arafat told him he was not a political amateur and was therefore not prepared to send letters to anyone. By doing this Arafat killed two birds with one stone. First, he did not send a letter and second, he indirectly informed the Israeli public that he agreed in principle and was prepared for the issues that had been discussed. But three hours after the working paper had been finalized, Faisal Husseini was arrested and, according to Israeli sources, Yitzhak Rabin ordered the brutal bombing of the Ain al-Hulwah refugee camp. Meanwhile, Amirav was supposed to travel to Geneva to meet Arafat.

Amirav's document which was published in *al-Shaab*, the Jerusalem Arabic daily, on 23 September 1987, contained the following principles:[1]

I. National rights including that of self-determination for both peoples in this country are undeniable.

II. The Palestine Liberation Organization is the sole legitimate representative of the Palestinian people and it alone has the rightful attributes to represent the Palestinian people at any negotiations with the Israeli Government. It affirms Israel's right to exist within secure and recognized borders.

III. Any attempt to achieve peace while excluding the Likud Party and the PLO are doomed to failure.

IV. The present circumstances do not admit of a resolution of the Palestinian–Israeli conflict.

We agree to the following:

1. Negotiations between the PLO and the Israeli government will be conducted in phases. A preliminary phase will lead to an interim agreement and the second phase will lead to a final peace accord.

2. The preliminary phase of negotiations may begin through another country to be agreed upon. The second phase of negotiations will begin one year after the implementation of the interim agreement. The negotiating parties will decide on the final format of the peace conference and the nature of the international guarantees required to consolidate the final peace accord. It is understood that the interim arrangement will last from three to five years.

3. It is understood that the interim arrangement will entail the establishment of a Palestinian entity in the territories occupied by Israel in

---

[1] Translated from Arabic.

June 1967. The administrative capital of the Palestinian entity will be located in the Arab part of Jerusalem. Palestinian residents of these territories will run their own affairs in a manner to be agreed upon during the first phase of negotiations. The legitimate rights of this Palestinian entity to natural resources and Israel's share in them shall be taken into account. The Palestinians will run their own affairs one year after the interim agreement is signed.

4. It is also understood that this entity will have the right to national symbols such as its own flag, national anthem, currency and an independent radio and television network. In addition, it will have the right to issue special identity cards and travel documents and other powers to be agreed upon at the negotiations, taking account of the fact that these powers do not prejudice the conditions of the desired peace between this entity and Israel.

5. A comprehensive agreement is to be reached regarding the establishment of this Palestinian entity, the status of Israeli settlements and settlers, the return of Palestinians, their rehousing, the sharing of resources, the economy, and commercial cooperation, etc., during the first phase of negotiations between Israel and the PLO.

In order to create an atmosphere conducive to the holding of negotiations the following is to be agreed:

(a) Israel will recognize the PLO as the legitimate representative of the Palestinian people and the PLO will simultaneously recognize the State of Israel.

(b) Both parties will declare their readiness to conduct direct bilateral negotiations in order to reach a settlement.

(c) Israel will officially declare a freeze on all settlement activities in the occupied territories and will cease all acts of violence against the Palestinian people and their property during the interim period. The PLO will announce a halt to all forms of violence against Israel, its people and property. It is understood that the final phase of negotiations will lead to the establishment of an independent Palestinian State.

Attempts with Sharon

Following the collapse of the Amirav–Nusseiba experiment we concluded that it had not been a total failure. When the details of this experiment became available to us, we found that Amirav had not attempted this move on his own initiative, but that he had had prior consultations with a number of Likud leaders, including Shamir's bureau chief, and that a number of Israeli Cabinet Ministers had also known of the talks. This meant that Likud was not averse to such initiatives in principle. Therefore we had to seek another way to resume the dialogue. We wanted this to happen with the cruellest and most hostile of Israelis, Ariel Sharon.

Sharon is a personality in search of a leadership role. His ambitions greatly outweigh his personal and political abilities, but he is an inspirational leader always looking for change, maybe to become Prime Minister one day. In the early 1970s he was a member of the Herut movement which itself was composed of small movements that formed the Gahal grouping. This grouping had participated in the coalition government formed in the wake of the 1967 war. Later, he broke with Herut and formed an independent group, Shlomit Tziom, which won two seats in the elections, one of which he took for himself. Then he rejoined the Likud bloc in which he enjoyed a leading role. This bloc formed the Cabinet after the 1977 elections. He twice attracted recognition, once when he breached the Egyptian defences at Deversoir on the Suez Canal in 1973 and when he invaded Beirut in 1982. He assumed the Housing portfolio and strove to erect settlements and other housing developments in a haphazard way, to realize his Zionist dream of complete Jewish domination of the occupied territories.

Following the fall of Likud at the Knesset's thirteenth elections in December 1992 he was one of four candidates vying for party leadership along with Shamir, Arens, and Levy, and it appeared that after the withdrawal of Shamir and Arens, he would win. However, he was beaten by Binyamin Netanyahu which greatly frustrated him.

MD, whose name we shall not reveal for his own good, made preliminary contacts with an Israeli intelligence chief, who had assumed the codename Bony, for a meeting with Sharon. Bony spoke Arabic very well and had a Master's degree in political science. They met at the Sheraton Hotel in Tel Aviv on 30 March 1992, and the following conversation ensued which, of course, is not verbatim.

Bony: How do you know Abu Mazen, and since when have you known him?

MD: I have known him for a long time, we went to the same school.

Bony: Who supports him in the Central Committee?

MD: He represents the faction that supports dialogue with Israel. This includes most PLO members.

Bony: What does he want to talk to us about?

MD: You know that the negotiations have not progressed. He wants the dialogue to be directly with the PLO. Everything is negotiable.

Another meeting took place on 25 April 1992 with another member of Israeli intelligence, and, after that, Bony and MD met again, on 2 May 1992, at the same hotel:

MD: I am a Palestinian and therefore have an interest in a solution. Our success will give me credit and enhance my reputation with my people.
Bony: Do you meet Abu Mazen in Jordan?
MD: Yes, I do.
Bony: We, the five chiefs, have met and evaluated the results and presented them to the Cabinet. Please, understand that if we do not offer a quick response it does not mean 'no'. We have told the Cabinet that Arafat is aware of these meetings.

These meetings paved the way for the first contact with Sharon through MD, a West Bank Palestinian who has a brother living in Israel. That first contact took place on 6 June 1992, when we posed questions and received answers as follows:

Q: Are you ready to discuss the peace process?
A: Yes.
Q: Are you ready to meet with us?
A: Yes.
Q: What is the topic of discussion?
A: It is open.
Q: Where?
A: This can be agreed.

MD then met Sharon for the first time. Sharon was fuming because the news had leaked to the press. 'They want to blackmail me and destroy my political future,' he said. 'We might deputize Sally Moridor to meet you, but they have to understand that no meetings shall take place if America is not in the picture. They are wrong if they think otherwise.'[1]

---

[1] Quotation is not verbatim.

David Kimche's Attempt

David Kimche is a famous name in Mossad. He is an expert on Iranian affairs and is currently in charge of relations with the Islamic republics of the former Soviet Union. He is of Iranian descent, and his family emigrated to Palestine before the creation of the State of Israel. He worked on African–Israeli relations, headed the Israeli delegation's refugee committee at the multilateral negotiations in Ottawa and played an important role in the Jewish immigration to Palestine. With his brother, Jon, he wrote a book about the illegal immigration to Palestine entitled *Secret Trails*. The brothers are the publishers of the *Jewish Chronicle* newspaper. At the time of the Camp David agreement he was Director-General of the Israeli Foreign Ministry and later became roving ambassador.

David Kimche is a member of Likud. The contacts that we made with Likud made no progress, because they were revealed at too early a stage. This was so because members of Likud were generally averse to contacts with the PLO, or because contact with one person to the exclusion of another invariably created bad feeling. The mere fact that these contacts did take place at all made us study Likud thinking to find out what made some people in Likud ready to sustain such contacts. The disposition of some conflicts starkly with Likud's known extremism.

I do not accept that all Jews share the same political ideas. Even Zionists are not alike in thought or in behaviour. This diversity also applies to parties in Israel. Not every member of a right-wing party is an extremist, nor is every member of a left-wing party a moderate. Likud embraced Ezer Weizman and Menachem Begin while they had different political outlooks (though it must be admitted that at one point they had to part company). There are many such cases in every party, and such differences do not necessarily imply a split. For many reasons, such individuals can coexist in one party; for example, Moshe Sharett and David Ben-Gurion, Abba Eban and Golda Meir of Labour. Personal circumstances and age also have a bearing on ideas and the ability to change them. Moshe Dayan who was implicated in the Lavon scandal in the 1950s was not the Dayan of the 1970s who sought peace and who resigned as Foreign Minister because of differences with Begin over ways of achieving peace with Egypt.

We often hear of different wings within the same party. Within Labour the group of seventeen 'doves' in the Knesset faced a similar number of 'hawks', the first headed by Shimon Peres, the second by Yitzhak Rabin. We often felt that in the coalition governments, Yitzhak Rabin's extremist positions were closer to those of Yitzhak Shamir than to those of Peres. And then came the day in 1993 when Rabin shook Arafat's hand on the White House lawn. There was also much talk within Likud of a moderate wing facing an extremist wing (led by the elderly). So lumping all individuals of a party or a group in one category is wrong. The biggest mistake of all is to make generalizations about Jews. If we cast our minds back to the beginnings of the Zionist movement, we find that Ahad Haam[1] who created the Moses' Children movement and established cultural Zionist institutions was in fact opposed to Herzl. He wrote in his book *Act of Conspiracy:* 'They fume with anger at those who remind them of the existence of another people living in Palestine and have no intention of leaving it. Herzl believed Palestine had no people and, like him, I imagined it to be swamp land. But I see a people, a civilization, children and oranges. If we take it and evict them we will be committing a grave injustice.'[2]

In this context we recall that Edwin Samuel Montague, the only Jewish Cabinet Minister in Lloyd George's Government, fought a losing battle with the Prime Minister and the Foreign Secretary, Arthur Balfour, over the now famous Balfour Declaration of 1917. He believed that it would not solve the problems of the Jews but was intended to benefit the British Empire. He said that the Jews had become a toy in the hands of the great powers, that they used them to preserve their colonies and guarantee their lines of communications. In private, Lloyd George himself used to say that leaving the holy places in Palestine to France's whims would strike at the heart of Britain's influence in the Middle East. If there is a fundamental difference in outlook between Herzl and Ahad Haam, the first founders of the Zionist movement, there is an even greater difference between Jews and non-Jews in their perception of Zionist ideology, goals and motivations. This is clear from Montague's attitude. It follows that a simplistic stereotyping of people does not help solve conflicts such as the Arab–Israeli conflict. Only through careful analysis of the past, the present and the ideologies of the peoples involved as well as their institutions, can one hope to understand the events that unfold in our region.

In the 1920s Vladimir Jabotinsky broke from the World Zionist Organization to create the Revision of Zionist movement. This movement forms the intellectual, political and organizational foundation of the present Likud bloc, or more accurately the Herut movement, Likud's backbone. His views diverged widely from Herzl's since he did not deny the existence of the Palestinian people in the land of Palestine, did not deny their rights within it and did not ignore their clinging to it as

[1] Known as Ashar Ginsberg, born 1886.
[2] Translated from the Arabic edition published by al-Fata al-Arabi, 1991, p. 52.

a homeland, even though he attempted to devise a formula that made Palestine a land for two peoples:

> First: the expulsion of the Arabs from Palestine is absolutely impossible in any form. There will always be *two* peoples in Palestine. Second: I am proud to have been a member of that group which formulated the Helsingfors [Helsinki] Program. We formulated it, not only for Jews, but for all peoples, and its basis is the equality of all nations. I am prepared to swear, for us and for our descendants, that we will never destroy this equality and we will never attempt to expel or oppress the Arabs . . . Compromisers in our midst attempt to convince us that the Arabs are some kind of fools who can be tricked by a softened formulation of our goals, or a tribe of money grubbers who will abandon their birth right to Palestine for cultural and economic gains. I flatly reject this assessment of the Palestine Arabs . . . Palestine would still remain for the Palestinians not a borderland, but their birthplace, the centre and basis of their own national existence.[1]

I am not setting out here the positive aspects of the thoughts and attitudes of some Zionist leaders, or to attribute merit to them. I am simply recording the facts as they are, so that we can deal with matters as they are. The Israelis know that Palestine was never a land without people. They also know that when they created their state they inflicted injustice on this people, harmed them and even tried to destroy them. The Jewish American peace campaigner, Hilda Silverman, says that in order for the Jews or Israelis to express solidarity with the Palestinians they must revise all the actions they took against them in the past and admit their part in the tragedy that has befallen them. She adds that insistence on the part of the majority of Israelis that what they did was right makes them persist in their extremism against Palestinians.

And so it was and so it still is for many Israelis, who totally ignore the victims, persist in negating their existence and refuse to revise their attitude for this would strike at the heart of Zionist thought, whether at the humanistic, intellectual, historical or even religious level. The foundation of this thought is the concept of 'Goyim' which is affixed to non-Jews including us, Palestinians. So when the Israelis recognize the 'Goyim', i.e. the Palestinian people, this will signal the beginning of change. Change is not restricted to a group, party or social or political section of society because it is a humanistic process that demands

---

[1] Vladimir Jatotinsky 'The Iron Wall (We and the Arabs)', *Rassuyet* (4 November 1923), quoted in Lenni Brenner, *The Iron Wall: Zionist Revisionism from Jabotinsky to Shamir* (London, Zed Books Ltd, 1984) pp. 73–4.

recognition of reality. It arises from reading, seeing and experiencing, or else from the daily clash with reality. This is what actually happened and may explain the contradictions which exist within the Israeli home, party, city, village and settlement.

This brings us back to the beginning of the tale, to Likud's David Kimche, the 'difficult-missions-man' who telephoned the British journalist, Alan Hart, and presented him with the broad outline for a scenario of secret coordination between Shamir and Arens, on the one hand, and Arafat on the other. Hart was uncertain of Kimche's intentions and words because he could not imagine a peace initiative to come from Likud. He expressed his doubts about what he had heard, but could not let such an opportunity to slip by, no matter how faint the hope. Jean-Claude Immetts shared his view and encouraged him to follow up the matter. So Alan Hart wrote a letter to Yasser Arafat saying that David Kimche had presented him with a broad outline of a scenario where a secret line of communication between Shamir, Arens and Arafat would be established with him (Hart) serving as the channel. He added that he did not claim to know Kimche's real intentions at this stage but that it seemed to him that there were are two possibilities; the first was that Kimche was playing a game of disinformation, the second was that he was serious. Alan Hart then mentioned that a common and neutral friend, Jean-Claude Immetts, shared his view and that the matter deserved testing Kimche's seriousness by asking him to arrange a special session between him and Arens. He asked Arafat for his view on this suggestion and said that he would await his summons to discuss this and other matters, including his first attempt to implement Hani al-Hasan's[1] idea (that of creating an independent working group consisting of prominent individuals representing all parties). He proposed that this group be called the Committee (or Institution) for Peace and Development in the Middle East and added that when they met, they should discuss the choice of candidates for membership of the Executive Committee of the Institution, Arabs, Jews, Europeans, Americans and so forth.

Other Attempts

In early December 1992 we made contact with Israeli groups associated with Likud and close to Sharon to see if we could open an informal channel for the stalled Washington negotiations. They welcomed the idea and a meeting took place in one of the European capitals, but we did not

---

[1] Hani al-Hasan is a member of the Central Committee of Fatah.

agree on a number of details which would require more than one meeting to work out. Eventually we decided that the venue would be the Palestinian Ambassador's residence in Rome. Meanwhile, the Oslo channel was starting up its initial activities. In spite of its unofficial and humble beginnings, at least on the Israeli side, we depended on it since to us it was a glimmer of hope that was not to be squandered.

When the messenger, whom I will call QD, returned to Tunis to get my opinion and decide on a date for the meeting in Rome the details of which had been fully agreed, he was surprised to find that I was against the meeting. I could not put a stop to it, however, without giving him convincing reasons, since he had visited Israel four times over the past months to arrange it. When he questioned me, I could not tell him the truth because of our determination to keep the Oslo channel secret. What I said was, 'Tell them I cannot meet them because of the reason they know.' 'What sort of a riddle is this that I'm supposed to convey?' he retorted. 'They will know exactly what I mean and will understand,' I replied.

I did not give this answer lightly. If they were senior state security officials, they would definitely be aware of a secret channel between us and their government, and if they were not privy to such secrets, there was no point them knowing about it because they might turn out to be supporters of the opposition who would expose it.

Our knowledge of the organizational and political situation in Israel made us wary of contacting and discussing everything with any Israeli, even if he was a senior state official, a Knesset member or even a cabinet minister. The conflict was not only between those who opposed peace and those who wanted it. The opposition was represented in all state organizations, not only among the coalition allies but also among Labour Party members. A notable example of this split was the attitude of Rabin and Peres. Each had his own vision, calculation and understanding of all the dimensions of the issues relating to a political settlement, and his own views about bilateral or multilateral negotiations. We knew that Rabin controlled the dossier on the bilateral negotiations, and that he did not permit any minister, deputy or official, apart from his most trusted colleagues, to have access to it.

Although I knew that all branches of the security apparatus were directly and personally linked to the Prime Minister, I did not give anything away because I believed that they might have other links and loyalties outside the framework of our venture in Oslo. Moreover, as we shall see later, the Oslo channel was opened, through an 'academic' who was associated with Yossi Beilin, the Deputy Foreign Minister who is very close to Peres. This might have meant that Rabin had not been aware of it yet, but even if he had, he may not have entirely approved of it. A situation like this could prompt Israeli intelligence to disrupt it (on the orders of Rabin) while encouraging the impression that the Palestinians could not keep a secret. This is why I spoke in riddles to QD, the messenger. I then awaited the reaction from Israel. If they knew of the Oslo channel, they would understand my message and remain silent. If they did not, then there would be no point in a meeting with them for the reasons just mentioned, but also because they could not be decision makers.

I waited for over a month. Finally, the messenger, QD, returned and quoted them as saying, 'We understand that the reason for his refusal to meet us is that he is angry at the deportation of four hundred Palestinians to Marj al-Zouhoor.' This answer confirmed my conclusion that the other side knew nothing of the Oslo channel and that there was therefore no point carrying on a dialogue with them. Courteously, I conveyed the message that the time was inopportune for meetings, but that we would remain in touch until the right moment arrived. Confirming our desire for peace, I said that we looked forward to further flexibility and under-standing on their part. I also conveyed the message that the Israeli side should not think that the hard time the Palestinian people were at present experiencing in the occupied territories would make them accept anything less than the minimum requirement for a settlement, since they were capable of great patience and endurance.

I did not meet QD again until June 1993 when he amazed me with these words:

> They are very reproachful; you say you know the Israelis well and have written many books about them, but you are mistaken. Don't you know that Rabin rules Israel? Don't you realize that the other ministers, including Foreign Minister Peres, carry no weight? They ask how you could make the mistake of opening up a channel with minor foreign ministry staff while abandoning the sources of decision and authority? They are waiting for you to agree to go through with the Rome meeting as soon as possible so that all the issues related to our common interests can be discussed.

After hearing this message I had no choice but to acknowledge that they had discovered the truth and that it could not be hidden anymore, so I said:

> It's true that we are meeting with some foreign ministry officials to exchange views. This has not reached the level of negotiations. I would like to say, however, that we regard the people we are meeting as representatives of the

official and legitimate establishment, and that any sensibilities that this may have aroused with the senior officials is an internal matter which they themselves must settle; that is their business, not ours. We agreed to meet and to open an official dialogue with them, and as long as the situation stands, we cannot ignore them and deal with another side that claims to be more influential. We respect our own credibility, even with our enemies, and will therefore not play upon internal differences. If we fail to achieve results with them, and the dialogue is officially suspended, we can then talk with this side and begin negotiations if possible. Let us wait and see. We are not in a hurry. We will not anticipate events, nor will we condemn our present talks as a failure before we have actually failed.

After QD had delivered this response to the Israeli side, the two of us did not meet again. Even though he saw them more than once, I was too busy to meet him to know their reaction until the Oslo mission had been accomplished and the Declaration of Principles had been signed in September 1993.

Oddly enough, at the same time that these contacts were taking place, and while Dr Usama al-Baz, President Mubarak's adviser on political affairs, was on a visit to Israel he suggested to a senior Israeli intelligence official that he should have a meeting with either myself or with the Palestinian Ambassador to Egypt, Saeed Kamal. The Israeli's initial reaction indicated a lack of interest though the idea was not actually rejected out of hand. When Dr al-Baz told me about this, I merely listened without commenting, since the Israeli noncommittal response did not invite comment.

Two weeks later I met Dr al-Baz who informed me that the official had now agreed to meet me in Cairo at a time to be agreed. I could only give one answer, 'yes' or 'no'. I had no reason to decline meeting him because we used to ask him on every occasion to help establish an unofficial channel between us and Israeli officials. So I said to Dr al-Baz, 'Please, don't forget that we are currently negotiating secretly with the Israelis in Oslo and you know about that. Although the level of Israeli negotiators may not reflect the Israeli Government's seriousness, and although they may represent only one faction in the Government, it is inappropriate for us to outflank them by opening other channels. I am also afraid that they are trying through these attempts to test our credibility and seriousness at Oslo. Don't you agree that it would be better to wait for the results of the Oslo channel?'

Dr al-Baz, who is an intelligent man and an able politician, agreed and said, 'It is better to wait. I will make the appropriate excuses for postponing this request to an unspecified date.'

5

Indirect Contacts with Labour

The Labour Party in Israel had been out of power since 1977 when Likud defeated it, divided it and managed to attract one of its stars, retired general, Yigal Yadin. The general succeeded in winning 17 seats through Labour's supporters and subsequently formed an alliance with Likud to become Deputy Prime Minister in a coalition government. However, his star faded fast, and he died a few years later, causing his grouping to scatter. Likud continued to benefit from this breach in Labour's bastion which remained in the doldrums for fifteen years in spite of its improved stature on the ground. This improvement in Labour's fortunes enabled it to share power with Likud after two elections. In the twelfth round Labour overtook Likud by one seat in the Knesset, giving it the first chance in years to form a government. Shimon Peres, the then Leader of the Labour Party, was invited to form the government by the President. He began consultations with various parliamentary groups and managed to secure 61 out of the Knesset's 120 votes in preparation for the vote of confidence which Peres was certain to win and so become Prime Minister. However, I knew from a trusted source, a deputy who was a member of Agudat Yisrael, that this would not happen.

Meanwhile, I was in Cairo for a meeting with the Egyptian Foreign Minister, Dr Ismat Abdel-Mageed. We discussed the formation of Peres's cabinet and I could see that the Foreign Minister was pleased with this development because Labour's assumption of power would greatly increase the chances of peace talks being started. I then surprised Dr Abdel-Mageed by saying, 'Peres will not be able to form a government because his calculations are inaccurate. He believes he will get 61 votes but I am certain he will not.' With the utmost speed Dr Abdel-Mageed telephoned Shimon Peres to inform him of this. Peres found this strange and seemed very self-confident. But he quickly asked the Egyptian Foreign Minister for any further information that might be available. I had nothing else to add and reconfirmed my information, suggesting that Peres should seek out the truth himself since I did not want to disclose my confidential sources. When Abdel-Mageed passed this on to Peres, Peres replied that he had investigated the matter thoroughly and had found nothing. Dr Abdel-Mageed told me this, but I remained silent.

When the vote of confidence took place, this Knesset deputy declined to support Peres on the instructions of Rabbi Abraham Verdiger who lives in America. This is how Yitzhak Shamir was subsequently able to form a government. The Israeli cabinet was formed on more than one occasion by either of the major parties. Each of the Likud and Labour leaders assumed the premiership for half the Knesset's four-year term. Some people believed such cooperation between the two parties would lead to a reasonable Israeli government policy, but their only achievement was to marginalize the position of the Opposition. The balance between the two caused total paralysis; when one party decided upon a certain policy the other would oppose it and stop it in its tracks.

Darawsha's Efforts

At the beginning of his political career Abdel-Wahab al-Darawsha was a Labour Party member. He was nominated on more than one occasion and succeeded in becoming a deputy in the Knesset under Labour's banner. However, he decided to leave Labour after the eleventh session of the Knesset to form an Arab party from among the Arab circles, which he called the Arab Democratic Party. His predecessors in the Arab circles, like the members of the Israeli Communist Party, which had represented Arabs for a long time, and the Progressive List, headed by the attorney Muhammad Miari, which included an Arab majority and a Jewish minority, fought him tooth and nail because he was competing with them for the Arab vote. However, he succeeded in establishing his presence and, as he was at the head of his roster, he gained a seat in the Knesset. In the Knesset's thirteenth session he won two seats, one for himself and the other going to the lawyer, Talab al-Sane, who provided the quorum necessary for the formation of Rabin's present Cabinet.

Because of the good relations with both Labour and the PLO – which began to develop after his Arab Democratic Party came into being – Darawsha wanted to mediate between the two at a time when Labour was in partnership with Likud in the Cabinet. Protected by his parliamentary immunity, he visited us in Tunis on more than one occasion. He also informed Rabin and other Israeli officials of his travel plans to further ensure that he would not be prosecuted.

On 12 April 1989 Darawsha arrived in Tunis bearing a political plan consisting of many parts and sections. This he informed us was Rabin's brainchild and after presenting it to us he gave us a general analysis and evaluation of Rabin's position and that of Labour generally.

Here we may note that Rabin's 1989 plan was not much different in its conception from what we eventually attained in Oslo in 1993, nor did it differ greatly from the main items in the American letter of assurance. This indicates that Labour had been preparing itself for a long time for the stage, reached at Oslo, and that there had been full coordination of ideas and formulas between it and the Americans. Yitzhak Rabin's plan included the following principles:

I   *The transitional period*

This will last for five years during which the following steps will be taken:
1. The Palestinians will establish a local authority which will handle internal matters such as housing, agriculture, post, finance, health and municipalities.
2. During the transitional period foreign affairs, security and the Jewish settlements will remain in Israel's hands.
3. There will be economic cooperation between the Palestinian entity, Israel and Jordan in various spheres like electricity, water, currency and labour.
4. There will be economic arrangements that will guarantee the interests of the Palestinian and Israeli sides.

II   *The permanent solution stage*

1. Three years after the start of the transitional period, negotiations for the permanent status of the Palestinian territory will begin.
2. During the first three years there will be understanding and trust between the two sides and a lessening of tension in the area.
3. Negotiations will be conducted on the basis of the following two conditions:
   (a) acceptance of United Nations Resolutions 242 and 338 and of the principle of the exchange of land for peace;
   (b) that the representatives of the Palestinian side in the negotiations be residents of the territories as well as Palestinians resident abroad, this to be agreed upon.

III   *The steps required to break the impasse*

1. In the event of an agreement between the two sides over this

comprehensive plan and the subsequent calm that is expected to prevail, elections will be held in the West Bank and the Gaza Strip not later than six months after the entry into force of this agreement.

2. The purpose of the elections is to elect political representatives and not local authority representatives.

3. The Israeli side is prepared to accept suggestions by the Palestinian side on the mode of the elections and electoral lists whether individual, by block or unified, this to be agreed upon by the Palestinians themselves.

4. The results of the elections will determine the local leadership for the transitional period.

IV *Mode and conditions of elections*

1. Elections are to be completely democratic, with the Israeli side stressing this.

2. Acceptance of international supervision of the elections, with preference given to American supervision alone, through a Congress decision. Europeans may participate but the participation of observers from Third World countries is rejected (because they do not practise democracy).

3. Suggestions about the mode of elections are welcome by the Israeli side.

4. Residents of East Jerusalem have the right to candidacy and elections. Voting, however, is to take place in Ramallah or Bethlehem.

5. After a permanent settlement has been reached, residents of East Jerusalem will have the right to opt for either Palestinian or Israeli citizenship.

6. The basic principles governing the system, mode and conditions of elections will be determined through negotiations between the two sides.

7. The Israeli side is willing to withdraw its forces from populated areas during the preparatory stage of the elections.

V *The framework for negotiations*

1. Negotiations are to take place within the framework of an international conference. The Israeli side prefers a reduced conference with the participation of the United States, the Soviet Union, an Israeli delegation, a Jordanian delegation and a Palestinian delegation.

2. However, an enlarged international conference is acceptable in principle.
3. Jordan is not a substitute for the Palestinians.
4. The Palestinian delegation will participate in the conference as an independent representative of the Palestinians.
5. The proposed plan is a comprehensive one, and the interim arrangements are an integral part of it.

Darawsha had presented Rabin with a number of demands designed to energize the peace process by improving the atmosphere; to this Rabin agreed but without linking his consent to a political plan. Rather, it was a token of goodwill in preparation for the launching of a mutual debate on the plan.

It was obvious that Rabin had considered and was prepared during his session with Darawsha for what he called the 'harbingers of openness': these included: the immediate opening of schools and universities and the release of a number of prisoners before the *Id-al-Fitr* feast and permission for free travel abroad for some of them. He also promised to respond to the wider issues immediately after his meeting with the military leadership and civil administration in the West Bank. Pointing out that he had already begun implementing a policy of normalization, he also promised that he would agree to the reopening of national institutions, to allow freedom of movement and political action and indicated his readiness to arrive at an agreement regarding the withdrawal of the army from residential areas and centres of population, in addition to easing the suffering of people (which was the result of increasingly oppressive policies).

On 17 March 1990 Abdel-Wahab al-Darawsha arrived in Tunis bearing one specific question on confederation and the extent of the PLO's commitment to it. It was a written question to which the Israelis requested a written answer. We provided the following written answer, which we read shortly afterwards in the Israeli press:

The Palestinian National Councils have since 1983 (the sixteenth session), the last of which met in Algiers in 1988, adopted the issue of confederation between Jordan and Palestine. The two sides began holding serious discussions a while ago to examine the extent of such a confederation, its legal boundaries and other issues. There is a great degree of interest on both sides about this issue because it is vital for the Jordanian and Palestinian peoples. This is the one and only choice and position of the PLO.

Kanaan's Efforts

In the period between the beginning of the thirteenth election campaign for the Knesset and Labour's success in the formation of the Israeli government, contacts were made by Saeed Kanaan, a prominent member of the Fatah movement in the occupied territories who had been jailed more than once and who had links with a member of the Knesset close to Rabin. These were followed by contacts through Amr Moussa, the Egyptian Foreign Minister, who conveyed a number of points which he had discussed with Yitzhak Rabin and Shimon Peres following their party's election victory.

Although these contacts did not produce immediate results, they contributed greatly to the mutual clarification of each side's viewpoints. These contacts may be considered preparatory steps for the Oslo negotiations. We were careful to maintain complete secrecy of these contacts so as not to embarrass the Israeli side which was mounting a crucial election campaign at the time. If news of these contacts had leaked to the media – Arab, Western or Israeli – it would have caused Labour to lose many of the seats it was seeking to form a government. Israeli parties watch each other's every move and hunt for any mistakes which they would magnify and use to hurt each other's prospects. Similarly, many journalists are expert at handling scandals. They wait for a scandal to break to influence public opinion. This was how Rabin's first cabinet collapsed in 1974 when he failed to declare a sum of money held in his name at an American bank while serving as Ambassador to the US. As though the fall of his Government was not enough, he also lost the 1975 Labour Party elections to his competitor Shimon Peres.

Here I will note in passing that Didi Tsoker, the RATS Party member and current Meretz Party deputy, visited us in Tunis in 1987. It was a secret and undeclared visit. He asked us not to mention it at all for reasons pertaining both to him and to his party which could not withstand any jolts. We have kept it secret until today. There were also subsequent meetings with him in different places in Europe. Both the PLO and RATS intended to convene an official public meeting but we could not agree on an appropriate outcome of the meeting. We therefore kept all contacts secret and refused to discuss them out of respect for the other side's wishes.

Most of what led to the achievement in September 1993 cannot be kept secret, but we felt that for our part we had to maintain secrecy. In political terms, secrecy implied mutual recognition, and was maintained in order to achieve tangible results that can then be made public. In effect, the Palestinian–Israeli contacts at the decision-making level implied mutual recognition. It is our duty now to clear away the haze shrouding this achievement. Furthermore, many people who contributed to this event in one way or another are entitled to receive credit for their efforts and good offices. What was considered a crime in Israel punishable by law (contact with the PLO) is today a heroic act that paved the way for the historic breakthrough.

On 10 April 1992 in Israel Saeed Kanaan met a prominent Israeli Labour Party figure (who is close to Yitzhak Rabin and who now occupies an important position), and passed on a three-point message from the Palestinian leadership:

1. We are pleased with your electoral programme.
2. What do you ask of us so that we can offer it? We are prepared to conclude an agreement.
3. We would like meetings to be arranged at the level of Y.R. or whoever he appoints.

The response came in the form of a sheet of paper written in Hebrew which this prominent Israeli dictated to Kanaan in Israel. When he had finished dictating a paragraph he would reread it to be sure of every word. Before he finished dictating all the reply, Yitzhak Rabin came in for a few minutes to give the impression that the Israelis were serious. He said:

1. We are serious.
2. There must be no leakage whatsoever of these contacts.
3. I am prepared to discuss any other letters.
4. Watch every word you utter. We are following all your statements. A real effort must be made to control each person's statements.

When Rabin left, this prominent figure resumed the message, making the following comments:

1. We are serious and mean what we say. We understand that this is real business.
2. We presume that Yasser Arafat knows about everything and that he is behind this contact.
3. We will not hold any meetings abroad before the elections.
4. We understand that only four of you know about these contacts, yourself, Yasser Arafat, Mahmoud Abbas and Saeed Kamal. Two people are aware of them and are following them up on our side: Yitzhak Rabin and this prominent Israeli figure.
5. We shall not permit the opening of any other channel and we trust you, Saeed Kanaan.

6. If any of these meetings are leaked we will deny them and we will hold you responsible for aborting these contacts.

7. We have only just now begun serious work. We hope the contacts will continue in complete secrecy. We are completely open and aware of the importance of what is happening.

8. We hope and assume that you are serious and dealing with us in a manner compatible with the issue's historical and fateful importance.

This prominent Israeli said he would leave on 20 April and return a week later and that he would await the response either before 20 April or at the end of the month. Here is the text of the letter from the Israeli side that includes answers to the points we had previously raised with them.

1. Please avoid any expressions of sympathy or support for us or the coalition of the left (Mapam, RATS, Shinui, etc.).

2. We are satisfied with al-Darawsha and Miari's forming of a unified list. If they do not unite they shall not achieve more than 1.5 per cent and their votes will go to Likud. Furthermore, we consider an agreement between them and Rakah over surplus votes as positive.

3. Generally speaking we are in favour of encouraging people to vote. You are in a position that allows you to encourage people to vote. Also, Islamists should be encouraged to vote because, in the final analysis, they will not vote in favour of the left, Likud or the Zionist parties. We do not mind you sending a clear, unequivocal message banning votes for any party that encourages the building of settlements. Likud is currently spending huge amounts of money, and David Magen is giving money for the building of mosques and academic scholarships. He is also giving cash to Arabs, bedouins and even the Christians.

4. You should not derail the Washington peace talks. At the same time you should not portray these talks as a resounding victory for Shamir. We also believe you should not go to Washington with issues that will provoke the Israeli people. There are two such issues:
(a) The issue of Jerusalem.
(b) The final status.
Bring with you to the negotiating table constructive and practical suggestions on:
(a) Autonomy (self-government authority).
(b) Political elections.

The two subjects are specified in the Camp David accords. Likud cannot offer a positive response in this respect, Israeli public opinion can be provoked to oppose Shamir.

If you raise the issues of Jerusalem and of the final status of a Palestine State you will do Likud a great service because it can then claim that there is no common ground for negotiation.

Finally, I would like to point out that raising the issue of halting the construction of settlements will in turn give rise to the issue of ending the Arab economic boycott of Israel.

On 20 April 1992 Saeed Kanaan conveyed our response, consisting of specific points, to the Labour Party leadership represented by this prominent Israeli figure. It included the following points:

1. Yasser Arafat is aware of all of these contacts and supports them.
2. We read your letter carefully and agree to its content. We shall endeavour to implement all the points regarding the elections.
3. We are proceeding with the political process with utter seriousness.
4. We feel that we are committed to the contents of the American letter of assurances which we know you are aware of. We hope your position is the same.
5. We understand perfectly that making a distinction between settlements for security and settlements for political purposes is a matter of electoral propaganda that there is no difference between the two.
6. We have read your statements about confederation with Jordan or with Israel and have considered them with complete seriousness. If you have other political or intellectual views on this subject, we hope you will inform us of them after the elections.
7. We have also fully understood what you said about your readiness to have a dialogue with the Palestinians and for establishing self-rule for a period of between six to nine months, and we consider this to be a serious and responsible political statement.
8. How do you see the situation between Shamir and Levy? And how far will it go?

Later on Saeed Kanaan conveyed the following remarks from this prominent Israeli figure at Rabin's request:

1. Great anger at reports in the French magazine about secret contacts between Rabin and Arafat via Saeed Kanaan.
2. We told you repeatedly that any leakage of these contacts would lead to their suspension.
3. The source of the leak is Tunis, so what is the meaning of this leak if not to derail the peace process?
4. Furthermore it proves that you are totally unconcerned about peace and are not serious.

5. Our experience with you regarding leakages is a bad one. You cannot keep secrets. Anyway, we shall turn a new leaf this time, but you have to understand it is the last time that we will allow leaks about our contacts.

6. We understood the issue of the 'Kitchen'. For our part, we do not mind, if you are serious, and suggest three of you and two of us; myself and Rabin.

7. Contact will only be made through Saeed Kanaan. Let us understand your view of the working mechanism and the 'Kitchen' contact. What are the powers of the delegation other than implementing what we will agree?

8. We will suspend all contacts through the London and Paris groups.

9. We will talk now on the transitional phase only. Let us finish it first and then talk about the final phase.

10. What are the confidence-building measures you suggest for the transitional period?

11. We are more than serious and you will discover that by yourselves. We mean to work quickly and hope you will respond in kind.

12. Please understand we are hostages to the Israeli voter, who has given us a chance that will never be repeated to implement [Palestinian] self-rule. This chance must be allowed to bear fruit or it shall never be given to anyone again. Understand that well and act on that basis.

13. The Jordanian option is dead and buried.

14. We are determined to negotiate with you about all that concerns the Palestinian issue. As for the joint delegation its concern is with Jordan and common issues.

15. The confederation we are talking about is that between you and Jordan. As for a confederation with Israel, this was a passing comment on Haidar Abdul-Shafi's statement. We attach no importance to this comment and we do not ask for such a confederation.

16. The issue of the settlements is a thorny one, and the matter will crystallize after Rabin's visit to America.

Here is the gist of the letter from us that included answers to the above questions:[1]

Now that the election results have come out, we wish to inform you that we felt anxious about Shamir returning to power which would have spelt the end of the chances for peace. We were therefore looking

[1] Translated from Arabic.

forward to Rabin's victory after having carefully reviewed the Labour Party programme, the substance of its conference debate, and Rabin's statements during the election campaign.

Although we did not succeed in uniting the Arab lists, we can say that the efforts exerted led, or contributed, to the final election result, the result that ended all of Shamir's hopes or chances of retaining power.

This prompts us to convey to Rabin our satisfaction at his success. We had hoped to say this in public. Thus in as much as he has a responsibility to the Israeli voter, he must have his responsibility to the Palestinian Arab citizens because he is a courageous enough Israeli leader to make peace. We therefore hope he will not disappoint both the Israeli voter and the Palestinian Arab citizen. If Mr Rabin wishes to measure the extent of our interest, he should know that we opened five operations rooms in different parts of the world to keep track of the details of the elections.

At this point we must refer to the publication in France of a report about the alleged meeting. We stress that it did not emanate from us. The way in which the report was published as well as its content shows that those responsible for it were Rabin's electoral adversaries who seemed to have made a guess from certain events in order to harm his electoral chances. They knew that . . . was in Cairo during Arafat's visit there and wrote the report in the light of this coincidence.

We totally agree to the reduction of the channels of contact and limiting them to whomever you feel at ease about. At the same time, we are eager for the 'Kitchen' to begin work at an opportune time for you although we imagine the sooner the better for all of us.

And as long as both of us desire a real and lasting peace, and as long as we have decided, without manoeuvre or deceit, to coexist we must begin building bridges of trust and confidence from now on and put aside all formalities, evasiveness and wile. Rabin's courage in presenting some positive ideas to achieve a solution during an election campaign, which was characterized by demagogy, bigotry and obstinacy, is surpassed only by the courage of the Palestinian leadership which succeeded in overcoming all obstacles on the Palestinian and Arab scene and declared openly and unequivocally its acceptance of international legitimacy. It also accepted the ideas put forth by President George Bush and the contents of the American letter of invitation and letter of assurances. It would be regrettable that such brave steps on both sides would be thwarted by adherence to principles that we both know are not conducive to the realization of security, stability and coexistence. Both of us once experienced coexistence in Andalusia with its ups and downs: there we lived together and were expelled together.

In regard to our view of the transitional period, this conforms with that defined in the letter of assurances: The peaceful and orderly transfer of power from the Israelis to the Palestinians to enable the Palestinians to control their political and economic decisions and the decisions that affect their future. Thus we shall request that Rabin makes this plain and, having been given a mandate by the Israeli voter – as he says – to implement self-rule for the Palestinians, that he proceeds to do so on the understanding that the transitional autonomy period will be an interim preparatory step leading to a final solution (his statements during his election campaign).

The demise of the Jordanian option in the Israeli mind is a healthy sign. To say that confederation with Jordan should be the 'ceiling' of the negotiations is proof that there is sound appreciation of the future of the region. We not only agree with this concept but allow us to promote it. Our question about a tripartite confederation that includes Israel is an indication of our real wish to strengthen the ties of coexistence and is a true expression of our desire for a genuine peace. The attainment of peace requires the will of all parties. It cannot be imposed. Perhaps the time will come when all parties will feel that their interest lies in peace and will then seek it.

We were disturbed by the announcement of Arens and Shamir that they intend to negotiate for ten years without achieving a result. Although we understood the intentions of the previous government we could not fathom such evil intentions: take the region to the abyss and risking the destiny of the people, including your own people, who, through the last elections, expressed views that were at odds with the position of that government. Thus, we are in complete agreement with you about the need for urgent and intensive action in the coming negotiations. You will find us completely responsive.

Our traditions and customs require us to respect our brave and intelligent enemies. Until this moment Rabin is classified as one of our enemies who are occupying our land and persecuting our people. Nevertheless, we consider him to be a capable military man and politician, who appreciates international changes and transformations and who possesses a comprehensive view of international strategy. He is therefore in a position to fully understand the meaning of security. If you, the Israelis, need it, and you have a right to it, then we, the Palestinians, need it too. In fact, our need for security by far surpasses your need and that is because of the huge difference between your capabilities and ours. Until the elements of trust are established between us the issue of security shall remain an obsession for both of us. What we cannot understand is how 'geography' can be confused with 'security' at the end of the twentieth century in the age of intercontinental missiles. Holding on to this idea for so long has increased the obsession with 'security' and this indicates to us that the true desire for peace remains distant.

This brings us to the issue of settlements to which Rabin referred in the elections. Though we appreciate that negotiations may mean bargaining for 'improvement of conditions', we cannot accept such electoral explanations from a strategist such as Rabin. When you say that you will freeze the settlements we welcome this as long as the moratorium applies to territories occupied in 1967 including Jerusalem. But you follow up this statement by saying that you will retain locations necessary for security especially in the transitional period. We view with much alarm the expression 'especially in the transitional period'.

We are in a state of war and as long as the occupation lasts we will fight the war with our own means. But we do not practise violence for its own sake but only to realize our legitimate rights which are established by international legality. We are a people like other people wanting to live a normal life. But to show you that it is with insight and discernment that we try to uphold our rights, we advocated self-restraint on the eve of the elections so that Shamir could not arm himself against you.

We understand your concern as regards security. But let us ask: is it not in your power to take measures that would make life easier for people and so remove friction? Furthermore, rapid progress in the negotiations will give people the impression that an end to their suffering is near. You must remember that our children who have been brandishing stones against your soldiers for five years now, understand the political significance of the olive branch they held up after Madrid. Is this not a political gesture directed at Israel's children, politicians and soldiers? What will become of the hope that shone after Madrid if our people realize that Shamir is trying to gain more time to build more settlements, commit further oppression and cause further displacement? How can our people believe that the government that is going to Rome is not the same one that went to Madrid and Washington? They cannot have confidence unless they see changes on the ground and unless their convictions change. It is in your hands. For our pact, we have given all we can. No matter how positive our information is about this prominent

Israeli figure, with whom we are negotiating, the issue hinges upon the instructions he will convey. If they are positive, then no doubt his personal merits will add strength to them.

Please allow us to comment on your statement that the road is long and difficult because of what you say about the political map in Israel. We understand the Israeli political map and know that extremism is to a great extent the result of competition to win over the man in the street to stay in power. This reminds us of Yitzhak Shamir's words on the eve of his election defeat, that the Israeli people had tired of the struggle for Greater Israel, that he had failed to convince the Israeli voter of his aims. We also recall what Moshe Arens said after his retirement from political life, that he had not struggled for Greater Israel and so on.

If we exclude the extremist Moledet and Tsomet parties, we understand the goals and demands of the religious parties, of which you are more aware. I hope we have understood the significance of the Israeli voters withholding confidence from Geola Cohen; they clearly voted for peace. Therefore we hope the issue of the 'Israeli political map' is not a pretext for delay. If one side has any reason to speak of the contradictions in its political map then that side should be us: on the Palestinian scene there is serious opposition to peace on ideological grounds and on the Arab scene there are supporters of these Palestinian factions who try to derail the peace process. All the same, when our legislative and executive institutions decided to pursue the blueprint for peace they did so in spite of all opposition.

Peace is indivisible. Israel has problems with both Syria and Lebanon on account of the Israeli occupation. The efforts for peace must be comprehensive and serious on all fronts. We understand that you want both of us to concentrate on arrangements for the interim period, but this should not detract from seeking solutions with the others.

We have conducted five rounds of negotiations, the last of which was in Washington. We share your view that we should begin in Rome where we left off in Washington DC. We have presented memoranda and other documents to the Israeli delegation with proposals on the transfer of authority, legislative elections, the issue of settlements and human rights, but the Israeli delegation has made no response. We have made sure that the texts of these memoranda and documents and memos are compatible with international law and practice as well as the American letter of assurance and the letter of invitation (which the Americans have confirmed do not contradict other letters they have presented to any other party, including the Israeli side). We have openly declared our adherence to the contents of these letters in full in spite of the reservations we had registered with the American Administration at the time. To retreat from that position would place us in a difficult situation with our people and we would lose our credibility. So we shall not do so. Thus the new Israeli negotiator will note that the proposals that we have presented are rational and realistic. You are therefore called upon to begin establishing confidence-building measures immediately and then to move straight away to the legislative elections and the agreement on the transfer of power.

To this letter was attached an appendix on confidence-building measures that included the following:

1. Release of all political prisoners.
2. Scrapping administrative detention and the emergency laws in effect since Mandatory times.
3. Shutting down the Ansar 3 and Nafha detention centres.
4. Lifting the ban and restrictions on political activity and affiliations.
5. Returning deportees to their homes in accordance with the Security Council resolutions.
6. Eliminating taxes imposed since 1967 (five kinds of taxes).
7. Putting an end to the confiscation of land and property and returning confiscated land and property to their rightful owners.
8. Facilitating the reunion of families.
9. Lifting restrictions on exports from the occupied territories and abstaining from obstructing development projects.
10. Cancelling restrictions on construction.
11. Cancelling the system of the green card and allowing free entry into Jerusalem.

The Egyptian Effort

On 9 October 1992 I met the Egyptian Foreign Minister, Amr Moussa, following his return from Israel. He said he had held separate meetings, first with Yitzhak Rabin then with Shimon Peres, and that a tripartite meeting then took place in Tel Aviv. Before he travelled to Israel we had presented him with a number of issues to raise with the Israelis, namely Resolutions to 242 and 338, multilaterals, elections, Jerusalem, the proposed 'Jerusalem Committee', the informal channel, Israeli settlements and security, confederation, the issue of Gaza, supervision, confidence building measures and timetables. The Foreign Minister had various comments about these issues to pass on to us and these are outlined below in no particular order:

1. *Reference to Resolutions 242 and 338*

Rabin said during the first meeting that Resolution 242 was not applicable to the interim period. When Moussa pressured him to make reference to it in one way or another Rabin stated he would discuss a general formula with his colleagues and inform him of it in the evening. In this connection, he said that if the Palestinians wanted to negotiate with him, then all issues should be dealt with at the negotiating table, but as he wished to honour President Husni Mubarak's positive role, he would come back to Moussa with a formula.

In the second session attended by the three men, Rabin offered the following formula: 'Negotiations on the final settlement of the Palestinian question which would start not later than the third year of the interim period will be based on the Resolutions 242 and 338.' Rabin added that he would either personally announce this formula or present it as an official document at the negotiating table.

2. *Jerusalem and the Palestinian Council (elections)*

Rabin drew Moussa's attention to the subject of Jerusalem. He said it was a highly sensitive issue which he could not at present discuss. Moussa responded with an idea involving a 'Jerusalem Committee' and that the elections take place in a mosque or church with this Committee having links with the elected body. Rabin commented by saying, 'I hope the Palestinians will negotiate seriously with me and not grasp at superficialities. I shall not discuss such issues before then. I find the Syrians more serious than the Palestinians.' He said that the members of the Palestinian delegation had their individual opinions and that all they were interested in was publicity. He added that he would not make a move if the attitude remained as it was, but would be prepared to help if the Palestinians were serious and committed.

With regard to his proposal on Jerusalem, the Egyptian Foreign Minister suggested the formation of two teams. The first team would discuss elections with the Palestinians offering their suggestions on Jerusalem. Rabin was prepared to accept the proposal on condition that the discussions are not conducted randomly or for propaganda purposes. 'Either they want to act or they do not,' he said, adding, 'I will lose nothing.' The second team would discuss the responsibilities of the Palestinian Council. At this point Rabin refused to discuss the subject and a heated discussion ensued. He then asked for time to think. After a while he proposed calling the Council the 'Executive Body'. Moussa however interjected with Egypt's suggestion that it be called the 'Executive Palestinian Council'. Rabin's response was: 'Let them present it at the negotiations without using this expression in the media.' After a long discussion about the number of members of the Council, Rabin said he had no objection to it being 27. But Moussa suggested double that number and for the door to remain open regarding this matter.

3. *The informal channel*

Rabin decided he could only accept Egypt as an informal channel for the Israelis and the Palestinians in case of complications as he could not be sure that there would not be leaks. Egypt's help would be sought whenever the need arose, especially for major issues.

4. *Multilaterals*

Rabin agreed that Palestinians from abroad could participate in the five committees according to the following guidelines:
(a) Members are not to be residents of Jerusalem.
(b) Members are not to be from the ranks of the PLO or its apparatus.
(c) The current members in two of the committees, Yusuf al-Sayegh[1] and Elie Sanbar,[2] may retain their membership in name only and would be permanently absent. (At this point, Peres said that there was another person.)

Rabin then said that everything he had said would be nullified if Arafat went through with what he had announced in Amman the previous day, namely the convening of both chambers of the Council. To this Moussa replied, 'The important thing is that Arafat does not implement what he announced. We will inform Israel of that.'

5. *The tripartite confederation*

When Moussa asked Rabin for clarification of statements made in regard to a tripartite confederation, Rabin replied, 'Yes, in principle I agree. Later on we can discuss details, whether it will be tripartite, Israel, Palestine and Jordan or bilateral, Jordan and Palestine.' Moussa concurred, saying, 'As you know, this is a good thing and must be examined with Jordan first.'

---

[1] Economic adviser to the PLO.

[2] Member of the PNC and Chairman of the Working Group on Refugees in the multilateral negotiations. He is also a Professor at the Sorbonne.

6. *Settlements and security*

When on a previous occasion we discussed with Amr Moussa Rabin's distinction between political settlements and security settlements (and we said that they were all expansionist settlements), we told Moussa that as long as Rabin was really concerned with security, then we were prepared to discuss the issue with an open mind because security was just as important to us as it was to Rabin. But why, we argued, should we discuss security from the perspective of common fear and not from the context of common interests? At the meeting between Moussa, Rabin and Peres in Tel Aviv, Moussa conveyed our attitude on this matter, to which Rabin said that he agreed in principle with this stance but that the issue should nevertheless be revised at the negotiating table. Moussa's comment to us was that the question of security could be discussed peripherally and implicitly within the framework of the official negotiations. 'If you have any proposals I am prepared to convey them,' he added.

7. *Timetables*

Rabin stated, 'If they are serious then we are ready to finalize the modalities by January 1993 and to hold elections in April or May 1993: then we would be prepared to agree on the list of Council members.'

8. *Supervision*

Rabin said that supervision as a whole depended on the permanent status negotiations. As for the interim arrangement, this would be decided by agreement between the Government of Israel and the elected Palestinian Council.

9. *Gaza*

Moussa did not bring up the issue of Israel's withdrawal from the Strip. But at a separate meeting between Peres and Moussa, the water crisis in Gaza was brought up. Peres said, 'The Palestinians bear the responsibility for the thirst in Gaza.' He called for the setting up of a desalinization plant in Gaza with the participation of Saudi Arabia, Europe and others. He expressed Israel's readiness to help and added that this water would be the property of the residents of the Gaza Strip and it was theirs to use. Any surplus, he added, they could sell, and Israel could buy.

10. *Confidence-building measures*

Rabin said he had taken many measures to demonstrate goodwill but had regrettably met with hostile reactions which had forced him to suspend the process for the time being.

At the end of our talk, Amr Moussa said that if one word of these discussions was leaked he would be forced to suspend such deliberations and would deny any statements attributed to him.

When Haseeb Sabbagh met Henry Sigman, the Executive Director of the American Jewish Congress, on 15 November 1992 Sigman delivered a verbal message to the PLO asking it to facilitate the Palestinian delegation's task and highlighted the important role American Jews could play in the peace process.

A few months after the initiation of the Oslo channel I noticed that many Israeli officials wanted to meet me specifying me by name. I found this rush rather strange and refused such proposals because of the possibility in my mind that Rabin's Government was testing us and our commitment to the Oslo channel, to see whether we might hedge our bets and contact more than one group or open more than one channel. This forced me to refuse to meet the Israeli Education Minister, Shulamit Aloni, who had tried to set more than one date and venue for a meeting. Mahmoud Darwish was the last to meet her in Rome on 13 July 1993. Basil Aql informed me that a prominent Knesset deputy, who was very close to Rabin, had expressed a desire to meet me. I asked him to meet Nabil Shaath which he did during the preparations for the tenth round of the bilateral negotiations in Washington. A short while later our Ambassador in Rome informed me that Yossi Sarid and deputy Didi Tsoker, both members of the Meretz movement, wanted to meet me in Rome. I apologized and told him to arrange for them to meet Nabil Shaath in Cairo instead, which was what happened. What alarmed me was that Sarid told Shaath that Rabin had informed him of the existence of a secret channel. When Shaath conveyed the minutes of the meeting and this piece of news to me, I told him Sarid knew nothing, that Rabin meant an Egyptian channel and that he was referring to the Egyptian Foreign Minister's visits to Israel. I added, 'These meetings do not amount to an official channel because Rabin has from the outset refused to open informal channels with us since he believes we leak news, do not keep secrets and have no credibility. Therefore don't pay any attention to such talk.'

Later on Basil Aql informed me that Henry Sigman wanted to meet me. He had already asked Aql what ideas we had for a settlement, and I had subsequently sent him a brief memorandum about them to which he had not responded. He was now asking for a public face-to-face meeting, if we so wished. I found it best that Nabil Shaath should meet him, and a meeting between the two actually took place in Cairo on 23 July 1993.

The Israelis who requested meetings with us used to support their requests with claims that they were close to Rabin. Others used to claim they were close to decision-making circles, as in the case of Yossi Sarid and Didi Tsoker. But we felt that Rabin had not asked anyone to contact us. Possibly the situation was reversed, that is they would suggest to Rabin that they would contact us, and he would not express any objections. There is, however, a big difference between the two situations, and I made sure that Nabil Shaath ascertained from them whether they had explicitly been asked to meet us or whether they themselves asked if they could. I also wanted to arrive at another truth: were the ideas that they were conveying to us ideas they had themselves presented to Rabin, or had Rabin asked them to convey these ideas? There is again a tremendous difference between the two situations because for someone to suggest to Rabin that they would travel to tell us something was not the same as Rabin calling someone in and asking them to deliver specific ideas or questions. We concluded that all these individuals had volunteered to come on their own initiative, bringing their own personal ideas, and that they were looking for a personal role, rather than Rabin or Peres actually delegating someone to discuss matters with us.

This strengthened my opposition to holding meetings outside the Oslo framework. My excuse was that the Washington negotiations were on track, and that we did not want to disrupt them or to disturb the negotiators in their task.

Ahmad al-Tibi's Efforts

On 25 July 1993 Ahmad al-Tibi arrived in Tunis. He is a Palestinian with Israeli citizenship from the town of al-Tiba, a politically astute man with a wide-ranging knowledge of goings-on in Israel. He had long-standing relations with a number of prominent Israelis, a man endowed with an active spirit, vitality and patriotism. The martyr Abu Iyad had described him in 1990 as a patriotic Palestinian and a seeker of peace. Tibi was on friendly terms with Ezer Weizman, Haim Ramon, the left-wing Labour Health Minister, and other members of Labour and Meretz. He also enjoyed friendly relations with a number of Palestinian leaders. He used to send verbal as well as written messages that were sometimes of a political and at other times of a humanitarian nature. He also played a part in attempts to arrange a meeting between Ezer Weizman and myself. It will be remembered that Weizman was once a Likud hawk, but during, or just before, the Camp David talks he began altering his position. The reason for the change is said to have been the extraordinary attention heaped upon him by the late President Anwar Sadat who used to call him 'My dear Ezer'. It is also said that there was a personal reason; his only son and heir had received a bullet wound in his head during the war of attrition, which had left him permanently disabled. The incident had greatly affected Weizman who began to realize in a powerful way that the continuation of war would hurt many other sons as it had done his. He therefore began to preach peace, left Likud for Labour, and then created an independent list before returning once again to Labour. Nor did he stop calling for peace.

But let us return to Dr Ahmad Tibi who contributed to our contacts with the Israelis. After several meetings with Haim Ramon, Rabin's closest cabinet colleague, Tibi arrived carrying several questions which required answers. Tibi's mission helped Arafat to no small degree. Whenever Arafat explained points which were discussed in the Oslo channel, but could not actually mention Oslo, he would confine himself to talking about Tibi's mission and would say that the whole issue began and ended with this mission. Eventually 'Tibi' became established as the codename of the Oslo channel.

Tibi told me that before coming to us he had met Health Minister Haim Ramon twice. He had recorded the minutes of these meetings, which he then presented to me. He also gave me a list of the questions which Ramon had jotted down himself after he had consulted Yitzhak Rabin.[1]

Protocol

Venue: Health Ministry – Director's Office
Date: 14 July 1993

Ramon: I know you are very close to Arafat.
Tibi: I'm meeting you after having obtained his approval. He is aware of this meeting.
Ramon: Rabin is not aware of it but, depending on the contents of our talks, I will inform him of it in detail.
Tibi: I'm authorized to hear your suggestions and convey them to the Chairman. I cannot make decisions nor give you immediate replies to political points, but I'll try to convince you and Yitzhak Rabin of the inevitability of negotiating seriously with Yasser Arafat. He is the only decision maker among the Palestinian people and the one who can sign an accord with you.

[1] The minutes and list of questions are translated from Arabic.

Ramon: My opposition to holding discussions with the PLO in Tunis is pragmatic and not ideological.

Tibi: I was told that you agree in principle to negotiate with the PLO, and that Rabin agrees to negotiate with it in order to conclude a joint declaration of principles.

Ramon: I have to be precise. My personal opinion is that if the PLO shows itself to be capable of reaching the point of signing a joint declaration of principles with us on a phased solution, then I personally agree to Shimon Peres and Abu Mazen, or anyone else Arafat chooses – Nabil Shaath or others – signing it. I would like to add that I believe that if Yitzhak Rabin sees that the PLO will definitely sign a joint declaration with us then Rabin, who is a practical man, will agree to the PLO signing the agreement publicly and at ministerial level. But Rabin is a very suspicious man, sometimes rightly so, and he must be certain of the intentions of the Palestinian leadership in Tunis to reach a serious agreement and sign it.

Tibi: There are many points of disagreement over a declaration of principles. The American proposal is rejected more or less in its entirety because it uses Israeli language and adopts Israeli positions.

Ramon: Ahmad, you understand Israeli public opinion. The issue of Jerusalem is a 'red line' for us.

Tibi: And for us too. We are talking about East Jerusalem and not West Jerusalem.

Ramon: I realize what you want and realize what you aspire to. We, in contrast to the former government, have given you much, but you are making a mistake in rejecting it.

Tibi: There is an impression that you are giving the Palestinian self-rule over the Palestinian people and not over the land.

Ramon: What are you talking about? What are you saying? We have given you authority over 60 per cent of the territories. It must be clear: there is no way that Israel will not control the settlements in the interim period. You know the opinions of the Israeli people.

Tibi: But you are making of the settlements an extraterritorial area.

Ramon: We are just talking about the interim period.

Tibi: Palestinian public opinion has lost confidence in the way the negotiations are currently being conducted. The Madrid formula should have been declared dead a long time ago. Practically speaking, the present negotiations served their purpose some while ago and there is now no chance of progress. The level of negotiations must be raised and talks should take place with the decision maker in Tunis.

Ramon: We have to ask the PLO if it is prepared to soften its position over the points of difference. But that must be done in a very discreet manner.

Tibi: What is required?

Ramon: There are several questions they must answer.

Tibi: Write them down and I'll pass them to the leadership in Tunis.

Ramon: I will write them on a blank piece of paper.

Tibi: Then you will not get an answer on official PLO stationery because you are not giving me the questions on official Israeli stationery.

Ramon: The aim is to get their response and then move forward. As far as I am concerned, let them answer on a blank piece of paper.

Tibi: I will put the questions to them. What are the questions?

Ramon: The questions are the following:

1. Does the PLO accept the principle of a phased solution?
2. Does the PLO accept leaving the subject of a final solution for Jerusalem aside until the beginning of the permanent status negotiation?
3. Does the PLO accept Israeli control of the settlements during the interim period?
4. Does the PLO accept leaving the external security of the territories in Israeli hands?

Tibi: I expect there'll be answers, and questions too, from the PLO. There are many points of difference.

Ramon: The gap must be bridged and a joint declaration of principles must be signed. I'd like to say that this paper you have written [Tibi had written the questions in his own handwriting on Ministry of Health stationery] I'll pass on to Yitzhak Rabin and get it back to you by the end of the week. This meeting is a secret meeting.

Tibi: Let's move to another important subject, which is the status of the Arab masses, especially the Arab graduates in Israel. You have to work on finding suitable employment for them.

Ramon: Haven't you noticed that our dealings with the Arab sector is completely different from that of the Likud government? We appropriate big budgets for local authorities now because of the injustice you have suffered. And there is a special committee at the Prime Minister's office to place Arab graduates in ministerial offices.

Tibi: The health bill that you are trying to finalize is a good bill. I hope you'll succeed in passing it in the Knesset.

Ramon: Give me all your telephone numbers.

Tibi: These are my home and office telephone numbers.

Ramon: I'll come back to you in a few days' time because at the moment Rabin is preoccupied with the situation on the Lebanese border. I feel that this is an important meeting.

Protocol
(Second Meeting)

Venue: Health Ministry – Director's Office
Date: 20 July 1993

Ramon: What do you know of the Egyptian channel?
Tibi: I only know part of it. I do not know everything.
Ramon: There is a channel in Cairo. You know it. Abu Mazen via the Egyptians – Amr Moussa and Usama al-Baz – with Arafat's knowledge. But the truth is that things have stalled on the issue of Jerusalem. If this matter is resolved many things will be resolved. Rabin and Peres are open to many things. I've just come from a meeting with Shimon Peres. What is of importance to us is the issue of Jerusalem, but that it is not to be discussed today.
Tibi: And jurisdiction?
Ramon: No. We do not even mention that. We speak about the settlements and security, and you link this with territorial jurisdiction. The Palestinians want a definition of autonomy that it should apply to all the territories occupied in 1967. And so we return again to Jerusalem. What did they tell you in Tunis after our first meeting?
Tibi: I told Chairman Arafat there was something important, and he's awaiting the outcome of this meeting. Because you told me you would chase it with Yitzhak Rabin. You told me Rabin is a pragmatist, and that if an agreement is reached or almost reached Rabin would agree to the PLO signing the agreement in public.
Ramon: Yes. This is what I say. This is my opinion. Making public in exchange for substance.
Tibi: You mean reaching an agreement in principle?
Ramon: Yes, yes. Agreement on territorial jurisdiction and the issue of Jerusalem. If it is a clear agreement. But Rabin does not think that there should be a public announcement without signing. The Palestinians come off better than us because the meetings take place before the signing and the public announcement comes before the signing. We're afraid that a public meeting may not lead to an agreement. A meeting should take place only after making sure by 99 per cent that there would be agreement.
Tibi: You said that for secrecy's sake you would convey our previous exchange to Rabin and come back to me with questions for the PLO who will give you answers in return. I expect you to add some questions which are of importance to the Palestinian leadership, until we arrive at a point where you or someone else designated by the Prime Minister, someone of ministerial rank, will hold a meeting with . . .

Ramon: Someone comparable from the leadership in Tunis?

Tibi: Yes.

Ramon: I am trying – because it is a serious issue – and I met with Rabin – I am trying to be cautious.

Tibi: What is important to us is Rabin's opinion because you will get Arafat's opinion.

Ramon: Rabin is prepared for many things which the Palestinians in Tunis know. What Shimon Peres is doing in Cairo is not against Rabin's wish but in coordination with him. And they know that.

Tibi: The Egyptian channel is there all the time. It is important for the PLO and important for all parties. But the PLO wants direct contact. Even the Egyptians publicly demand this. I support the Egyptian channel. But Tunis prefers direct contact with those concerned.

Ramon: I concur with this. I have no problem with this. What you are saying about 'going public' or what Nabil Shaath has said about the need to raise the level of negotiations, that is direct contact in the talks in Cairo, we did not think that this is a central matter for Tunis. Between us, I tell you that if this is not as important as I thought, then what is the issue? My main card is that high-level meetings should take place in public. Over here it is said at the highest levels, at 'the top of the pyramid', that it is not clear that the PLO is really concerned with holding high-level meetings in public. This worries me. So, the other channel, the Egyptian channel, is more practical because there is no such talk there. Between you and me, what we are saying here is that the PLO is going to soften its position on Jerusalem.

Tibi: No. It is not so. I am saying that the PLO will convey to you its position in this respect in writing first, thereafter by personal contact. It is possible that the two positions would come closer. This is my opinion. The leadership in Tunis, especially Arafat and Abu Mazen, is interested in direct negotiations with Yitzhak Rabin or whoever he appoints. Abu Mazen and Arafat coordinate everything together. What is happening in Cairo is a collective decision.

Ramon: We know that. We know that.

Tibi: Regarding the contacts via Cairo, Abu Mazen is the man.

Ramon: Of course. This is what I'm saying.

Tibi: When a direct channel does not exist then the only way is through a side channel, a third party. The PLO will sometimes use the Tunisian Government to send messages to the American Administration – mostly through Egypt – and sometimes via the Palestine Delegation. It would have been better if there was direct contact between the PLO and the American Administration.

Ramon: The Egyptian channel is mainly managed by Shimon Peres.

Tibi: I understand from what you are saying that it is Shimon Peres who fears direct contact with the PLO so that it should not taint the channel he is running. It gives him the possibility of controlling matters and, moreover, is afraid the Egyptians would not look favourably on that. But on the contrary, the Egyptians will be happy if face-to-face meetings take place; they have often said so.

Ramon: We have arrived at a decision to hand questions to you. But I don't want you to send them by fax, so when will you travel?

Tibi: If the questions are ready today, I will leave within forty-eight hours.

Ramon: Yes, you'll get the questions today.

Tibi: I'm interested in what you have said about Rabin's pragmatism. Will he agree to sit with the PLO?

Ramon: My estimation is that he will. Rabin's preoccupation is with the issue of Jerusalem and security. In other matters he is open to everything.

Tibi: The Palestinian side is concerned with 'phased arrangements' in East Jerusalem during the interim period as well as with the permanent status [of the territories] during the negotiations for the final solution. I hope we can arrive at an agreement over this point.

Ramon: What you're saying is that the Palestinians are essentially interested in the issue of East Jerusalem.

Tibi: Essentially.

Ramon: What do you mean by 'phased arrangements' in Jerusalem?

Tibi: There are a number of points, which should be dealt with in the detailed negotiations. I would rather consult the leadership and then come back to you.

Ramon: Give me an example.

Tibi: I haven't got the authority to talk about this. Give me a chance to check with the leadership in Tunis. We'll be meeting in Tunis at the end of this week.

Ramon: By the way, Nabil Shaath's statement yesterday was good. Television has been showing openness of late, has it not?

Tibi: Yes, there is some change.

Ramon: How do you want the questions, typed or handwritten?

Tibi: As you wish.

Ramon: I'd rather they were not handwritten. I'll give you the questions typed on a blank sheet of paper and wait for the response from Tunis.

Tibi: There might be a need at some stage for a meeting between you and Abu Mazen or others whom Arafat chooses.

Ramon: Abu Mazen has not held meetings to date. There have been embarrassing incidents in the past, and I am putting it delicately. There have been people who claimed that Abu Mazen was interested in meeting them, but did not, or were not permitted to, while others were allowed to but the meeting never took place. I don't think Abu Mazen wanted to meet them.

Tibi: You are right. Abu Mazen did not request a meeting with anyone. It was your side which asked to meet him.

Ramon: Practically speaking, if there is progress and a need for a meeting arises, and Abu Mazen agrees to a meeting, and Rabin is sure that Abu Mazen wants a meeting, then Rabin will agree. This must proceed in this way because of the claims by some that in the past Abu Mazen wanted to meet them but that no meetings ever took place.

Tibi: Please pass this on clearly to Rabin: in spite of Abu Mazen's flexibility and pragmatism he is not interested in fruitless meetings with Israeli officials. Whoever claimed to Rabin that Abu Mazen had asked to meet them, did so on their own initiative.

Ramon: I will convey that to him. I believe Rabin knows that. Rabin must be completely convinced that any proposed meeting has been agreed upon by Abu Mazen and Arafat. Why did I come running to this meeting with you? Because I took part in important meetings for two days before meeting you. It must be clear to you and to them that we do not want this particular channel to harm the Egyptian channel, because we are comfortable with it. I am being honest with you. The issue of peace is one of the most important issues for me. I'm not looking for personal benefit. It is important that we do not harm the Egyptian channel. I say it openly. There's another point that relates to you personally. Rabin has not met you in the past but he knows you and he says you are close to Arafat but that you have no great influence on him, you cannot pressure him like the Egyptians can – honestly.

Tibi: Tell Rabin I wouldn't try to pressure him because I honestly don't have the ability nor do I want to anyway, but the importance of this channel is that it is more direct than the other channel and is more 'primary' and it will lead to a Rabin–Arafat encounter sooner.

Ramon: It is possible that this present channel is more 'primary' and quicker and could bring Rabin and Arafat together but the Egyptian channel is important to us.

Tibi: I'll pass on your concerns. In the past, no one channel had a negative effect on another.

Ramon: We don't want this channel to affect the progress achieved on the other channel especially since the Palestinians have not suggested holding a face-to-face meeting.

Tibi: The importance of direct contact is that the government of Israel will talk with a national liberation movement. You're talking to me while I'm not a decision maker. I told you what the next steps should be; the gradual way is the right way. I express my viewpoint to the leadership and it is sometimes accepted and sometimes rejected. I'm no substitute for the leadership in Tunis, I am its temporary representative at this meeting.

Ramon: This is the advantage you have. When we meet you, we don't regard you as a substitute for the PLO, but when we meet Faisal Husseini it should be said that we are meeting people of another leadership – or that is what Arafat thinks.

Tibi: It has been proved to you that there is no other leadership and there will not be another leadership, and Husseini himself and his colleagues in the delegation have said so.

Ramon: That is clear today.

Tibi: Do you see a possibility for an Arafat–Rabin meeting?

Ramon: If there's agreement on the issue of Jerusalem then the subject is open for consideration.

Tibi: What about the confederation?

Ramon: I don't want to talk about issues concerning the permanent status; let them ask this question. This anticipates the talks on the phased solution.

Tibi: The permanent status negotiations can start quickly with the signing of the declaration of principles for the interim period.

Ramon: Not with the signing of the declaration of principles, but when self-rule has actually begun or the agreement for it has been signed. You have to inform Tunis that if the indirect channels have proved to be more effective than the direct channels then why the need for direct contact. The Madrid conference took place after pressure by the American Administration and Egypt because they can pressure. You see, you neither want to use pressure nor are you in a position to.

Tibi: Which is why Arafat is comfortable with this channel.

Ramon: By the way, are the authorities harassing you as they did during Shamir's partnership.

Tibi: No. Shamir stopped me from travelling on three occasions on the basis of a law from the days of the British Mandate. At least Rabin permits freedom of movement for everyone. Facts must be admitted.

Ramon: At least this is proof that we are better in this respect than the previous government.

Tibi: That is certain. Goodbye.
Ramon: Call me as soon as you return. Goodbye.

The questions that Haim Ramon had asked and that Ahmad Tibi conveyed to us are as follows:

1. Does the PLO accept in principle the concept of a phased solution involving an interim arrangement to precede a permanent settlement?
2. Does the PLO accept the principle that the permanent status of Jerusalem is to be discussed and determined within the framework of the permanent settlement?
3. Does the PLO accept the principle that responsibility for Jewish settlements during the interim period shall be in Israel's hands?
4. Does the PLO accept that overall security in the territories during the transitional period remain in Israel's hands?

The answers to these questions were passed on to Haim Ramon by Ahmed Tibi and were received by Ramon on 26 July 1993. Their substance is as follows:

1. *The two stages*
   We agree to two stages, transitional and final. The issues for the permanent status negotiations are to be specified in the declaration of principles so that the two stages are linked. These issues include: Jerusalem, refugees, settlements, security arrangements, borders and other issues.
2. *Jerusalem*
   We agree that its permanent status is to be discussed within the framework of a permanent settlement. Position at present: there should be full participation in the elections by candidates and voters. There should be linkage between the Jerusalem institutions and the interim authority which will oversee them.
3. *Settlements*
   We agree that their final status is to be discussed at the permanent status negotiations. Position at present: that they remain the responsibility of the Israeli army. Because of the complex nature of the settlements, a special agreement should be concluded for dealing with it during the interim period.
4. *Security*
   External security will be Israel's responsibility during the interim period while internal security will be the responsibility of the

Palestinian authority. A joint liaison and coordination committee is to be established to deal with issues requiring coordination, other issues of common interest, and disputes.

5. We believe that any agreement on a declaration of principles must be accompanied by a significant moral step to be taken by the PLO and the Government of Israel regarding the announcement and signing of the declaration of principles.

On 1 August 1993 I received the following letter from Ahmad Tibi:

Greetings. As I informed you yesterday the response was generally positive and clear. We were not asked to make changes to the text, but the question put by the first official is: will additions to this 'skeleton' contradict the content of the four points, specifically that regarding territorial jurisdiction.

The first official says that Abu Mazen's position will be as follows: territorial jurisdiction is to apply to all the territories occupied in 1967. There are points of exception: Jerusalem and settlements.

The first official says this text raises a certain contradiction in the answers to the four questions. So what do you suggest should link the issue of jurisdiction and the issues of Jerusalem and settlements in order to refute the allegation about there being a contradiction? For example: the territorial jurisdiction will apply to the territories of the West Bank and the Gaza Strip with the exception of Jerusalem (here your detailed response about Jerusalem and the settlements come in); or any other suggestion you deem appropriate.

On 18 August 1993 Tibi responded to the answers that we had provided to the questions raised in the previous letter:

Greetings. The first official's reaction over here was positive regarding the answers. He requested two weeks before making a final decision on the fifth point (i.e. direct negotiations). This was after he understood that the answers are an indivisible part of the negotiations with the PLO. The man wants this time to make a decision he described as different from all other past decisions in the light of the severe coalition crisis with the Shas movement. He is afraid of losing his majority in the coming ten days.

Therefore, in my opinion, the coming round of negotiations should be held for the sake of formalities only. There is more than a good possibility for success here. The third person has come to share this view after the fourth meeting which they held last evening.

Shamir's Attempts to Obstruct Contacts with the PLO

On 31 December 1989 Shamir announced that he had expelled Science Minister Ezer Weizman from the Israeli Cabinet and that the decision was to take effect within 48 hours, that is by noon on Tuesday, 2 January 1990. Weizman was accused of contacting an important PLO official and sending messengers bearing letters to Arafat.

According to *Haaretz*, Israeli intelligence had reported to Shamir on 31 December 1989 that Ahmad Tibi had delivered letters from Weizman to Arafat. Shamir was furious because he believed that such contacts had contributed greatly to the PLO's positive decision regarding the Baker plan and had prompted the Palestinians to become partners in the peace process. Weizman favoured direct negotiations with the PLO and regularly called on Labour to quit the government of national unity in order to relaunch the Middle East peace process from the Opposition benches.

Shamir also saw an opportunity in the Weizman incident to defeat Labour, which had sunk to its lowest point and had become so dispersed that it seemed to have nothing to offer voters in elections. If Labour supported Weizman, then it followed that Labour considered contact with the PLO as legitimate but did not seem to have enough courage to pursue that course, at least in the case of Peres and Rabin. So Shamir headed off Labour by accusing everyone who contacted the PLO of treachery and hoped to win Israeli opinion over to his side. Striking at Weizman also meant reining in shifting views among the population at large. He also wanted to show America that he was firmly in the saddle and therefore irreplaceable. In this way, he thought he could counter American pressure as well as pressures from within and force Labour to tread the path laid down by Likud.

At the time the view from our side was that Israel was experiencing a serious political crisis, and that this situation should be taken advantage of by highlighting through the media the Palestinians' desire for peace, and the PLO's predisposition to have a dialogue with all Israeli parties and factions. It was considered that negotiations should take place at an international conference, and that high-level diplomatic contacts were needed to breach this new Israeli iron wall behind which the government was stifling factions that were tending towards peace through dialogue and negotiation.

Weizman had expressed a readiness on more than one occasion to meet Arafat and to recognize the PLO, stating that he was in favour of a peaceful solution based on respect for the interests and rights of both peoples. But whenever the opportunity arose for a meeting with us he would back down so as to avoid problems with his government, especially since Labour did not approve of anyone having such meetings. Weizman thought he would lose his cabinet portfolio if he did go ahead with such a meeting, something he did not relish. So he dallied until one day he met Nabil Ramlawi, the PLO representative in Geneva. Mossad found out, and Weizman suffered a blistering attack that nearly brought about the downfall of the national coalition government. The matter was finally settled when it was agreed that he should remain in the cabinet but barred from attending cabinet sessions for a year and a half.

Following the so-called Weizman scandal, Weizman travelled to the Soviet Union, which had been a long-time dream of his. He asked us to arrange a meeting with a Soviet politician, and to his pleasure he met Eduard Shevardnadze. At this encounter Shevardnadze informed him that the representation of the PLO had been raised to ambassadorial level, a fact the Israeli minister did not approve of. But Shamir accused him of collusion and of being in agreement with the Soviet minister on this matter. He was also accused of being conspiratorial for having refused to take the Chargé d'Affaires of the Israeli Consulate in Moscow with him to his meeting with Shevardnadze, as if he had intended to say things Tel Aviv should not hear.

In a statement he made in Moscow to the daily newspaper *Izvestia*, Weizman said:

> What I have done is not wrong. On the contrary, it is right. My actions will bring benefits in the future for my country. The general international climate is forcing the government of Israel to understand that time is not on our side. The quicker we understand that the quicker we sit at the negotiating table. At the same time, we have to find people in the Arab world capable of shouldering the responsibility and conducting negotiations with us. I am certain they exist. They are the PLO, with whom it is necessary to establish links. [1]

Subsequent events proved how right Ezer Weizman was. As it turned out it was a Likud government which represented Israel in the Madrid conference.

[1] Translated from Arabic.

6

The Madrid Panel

After achieving two victories during his presidential term in office, one in the Gulf and the other in Eastern Europe where the breakup of the Soviet Union and its Socialist allies made the United States the single unchallenged superpower, former US President George Bush found it appropriate to follow up his victories by turning his attentions to the Middle East. This was not simply to score further victories but to confirm US credibility following the speedy implementation of the UN resolutions on the occupation of Kuwait. His aim now was to try to implement UN resolutions concerning the other major problem in the Middle East. Naturally one cannot expect the same enthusiasm with which the United States prosecuted the war in the Gulf to apply to the search for a settlement of the Palestinian question. Still, there are parallels. While there were over thirty countries involved in the Gulf war, a similar number was involved in the multilateral Middle East peace negotiations. It was an international demonstration of the desire for peace.

On 6 March 1991 George Bush announced his four-point initiative to solve the Middle East problem: implementation of Resolutions 242 and 338; the acceptance of the principle of 'land for peace'; the legitimate rights of the Palestinian people; peace and security for the State of Israel. The Palestinian leadership immediately welcomed the contents of this initiative. The American Administration showed willingness to have dealings with Palestinian residents in the occupied territories through a joint Jordanian–Palestinian delegation and sent Secretary of State, James Baker, to the area. We were then faced with two problems which most members of the Palestinian leadership recognized. The first concerned the representation of the Palestinians at the peace conference. Only Palestinians from the occupied territories, other than Jerusalem, could qualify. This condition we rejected. The second problem was that representation had to be through a joint Jordanian–Palestinian delegation. This too we rejected.

We sought participation in an independent Palestinian delegation or in a joint Arab delegation, but both America and Israel rejected the first proposal while the Arabs themselves rejected the second. The participating Arab states, Syria, Lebanon and Jordan, rejected the participation of Palestinians on the grounds that this would be an obstacle to their achieving regional solutions because of the intricacies of the Palestinian issue. Therefore everyone without exception told us that the idea of a joint Arab delegation was impractical. When we realized that both our proposals would not be accepted, we agreed, after a prolonged debate, to open negotiations with Jordan to determine the nature of the joint Palestinian–Jordanian delegation.

We had no demands regarding the peace process, but we did ask the Soviets to obtain a letter of assurance for us from the Americans defining their views about Palestinian rights based on 'international legality'. Alexander. Bessmertnikh the then Soviet Foreign Minister, was enthusiastic about the peace process that seemed to be starting and presented the request to James Baker. The US letter of assurance was duly supplied to each party.

Yitzhak Shamir's government rejected European participation in the peace process and would not allow the United Nations any role in it, no matter how small. At the same time it rejected the idea of an international conference, insisting instead that it be a regional conference. Bessmertnikh played a salutary role in the rapprochement of views during a meeting held at the Soviet mission in Geneva on 14 May 1991 with a Palestinian delegation led by Arafat and included Abu Mazen, Suleiman al-Najjab, PLO Executive Committee member, Yasser Abd Rabbo, also a PLO Executive Committee member, and Nabil Amr, PLO representative in Moscow. The problems that this meeting tackled were those that had been raised by the parties concerned with the peace process. The answers to these problems were as follows: the conference was to be called: The Peace Conference; Europe would participate as an observer in the process; the United Nations would also participate as an observer; the agreements were to be consigned at the United Nations; and the United Nations would ratify any agreements arrived at.

James Baker felt it necessary to assure Shamir's Cabinet that the Palestinians who would conclude the Jordanian–Palestinian agreement would be Palestinians from inside Israel. He therefore continued to insist that Faisal Husseini, Hanan Ashrawi and Zakariyya al-Agha should travel to Jordan on different occasions to meet King Hussein or the Jordanian Prime Minister, Taher al-Masri. His intention was to reassure Shamir's government that the PLO had no role in this process, and that only those three figures were involved. Meanwhile, Shamir had been threatening the

Palestinians inside Israel that he would implement the Knesset legislation of 6 August 1986 which stipulated that anyone contacting the PLO would be liable to imprisonment.

On 23 October 1991, a week before the Madrid conference, we were in Amman to put the final touches to the Jordanian–Palestinian agreement. This coincided with the arrival of Husseini, Ashrawi and Agha. Upon Baker's instructions, Husseini's delegation was placed under the spotlight while the PLO delegation drifted completely out of the picture to give the impression that the agreement would be concluded with Husseini's delegation and not ours. We therefore agreed that Husseini and his colleagues should go to the office of the Prime Minister, be officially welcomed there and then confirm to journalists that the agreement had been concluded. We would then go in to complete the process. This is how the Jordanian–Palestinian agreement which allowed us to participate in the Madrid conference was reached.

The Jordanian–Palestinian agreement was a necessary starting point for the launching of the peace process in Madrid. James Baker had camped in Jerusalem waiting for a smokescreen to form, knowing that without such a smokescreen (agreement with Jordan) there would be no Palestinian participation in the negotiations; he also knew that without the PNC's adoption of such a course the Palestinians inside Israel would not consent to participating. Baker was confronting very difficult and complex formulas in terms of stages, since the agreement had to be concluded between the PLO and Jordan without the PLO being seen as a party to it. It also required PNC ratification without the PNC admitting to its existence. Our Palestinian friends on the inside were awaiting its ratification without saying they were awaiting it. Finally, the PLO leadership had to determine the names of the members of the delegation without saying so. Everyone knew this and everyone had to claim they knew nothing. Israel too was aware of this scenario and turned a blind eye. Baker knew everything and claimed to know nothing. The friends on the inside awaited instructions from Tunis, but had to claim sole responsibility for any decision. In fact the PLO was running everything but announcing nothing. While I was in Amman negotiating with Prime Minister Taher Masri it was announced that negotiations with Faisal Husseini and his delegation were under way. In Tunis the PNC was discussing the terms of the Jordanian–Palestinian agreement but saying nothing about them. In Jerusalem James Baker sat with our Palestinian friends allegedly choosing the names of the Palestinian delegation, while in reality the names were being chosen in Tunis.

Shamir's sterile policy made this beating about the bush necessary, something we had to tolerate patiently. We had to endure this rigmarole because the end was nobler than the means.

A committee composed of members of the PLO leadership was formed to follow up the negotiations and to supply the delegation with directives and to prepare the studies it would need at the negotiating table so that it may perform its duties well and avoid contradictions and embarrassments; moreover it was to circulate the results of the negotiations to our embassies and bureaux involved. So we set out to prepare for this task thoroughly in order to supply the delegation with all the documents and studies as and when they were needed.

The Jordanian–Palestinian agreement stipulated that the Jordanian team in the joint delegation would deal with the Jordanian track and Jordanian issues, while the Palestinian team would handle the Palestinian track and Palestinian issues. We thought that the American Administration and consequently the Israeli Government were aware of this agreement and had approved it in principle, especially since Secretary Baker had firsthand knowledge of the negotiations in Amman that had led to this agreement. It was inconceivable that our brothers in Jordan would sign an agreement that we did not approve or one that the American Administration did not approve. Hence, we were secure in the knowledge that the launching of the negotiations in Washington would not be blocked in any way by the Israelis, and if it was, then the American Administration would immediately intervene.

However, the Israelis insisted on negotiating with the joint delegation over both Palestinian and Jordanian tracks; this forced our delegation to withdraw from the negotiations for a whole week, a move which was supported by the Jordanian delegation. The issue was finally resolved when the Israelis accepted a proposal which called for the Palestinian delegation to be headed by Haidar Abdel-Shafi and to include two members from the Jordanian delegation, while Dr Abdel-Salam al-Majali would head the Jordanian delegation that was to include two Palestinians from the Palestinian delegation. This formula expressed the solidarity of the joint delegation.

We began the negotiations in the corridors of the US State Department; hence the label 'the corridor negotiations'. The Syrian and Lebanese tracks had begun on time, on 10 December 1991, while we and the Jordanians began on 18 December 1991. The initial rounds took place while the Likud were still in power in Israel. The negotiations during the first five rounds centred on specific issues. Very soon we noticed that each side had to halt at a certain point unable to progress further because the Israeli delegation would always block any positive step forward. Neither side was able to agree on an agenda for the negotiations and both sides had to resort to sending memoranda to each other expressing their respective viewpoints and demands. The Israelis could not accept our proposals because of their conviction that the land of Palestine was theirs and that we should come to terms with this reality. We therefore tried to seek partial victories in peripheral matters. In matters of substance, there was no meeting ground. There was a slight improvement on the matter of Palestinian representation in the fourth round. On 10 February 1992 Secretary of State James Baker sent a letter to Faisal Husseini in his capacity as the head of the Palestinian team in the peace conference. We considered this a positive step taken by the American Administration regarding Palestinian representation at the conference.

One of our most important tasks was to keep track of the many Israeli factions that formed the Knesset. We followed every minor and major event among those parties, whether relating to alliances, divisions or links among them. We had been trying since 1977 to encourage certain small left-wing factions, and others that called for peace between the two peoples, so that these parties could enter the Knesset and vote within it. This would mean new voices within the Knesset, different from the voices we had become accustomed to hearing ever since the State of Israel had been created, or even before. The word 'Palestine', or 'Palestinians', was one of the harshest to Israeli ears. It reminded them of the people who had lived on the land that was Palestine, the land that had been transformed to become Israel. They went along with what had been inculcated in their minds by the leaders of Zionist ideology since the turn of the century, the ideology that proclaimed: 'A land without people for a people without a land.' And as long as Palestine was imagined to be a land without people, then the word must be erased, and anyone connected with it must also be erased. Thus 'Goyim' became an inseparable part of Zionist ideology, both in theory and in practice.

In the early 1920s a Dutch Jew called De Haan came to Palestine and discovered after a few years that stability in the land of Palestine was impossible without coming to terms with its original inhabitants. He began therefore to call for understanding and coexistence with them, but was assassinated in 1925 in order that such calls would not be repeated by others. Likewise, we, the Palestinians, did not accept the presence of Jews on our land. When they declared the creation of their State, we refused to recognize its existence. Two-thirds of our people left their land in 1948 and there the situation stood. Then the PLO was created, and the Fatah movement launched in 1965, and the call for the liberation of all Palestinian soil went on.

A political pause was necessary. What if we stretched out our hand to the Jews? This question struck a number of people on both sides like a thunderbolt. We tried at this stage to seek a faction in Israel that would talk to us, one that carried weight in Israeli politics and at the highest political level, the Knesset. Uri Avniri, General Metitiahu Peled and certain Arabs allied with them, succeeded in entering the Knesset. We felt that this augured well and so we began to follow up every subsequent round of Knesset elections. During the twelfth Knesset elections we made several attempts to encourage the Arab parties to conclude agreements amongst themselves. However, all our attempts failed, with each side clinging to its position; as a result Rakah won four seats and both the Democratic List and the Arab Democratic Party ended up with only one seat. Their disagreement meant that they lost two seats which were won by Zionist parties, giving Likud the advantage over Labour.

Likud was in power when negotiations began in Madrid and Washington. We knew that Likud would not take one single step towards a settlement, and so we became doubly interested in the preparations for the elections that were announced in June 1992. We made exhaustive efforts with the Arab parties that were taking part in the elections, since their success would have a significant impact on the overall results. If the result was positive, then it would herald a new era in Israel, for the country would be governed by Labour with some of its allies such as the Meretz movement, a coalition of left-wing parties that advocated progressive views regarding the Palestinian issue. This view was bolstered by the decisions taken at the Labour Party conference which indicated a certain political development in Labour's stance that clearly differentiated it from Likud. In the electoral campaigns in Israel, accurate calculation is necessary because of the importance of a few votes in the overall outcome. We are able to influence the Arab sector not only because it has a natural leaning towards us but also because it needs our assistance, especially in the case of candidates requiring considerable resources to achieve the minimum number of votes required for success.

Until the twelfth Knesset, Israeli electoral law set the determining number of votes at 20,000. This meant that any list which achieved this figure would gain one seat, with the number of seats increasing at each doubling of votes. But the law was changed to eliminate the weaker lists which squandered votes, and the crucial number was raised to 40,000, giving two seats in the Knesset for those achieving this number. Anything less than this figure meant that it lost everything.

The Arab sector, which numbers some 700,000 people, has more than 300,000 votes that can in theory elect 14 deputies to the Knesset. But this figure is purely hypothetical because 30 per cent of them do not exercise their electoral rights. A similar proportion goes to the major parties, namely Labour, Likud and Meretz and to the party to which the Interior Minister is affiliated, because the social services for Arab villages come under his jurisdiction. The remaining votes are divided among the Arab parties and among the parties with Arab leanings such as the Communist Party.

Here we must not neglect to acknowledge an important personality. The Egyptian Government, in the person of Dr Usama al-Baz, was aware early on of the need to organize Arab ranks in order to gain as many votes and seats as possible. He expressed readiness to provide assistance to the Democratic Front for Peace and Equality which groups the Israeli Communist Party and a number of its supporters. Its members are Arabs and Jews. There was also the Arab Democratic Party headed by Abdel-Wahab al-Darawsha and the Progressive List which is headed by the lawyer Muhammad Miari. During the meetings with these three factions, we set guidelines for them which would eliminate competition between them for the Arab vote and avoid mud-slinging. These guidelines are as follows:

1. That the factions draft among themselves a charter of honour promising not to attack each other and to avoid mud-slinging in the media.
2. That the Arab Democratic Party and the Progressive List form a united electoral list.
3. That an agreement on the surplus votes be concluded between the Democratic Front for Peace and Equality and the above-mentioned parties' joint electoral list.
4. That we would work to convince the fundamentalist element within the Islamic tendency of the necessity of casting its vote since abstention would merely serve the interests of the Zionist parties.
5. We undertake to offer them political and media support.

Accordingly, a draft agreement, which aimed at preserving the rights of the Progressive List and the Arab Democratic Party, was presented along the following lines: if the head of the list was from Party 'A', then Party 'B' would get the second and third seats while the fourth seat would go to list 'A' or the independents and so on.

It was the Arab vote that gave Rabin the determining margin and allowed him to overwhelm Yitzhak Shamir and form a government.

Having said that, the importance of the Arab vote lies in the fact that it prevented Shamir from forming a government. But no Israeli leader can expect to depend on the Arab seats to achieve a quorum because they are historically outside the framework of national consensus, despite their numerical weight.

After the announcement of the election results, the ranks of the Right which had governed Israel for fifteen years collapsed, and Shamir announced his intention of retiring from politics. To the Israelis his retirement heralded the demise of the Zionist dogma. He was followed by Moshe Arens who confirmed that he, too, was retiring. He tried to shirk responsibility for Likud's short-sighted policies over the past years by blaming Shamir. He said that Israel must not continue to occupy all the territories, and that Shamir was behind the procrastination in the negotiations, and that this had brought about Likud's defeat. Arens added that he had never been a fighter in the movement that supported Greater Israel, i.e. that included the occupied territories.

So much for the Likud. As for the rest of the religious and right-wing parties, most of them quickly sought to negotiate cabinet seats with Rabin, especially religious parties like Shas and Yehudat Hatorat, which seek financial gain to finance their religious schools and institutions.

During the thirteenth Knesset elections, and after the results were announced, we began to promote the idea of the informal channel which could be used to support the Washington negotiations. (Our attempts to realize this idea are described in other parts of this book.) It was the bitter experience of five rounds with Likud that forced us without further ado to seek an unofficial channel through which ideas could be presented freely, without censorship, even though we expected that the victory of Labour and its allies would bring in a new style of negotiating and novel ideas to it. In this our expectations were misplaced.

The Cabinet changed, but the negotiating delegation did not. That was a bad sign and an ill omen – because Elyakim Rubinstein, who had negotiated with us when Likud was in power, was now negotiating with us still. No matter how hard he tried to shed his skin and change his tone and his ideas, he would still not empathize with the new spirit. Even as a civil servant (which he is) who is given his orders and obeys them, the personal element continued to influence his behaviour however hard he tried to play along with the ideas of his new bosses. I remember that on one occasion in Cairo I met Steve Cohen who is close to Shimon Peres. We discussed the Washington negotiations and agreed over certain ideas relating to the terms of reference of an agreement and the name and powers of the proposed elected Palestinian Council. I asked him to pass on these ideas to Peres, and if Peres agreed to them, then Cohen would travel to Washington to inform our delegation and the Israeli delegation about them. Perhaps these ideas would signal the beginning of an understanding over simple points that both sides could begin with. I hinted to Dr Nabil Shaath that he should accept these points when Cohen presented them to him, which is what in fact happened. But when Cohen presented the points to Rubinstein, the latter steadfastly rejected them, swore at him, and said he did not accept instructions from either Cohen or from Shimon Peres, and so the initiative ended.

I used to believe that in countries with strong institutional traditions the personal element would not exist. I also used to believe that the personal touch was a trait common only in countries from the Third World. But I now believe that the personal element is present everywhere and comes in different forms and has varying effects.

With the holding of the sixth round of negotiations on 24 August 1992 an atmosphere of optimism reigned in international circles as well as in the Arab world. This was due to the victory of the political alliance in Israel, which arrived bearing a programme based on the need for direct negotiations with the Arabs in accordance with Security Council Resolutions 242 and 338, and also concessions on all fronts. Political circles believed that this change had to be accompanied by fundamental changes in the established track of the negotiating process. This gave the sixth round a distinctive character, especially as the Israeli Government agreed to the negotiations continuing over a much longer time-frame than its predecessors had. It also agreed to relocate the negotiations to Washington after it had been agreed that they would be held in Rome. This increased the degree of optimism since not only was the American Administration one of the co-sponsors, with a special role in the negotiating process, but also the negotiations were being held on the eve of the presidential elections in the United States.

But things followed a different path after the American Administration announced its consent to release $1 billion in loan guarantees to Israel and that it would allow the Israeli Government to finish building 11,000 residential units in settlements in the occupied territories, including Jerusalem. This decision was an early blow to the Palestinian side. The American elections then cast a shadow over the seventh round of negotiations when, following Clinton's victory, the negotiations had to be suspended for ten days until the new American Administration was installed to replace the one that had sponsored the political process from its inception. We had thought that the changeover could not alter the incoming Administration's view of strategic issues, of which the political process in the Middle East was one. But the Israeli delegation used this transitional period to manoeuvre, stall and evade serious discussions of the issues on the negotiating table.

In the countdown to this round the Palestinian leadership held lengthy meetings and arrived at a decision in which the Palestinian delegation was called upon to concentrate attention on the inclusion in any agreement of the implementation of Resolutions 242 and 338, since they were prerequisites of a comprehensive settlement. Furthermore, it was to make sure that the interim arrangements for a Palestinian Authority would lead to a final phase requiring a full Israeli withdrawal and the creation of an independent Palestinian State.

This direction was one among a number of other reasons that made us think carefully about a negotiating style other than the one currently employed. We felt that the route to success was likely to be in negotiations through a side channel.

In this type of negotiation there would be a minimum of formalities and no taking of minutes so that everyone could talk freely and probe matters without inhibition. In this way, it would be easier to arrive at some common ground on specific issues which could then be forwarded to the official negotiating sessions. Needless to say, the official negotiating course would continue as normal but in tandem with the unofficial talks. The Israeli side welcomed our proposal and agreed to it, whereupon three unofficial committees were formed to discuss the following issues: the concept; land; the economy and human rights.

The minutes of the sessions of the seventh round reported that there were several meetings of these committees, and that the aim of the Palestinian delegation was to sound out the Israeli position. The Palestinian position in most of the unofficial meetings centred on the topics of the negotiations plan. It proceeded on the basis that all the land was ours and that the interim period would mark the beginning of an irreversible process. The interim arrangement would lead to the final status which would embody our right to self-determination and our right to legislate; the jurisdiction of our legislative council would cover all Palestinian territory, including Jerusalem; authority would be transferred from the government of occupation to the transitional government in all spheres with the exception of what would be agreed upon in the spheres of external security and foreign relations. The delegation's motto in the negotiation was that everything was ours and that we would discuss the exceptions if they wished. This was the thread linking discussions of all these subjects.

The seventh round of negotiations went ahead without us noticing any progress. Furthermore, the experiment which we had hoped would change the method of negotiations did not succeed. The unofficial committees had no effect on the method and style of negotiating, and all that happened was that both delegations subdivided themselves into three sections, each of which handled one of three issues. This was done within a rigid framework of meetings whose duration, venue and composition were set in advance. Even minutes were taken down. Thus these experimental meetings on the side failed largely because neither party really understood the main purpose behind them.

As a result of the failure of the negotiations, and after realizing that the Israeli position was to reject the simplest of conditions such as a commitment to the terms of reference for the negotiations themselves, the Palestinian leadership decided to reduce the membership of the delegation to only four or five delegates as an expression of protest at the barrenness of the previous rounds and the inflexibility of the Israeli positions. The reduction in the membership also served as a demonstration of our dissatisfaction with negotiations that had been going for a year, the time specified in the letters of invitation and assurances.

The eighth round was limited to eight days of negotiations because of the break requested by our delegation to mark the fifth anniversary of the uprising. The Arab delegations also responded to the occasion and all talks were suspended. There was another stoppage at the end of this round when the Israeli authorities deported 415 Palestinian members of Hamas (Islamist movement) across the Lebanese border on 17 December 1992. Thus the eighth round was overshadowed by this event, which at the time was placed on the agenda of the two meetings that were held with President Bush and the Department of State. Our delegation also followed up the debates in the Security Council and worked to secure the adoption of Resolution 799 regarding the return of the men who had been deported to Marj al-Zouhoor in southern Lebanon.

The delegations left the eighth round without fixing a date for future meetings. It was obvious that the break would be a long one. The stalemate meant that a general gloom would hang over the Middle East, and that the uprising would continue and tension would rise day by day. The Israeli leadership was aware of the situation. It too worried as much as others for the problems facing Israel were not so very different from ours. In fact the disagreement between Rabin, who controlled the bilateral negotiations, and Peres, who was prevented from following these negotiations, but controlled the multilateral negotiations, was apparent to everyone.

For our part we realized that the Washington negotiations were headed for a crisis and sent word to Rabin and Peres asking them to open informal channels that would save these negotiations from floundering, but Rabin rejected the idea. We also asked the Egyptians and the Russians to mediate.

Despite the diminished role of Russia in world affairs we maintained our good relations with it and took it seriously as a co-sponsor of the bilateral and multilateral negotiations. Because Russia had direct and formal links with the negotiations and spoke to us on an official level, we tried to use it as a channel through which to convey messages to the Americans and Israelis. The Russians relayed our messages honestly and tried hard to convince the parties concerned to accept the proposals we had asked them to communicate. We asked them repeatedly to talk to the Israelis about an informal channel to be located in Moscow and sponsored by the Russians. Peres's answer came when the Oslo channel had started. He said that what was available was sufficient, which the Russians naturally understood to be the negotiations in Washington. All the same, I thanked them for their efforts and did not comment on Peres's response.

During the lull in the negotiations, the Americans' policy *vis-à-vis* the peace process remained unchanged and stood by their letters of invitation and assurances. Their view was that the goal of the negotiating process was to grant authority to the Palestinian people, to end the Israeli occupation, to establish new relations between the two peoples, that the interim arrangements be an integral part of the overall peace process and that the overall settlement should be based on UN Resolutions 242 and 338. They also emphasized the importance of a Palestinian elected body, because elections were a practical means of achieving political authority. They held that the legislative task should not be confused with legislative authority. During the meetings with the American State Department certain issues that were outside the framework of negotiations were discussed, such as the despotic practices of the Israelis in the occupied territories and their effect on the negotiations and the peace process as a whole.

In this gloomy atmosphere, Shimon Peres resorted to an adventurous move by sending two of his men to contact the PLO delegation at the multilateral negotiations in London. They were to initiate an unofficial dialogue after presenting themselves as academics who wished to push the peace process forward. This is how Oslo came to be. During the long break there was plenty of time for each side to test the other, well away from the sight of Washington and its negotiators and without any prior commitment. The five months that separated the eighth and ninth rounds were enough for the parties to probe the depths of the problem and scout their respective positions and intentions. The rest is history. The ninth round of Washington negotiations began after we had in fact completed four months of intensive and in-depth negotiations in Oslo.

August 1993 was a critical month, for the negotiations that took place in Oslo during that time ended in a serious crisis. On the Washington front there was complete darkness with the Americans quite unable to stimulate matters in any direction whatsoever. Secretary of State Warren Christopher's mission to the region had failed to promote the American peace plan. Indeed we were beginning to lose hope in both channels, and it seemed that we had reached complete deadlock.

In Israel a silent battle raged between the Washington and the Oslo groups. Rabin who was the centre of decision making believed, until Warren Christopher's visit, that he should depend on the Washington channel which offered fewer risks than Oslo. The Washington negotiations were espoused by the American sponsor for several reasons: first, they followed the conditions set in Madrid which Likud had approved and which Labour had upheld; second, the PLO was excluded from them, at least in appearance, and third, they were conducted on the Palestinian side by Palestinians from inside Israel. In the ninth round the Americans introduced a draft proposal, and in the tenth a blueprint for it. We were convinced that such proposals could not achieve the results we desired and we wanted to convince the Israelis of that too. I believe that they finally arrived at the same conclusion and realized that the hopes for a solution lay in Oslo after all, especially as the negotiators had already laid a solid foundation. All they had to do now was to deal with the remaining set of points which would put the finishing touches to the draft Declaration of Principles and so make it ready for signing. This did not mean, of course, that either party could not disrupt this draft, if it so wished, over a single point (whether vital or minor) if such a party was less than honest in its intentions, particularly if it hoped to keep its options open. However, there were no other options, and having turned down the American proposal, the two sides turned their sights on Oslo.

The Arabs by then did not view the multilateral negotiations with the same enthusiasm as they did the bilaterals. The Syrians and then the Lebanese refused to participate in the multinationals without giving specific reasons and tried to enlist wide Arab support for their position. When no one responded, they began to encourage the Palestinians to reject negotiations in order to form a wider front that would strengthen their own position.

Palestinian participation in the activities of the working groups involved presenting the Palestinian position to each working group. The Israeli position was negative and defensive. The Israelis often absented themselves and also withdrew from the activities of the refugees and economic development working groups. The six working groups met during the period between 11 and 27 May 1992 in Brussels, Washington, Vienna, Ottawa, Tokyo and Lisbon. They handled the vital and crucial issues of the Palestinian–Israeli and Arab–Israeli conflict; the issues of water, refugees, economic development, environment, security and arms control.

The PLO had a prominent presence in the activities of the groups. The heads of the Palestinian delegations to these committees were prominent Palestinian officials of high standing in the PLO structure, as in the case of the economic development group and the refugees group. When we were denied participation in the security and arms control group we sent a delegation to the meeting. Although it did not enter the meeting room it contacted the other participating delegations, including the American delegation, to explain the risks of excluding the Palestinian delegation and the importance of its participation in this group.

The working groups met during the second round of multilateral negotiations in six world capitals during the period between 18 September and 4 December 1992. During the meeting of the security and arms control committee in Moscow on 18 and 19 November 1992 the Palestinian side was excluded on the grounds that it was restricted to sovereign States whereas the Palestinians were not representatives of a sovereign State. During the proceedings the Americans informed us that they were prepared to accept our participation and that of members from the diaspora if we agreed to freeze the membership of the heads of the economic development committee (Yusuf al-Sayegh) and the refugees committee (Elie Sanbar). They claimed that these two men were important members of the PLO and therefore their presence on these committees would prevent Israel from attending. The Americans quickly withdrew this offer before we could express an opinion one way or the other. When the Egyptian Foreign Minister, Amr Moussa, visited Israel he raised this matter with his Israeli counterpart, Shimon Peres, who then set three conditions for Israeli participation in these committees. Palestinians from the inside and from the diaspora were allowed to attend provided that the Palestinian delegation would not include people from Jerusalem, that it would not include people from the PNC and that Sayegh and Sanbar would step down as committee heads but could remain as delegation members.

The Palestinian leadership discussed these conditions, and on 20 October 1992 duly sent a letter to Amr Moussa for transmission to Shimon Peres. It did not refer to the discussions that took place in Washington between the Palestinian negotiating delegation and Dan Kurtzer of the US State Department, concerning Palestinian participation in the multilateral committee. We offered the following: the heads of the two committees would forgo one round only and, in exchange, the Palestinian side would participate in all six multilateral committees, including the security and arms control committee.

The letter was signed by Yasser Arafat and sent to the PLO Ambassador to Egypt, Saeed Kamal, for action. Shimon Peres's reply was that Israel would attend only this round of the multilateral negotiations and would discuss Israel's position for the next round in light of what would transpire between now and then. Based on this exchange of letters a formula for Palestinian attendance was arrived at, with the result that the Israelis attended the economic development committee which they had previously boycotted.

During these two days important contacts and meetings took place with the American Administration, the most important of which was the meeting at the American Department of State between Edward Djerejian and Hanan Ashrawi on 21 October 1992, in which discussions centred on the substance of Palestinian participation in the multilateral negotiations. The meeting went something like this:

Djerejian: We heard some very interesting things from the Russians about their consultations with Palestinian leaders in Moscow.
Ashrawi: Do you mean Abu Mazen?
Djerejian: Yes, with Abu Mazen on the issue of the Palestinian participation in the multilaterals. We want to hear about what's happening. There are many variations on the theme. If the purpose is to confuse the sponsors then you have succeeded.
Ashrawi: I don't know if you want an answer from us about this now or if you want to postpone the matter until a later time.
Djerejian: I hope you have a position.
Ashrawi: We have a position. We have discussed this matter. Whether through you or in other places, this matter was brought up. We are about to settle the matter. We have a different text from what we got from Amr Moussa. The matter of 'for one time only' remains.
Djerejian: Are you going to continue to insist on this point?
Ashrawi: Yes, but we can discuss this later on today.
Djerejian: [Refering to internal security.] Security is an important

matter. We discussed this before and after Madrid. We have reason to believe that the Israelis are prepared to discuss this issue with you. In this respect, we have spoken to your people in Jerusalem about advanced training of the Palestinians in general administration. We are planning to push in this direction in Paris as part of the working group on economic development, and bilaterally between the United States and the Palestinians in the event of success. You will have to start shouldering some responsibility. You do not possess the structure at the moment to handle that. Back to the multilaterals. I hope you will clarify matters.

Ashrawi: About the multilaterals, in their discussions with Amr Moussa the Israelis said two people who are members of the PNC must not attend the meetings, and that a third [unnamed] person is unacceptable. This is an unofficial draft [Ashrawi read from the unofficial draft which referred to the activities of Palestinians from the diaspora in all working groups]. The people in Paris have agreed to this. Our people are still worried about the ambiguous drafting. We thought that as long as the issue is going on there is no need for an immediate answer to the issue of security, disarmament and water.

Djerejian: Your position is that the PNC members will be absent for one time only.

Ashrawi: We refuse to allude to the PNC in any way. We intend to make it clear that we will not accept any preconditions and we say that there are no preconditions.

Kurtzer: The group on the environment meets on Monday and the one on the economy Thursday. You have Palestinians from the diaspora, including PNC members, and the Israelis have yet to inform us [of the formula]. We told the Israelis that we will not play the role of the policeman in the implementation of an agreement whose content we are not aware of. As of Monday, if Palestinians from the diaspora arrive for the meeting on the environment, we shall not permit them entry. Your reaching an agreement will be something great.

Ashrawi: We might know today or tomorrow. There is a problem. Did Peres announce that they would be going to Paris?

Kurtzer: They do not have an answer to the question of the PNC members being in the conference room. We told them that if Yusuf Sayegh comes we shall not throw him out.

Ashrawi: We will try to settle the matter. The idea of 'for one time only' poses a problem. We will not talk about comprehensive issues. Our discussions dealt only with Yusuf and Elia; they mentioned a third person.

The Canadian capital Ottawa hosted the meetings of the working groups on refugees on 11 and 12 November 1992. When the Israeli delegation arrived in the conference room where Dr Muhammad al-Hallaj, the deputy head of the Palestinian delegation, was present, they demanded his withdrawal on the ground that Hallaj was a PNC member. The Palestinian side refused. When both sides stuck to their guns the Israeli delegation boycotted the meeting. Dr Hallaj then made a statement on behalf of the Palestinian delegation at a press conference, and said in response to a question: 'Yes, I have participated in previous PNC meetings. That is a matter of public knowledge and is no secret. I have also not resigned or been expelled from it, and if I am invited to future PNC meetings I shall attend.' The American sponsors then suggested a way out of the deadlock to bring the Israelis back to the negotiating table. The head of the American delegation would say in the conference hall that Hallaj's membership in the PNC had in effect ended; Hallaj would respond that he had participated in the last session of the PNC, that his membership of the PNC was for that session only, but that this fact would not prevent him from attending future PNC sessions if invited. This is how the deadlock was broken:

The American: After far-ranging discussions with the delegations, we are pleased that the Israeli delegation and the Palestinian side of the Palestinian–Jordanian joint delegation are attending this meeting. I understand, according to these consultations, that the membership of Dr Hallaj in the PNC had lapsed at the end of the last PNC session in 1991 and he is therefore no longer a PNC member.

Hallaj: As the sponsor said, I attended the last PNC session and, according to the PNC's method of operation, my membership was for that session only. This does not preclude my participation in the future PNC sessions.

The Israeli: According to what I have heard from the sponsor about the lapse in the membership of Dr Hallaj in the PNC, Israel is pleased to attend today's meeting.

The multilateral negotiations began to move forward after the Moscow meetings. We participated in the committees, with Palestinian representation developing to include Palestinian delegates from outside the PLO and those representing the PLO. Thus our delegations to the various committees were able to effectively present the different concerns of the Palestinian people. As the multilateral talks progressed – making gains as well as losses – the people who had opposed the multilateral talks began to forget why they had opposed them in the first place.

7

Norway's Role

It might seem strange and disagreeable to say that the minnow was able to perform the miracles which the whale could not. Norway is not on the list of influential countries which have capabilities and influence in the new world order or the old. In spite of this Norway achieved what the giants could not and accomplished what the great ones could not. We record that the events in Oslo that led to the historic Declaration of Principles were one of the twentieth century's most notable milestones. We must give this small country full credit for assuming an outstanding, positive and effective role in bringing this document to the lawn of the White House.

It was not our choice nor, I believe, was it the Israelis' choice that Oslo should host the secret channel for our negotiations. It was a Norwegian initiative that was directed initially at the Israeli side, which accepted it in principle. Then the London meeting was arranged at which under-standing between the two sides was achieved, and it was at that point that we realized how perfectly the Norwegians had played their hand in bringing about a meeting between the two adversaries on their soil. But the idea of a secret channel was not, in principle, new to us or to the Israelis. It had been proposed in the past in different ways and through different parties such as Egypt and the Russians. But it had still to mature, until the Norwegians adopted it, worked on it and acted on it.

It was a difficult task that required the maintenance of absolute secrecy on the part of all three. It imposed on the Israelis and Palestinians complete secrecy of movement, but it also burdened the Norwegians with the even greater responsibility of controlling these movements on their territory in order not to attract the attention of foreign embassies, the media and the various intelligence services. It was an apparently impos-sible mission, but it was accomplished. The Norwegians continually moved the venue of the negotiations from one place to another, so that no two consecutive meetings were held in the same place. They also restricted the number of people who would be responsible for the whole operation, who concealed themselves behind a wall of mist to prevent leaks to other Norwegian Foreign Ministry staff.

Fortunately, the team that sponsored the Norway negotiations possessed a high degree of vitality, enthusiasm and concern. They also had a profound desire to succeed. Cynics may say that they were motivated by the hunt for political credit and an enhanced international reputation for Norway, but this is not enough to explain the efforts that were exerted by them. It was an undertaking that entailed a drastic change in their lifestyle, not a mean sacrifice for the orderly Scandinavians. But they adapted quickly to our working ways and adjusted to our circumstances. They worked at night and sometimes well into the next day in order to keep up with the process of negotiation. Thus to attribute the concern they showed to a desire for personal polit-ical credit or an enhanced international reputation for their country is clearly not right. We sensed an inner motivation and a real desire to bring about peace in the Middle East. The Norwegian peacemakers would often be frustrated or disappointed when negotiations reached an impasse. But they never lost hope, not even for a moment.

The two main conditions for the success of any venture were present in Norway: first, when it is sponsored by the State, and second, when the people assigned to its service are dedicated to it, have enthusiasm and a true desire to succeed. We saw them go beyond the role of host providing conditions of comfort and total secrecy for the negotiators, right up to direct intervention between the negotiators: to reconcile viewpoints and provide suggestions, alternatives and sometimes different scenarios. They adopted the role of a full partner in the negotiations. Nor was their role limited to within their own borders but they were willing to go further, travelling to Tel Aviv, Tunis and Washington whenever necessary, so that the momentum and continuity could be maintained. Sometimes they would travel to gain first-hand understanding of the thoughts of the leaderships of the negotiating teams and to try to convince them of what their representatives had brought to the negotiating table.

The Norwegian Foreign Minister, Johan Joergen Holst, was in charge of the team assigned to this mission and rather than leave matters to his capable senior staff, he personally followed the negotiations and kept himself informed of developments. He contacted the parties concerned abroad and travelled to meet them, though without drawing attention to his real mission, managing to keep the reasons for his travels from the media and the international intelligence services. He was brilliant in coming up with reasons to cover his trail. The Norwegians also succeeded in creating the appropriate atmosphere for the negotiators, not only by their attemps to reconcile both sides' viewpoints but also by creating friendly relations and a friendly climate. It must be noted here that negotiations do not consist merely of a dry political dialogue. They reflect a mixture of different interests, feelings, senses and emotions which all interact to lead either to complete understanding or total alienation. If the human element is taken out of negotiations, they become soulless, even if they do lead to agreements. Agreements reached in this way will always need something else to support, consolidate and deepen them. Without a doubt, a thorough understanding of the psychology of negotiation contributed to the success of the mission undertaken by the Norwegian team. There was no divergence between Holst and his team (who shared the responsibility and followed up the process with him) in the degree of enthusiasm and desire to achieve results. They were not trying to flatter their boss, or go along with him in this venture. They shared his enthusiasm and genuine desire. Terje Larsen, the social scientist, and his wife Mona Juul, Holst's bureau chief, were perfect examples of those honest Norwegians who considered the success of the negotiations a personal success. I shall never forget that on one occasion Terje Larsen was in tears when he felt that failure was threatening the process. I do not believe he felt downcast because his own mission was about to fail, but because the peace process in which he believed was going to fail. This was the human element that enhanced the character of the negotiations, providing a congenial atmosphere conducive to success. The credit goes to those Norwegians. The negotiating process spread beyond their persons to their homes, their families and children who shared the experience of the negotiators. No doubt they contributed to these crucial moments in history. When they invited the two adversaries into the family atmosphere with such warmth and kindness, all formality disappeared. Such human touches left a lasting impression on us all.

Foreign Minister Holst was twice admitted to hospital with serious health problems, but did not allow his condition to prevent him or his colleagues from pursuing the peace process. Their moral and political responsibility did not end with the signing ceremony in Washington on 13 September 1993, but extended to beyond this date persuading and encouraging both sides to remove the obstacles in the way of implementation. If it was the Palestinians and Israelis who were celebrated on the White House lawn, and if it was Bill Clinton and his Administration, together with former American leaders, who were the hosts of this celebration, then Johan Joergen Holst was the godfather whom everyone looked up to with admiration and gratitude.

A Palestinian friend once asked: 'The Covenant of the PLO says that a Palestinian is defined as the descendant of Ottoman parents. Does that mean that Palestinian nationality is limited to descendants of Palestinian origin?' I replied: 'After these prolonged efforts that have involved both Arab and non-Arab as well as individuals who sacrificed their time and their money, I don't think Palestinian nationality can be restricted to those of Palestinian descent because "Palestinianism" has become more a belonging and a commitment rather than attachment to blood and descent.' We owe much to the states and to the individuals who have served and made sacrifices for the Palestinian Revolution, sacrifices that will be remembered for generations to come. We have to give them credit in different forms and ways as an expression of our loyalty, gratitude and appreciation. I shall not name or count them all. I leave this task to others to do what duty demands.

Johan Joergen Holst arrived in Tunis on 16 July 1993 at the head of a high-level official delegation on a state visit to the Republic of Tunisia, an occasion which he used for a meeting with Arafat to discuss the Oslo channel. Because he was visiting Arafat officially he was accompanied by a member of staff who knew nothing of the Oslo channel, while, similarly, there were people with Arafat who knew nothing either. Two meetings were arranged; the first plenary and the second between the two men alone. The first lasted for twenty minutes after which Holst and Arafat were left alone. After the meeting, Holst sent a detailed letter to Shimon Peres which was conveyed by Terje Larsen and Mona Juul. Holst had noticed that Arafat was making a great display during the plenary meeting of speaking more to his colleagues than to the Norwegian side. But things changed when the two were alone. They discussed the Oslo channel in detail, the importance of continuing to support it in order to achieve positive results, and the need to keep it secret lest it should break down. They also touched on various details related to the articles of the Declaration of Principles, especially the points of disagreement. Holst's letter therefore tried to present an encouraging image of his meeting with Arafat to reassure Peres that his adversary's intention and desire to achieve peace were genuine.

On 19 July 1993 Terje Larsen delivered Peres's reply, in which the Israeli leader expressed appreciation for Holst's efforts and Larsen's consultations in Tel Aviv. Peres and the Israeli Government were apparently encouraged to follow up the Oslo channel and to speed up the search for solutions to the obstacles still facing the negotiators. Peres's letter stressed that, in the light of Holst's letter and Larsen's consultations, a historic breakthrough would take place and indicated that the two leaders would meet in August.

Holst remained in Tunis to wait for his envoys to return from Tel Aviv. After the Norwegians had evaluated all available data on 20 July 1993, Holst wrote down a number of points that would need to be raised during his second meeting with Arafat. These included the following:

1. Leaks in some Israeli and Western newspapers about the Oslo channel and the means employed to deny its existence and cover its trail.

2. The Israelis favour the Oslo channel and wish it to continue provided it does not last for too long. They see in it the only and final hope.

3. The Israelis want the next round in Oslo to be the decisive round. This is Rabin's opinion as well as the opinion of the reduced Israeli Government.

4. The Israelis are showing some flexibility over Jericho.

5. The Israeli obsession is with security. Therefore, they are prepared to grant the [proposed] Palestinian Authority all the facilities for the creation of a skilled and able police force.

6. Jerusalem is one of the very sensitive issues. Therefore it is preferable to postpone discussing it and other issues until the final stage.

7. The Israelis show a readiness to discuss economic issues within the framework of the Declaration of Principles.

8. Concentration on confidence-building between the two sides. Holst believes that the implementation of the first phase will change many of the two sides' convictions.

9. Norway has no personal interests and its role is one of facilitation. In Holst's opinion, the most successful negotiations take place directly between adversaries.

10. The agreement requires courage from the leadership. Holst sees this in Arafat and that Arafat is able to give legitimacy to any agreement in Palestinian popular circles.

11. Holst feels that conflicts lasting for a long time make it difficult to remove the stumbling blocks of symbols and slogans, and he advises some other expressions be employed that would reassure the other side. He concludes by pointing out the need to talk about the Palestinian Covenant [founding the PLO in 1964], since many of the Israelis find its provisions frightening. He is in favour of Arafat repeating the statement that the Covenant is outdated.

Holst then left Tunis for Paris from where he sent another letter to Peres on 21 July 1993 which included remarks about his meeting with Arafat and suggestions relating to the continuation and success of the channel. In this letter he repeated the points he had raised during his meeting with Arafat and quoted Arafat on the following points:

- Arafat considered that achieving an agreement will be an historic breakthrough.
- He promised to prevent the leaks previously made by Dr Nabil Shaath.
- He stressed the Gaza–Jericho plan and explained his viewpoint in detail and the importance of this plan in promoting the Declaration of Principles.
- He spoke of his relations with Jordan.
- He believed that the Palestinian–Israeli agreement will pave the way for other agreements with Syria, Lebanon and Jordan.
- He concentrated on his need for strong security forces to control the situation in the occupied territories.
- He accepted the idea of a joint statement on the points agreed upon, but Abu Ala [chief PLO negotiator in Oslo] objected and demanded that a Declaration of Principles be produced.
- He accepted a somewhat ambiguous position on Jerusalem expressing his understanding of Israeli sensitivity regarding this issue. He demanded some sort of reference in the Declaration of Principles to the religious sites.
- Arafat indicated his desire for a speedy conclusion of an agreement because of the bad conditions in the occupied territories and stressed that peace was necessary for both sides and that the Israelis and Palestinians must learn to coexist.
- He emphasized that he was prepared to repeat what he had said about the Palestinian Covenant being outdated, something he had already declared in Geneva. He provided evidence in this respect such as the recognition of two States and the acceptance of Resolutions 242 and 338.

These intensive contacts undertaken by Holst took place just one month before the final draft of the Declaration of Principles was initialled in Oslo; they contributed to the speed with which both sides concluded their tasks. They also contributed to the reconciliation of viewpoints. Holst's honesty in relaying ideas and in choosing the subjects he discussed with both sides played an important role both in laying the groundwork for mutual trust and in consolidating that trust, a vital ingredient in reassuring each side of the other's intentions.

Holst used the occasion of a visit by the Israeli Foreign Minister to Stockholm to meet him there on 17 August 1993. He telephoned us from Sweden and mediated in the talks between the two sides. The talks lasted from 10 p.m. until 5 a.m. the next day, and all the unresolved points of difference were finally resolved.

His mission did not end with the initialling of the Declaration of Principles. It took three further weeks to secure mutual recognition between the two parties, a task which obliged Holst to travel continually between Oslo, Paris, Tunis and Tel Aviv until it was signed on 10 September 1993.

Everyone who followed the peace process and witnessed the signing of the Declaration of Principles on 13 September at the White House believed the role of the mediators and sponsors had come to an end, and that all issues pertaining to its implementation had now become the signatories' business. Indeed, whenever America's intervention was requested to remove obstacles, it refused, insisting that this was a matter for the negotiators. But not so with Johan Joergen Holst. Having carefully followed the Taba meetings in Sinai and the Arafat–Rabin summits in Cairo, which were unsuccessful and threatening the accord itself, Holst again stepped in to save the whole peace process.

At 2 a.m. on 20 December 1993 the Norwegian Foreign Ministry rang me at home to say that Minister Holst was on the line. His voice was shaky and sounded exhausted as he had only just on that day been discharged from hospital following his first heart attack. He asked me to meet Peres in Oslo in order to save the accord and was so insistent that I should agree that I felt ashamed of myself. At 4 a.m. on 22 December 1993 Terje Larsen telephoned me at the Rabat Regency Hotel in Morocco to tell me that Holst had gone to hospital yet again due to exhaustion, but that the arrangements he had initiated for a meeting in Oslo were proceeding and that he wanted it to take place.

Thus Norway's good offices continued until the Palestinians and Israelis met again to examine the obstacles to the implementation of the accord. It was decided to continue the meetings in Paris and then in Cairo where the joint follow-up committee met with all members attending. It did not reach a final agreement but arrived at ideas that could be developed further.

It was an unhappy coincidence that as I was writing this chapter on 13 January 1994 I heard of the death of the Foreign Minister of Norway, Johan Joergen Holst, at the age of fifty-six. On 13 September 1993 on the White House lawn he had attended the signing of the accord which he had sponsored and had helped to shape. A few months later he died, his hopes frustrated. The news was shocking and it was difficult to express our profound sense of loss. His example is his legacy.

8

The Oslo Channel

Any Palestinian leader who wants to embark on secret negotiations with the Israelis will face violent Arab and Palestinian opposition, because he would be departing from the norm in dealing with the Palestinian issue – an issue of interest to all and about which all have the right to express an opinion and to contribute to its resolution. The leader or official who attempts such an act needs a unique blend of daring, protection and immunity, without which it is impossible to set forth on such a dangerous path.

There have been positive developments in the Palestinian situation, specifically in respect of a diminution of geopolitical influences, whose restrictive effects have in the past often caused the Palestinian leadership to waste many historic opportunities. By regarding the question of Palestine as an issue for all Arabs and Muslims, any Arab or Muslim faction, of any importance, could demand a share in the Palestinian decision-making process. This state of affairs has considerably changed at all levels – Arab, Palestinian and international – allowing much greater room for manoeuvre on the part of the Palestinian leadership.

Even so these developments did not completely prevent either Arab or Islamic groups from expressing their great anger at those who had 'forfeited' Arab and Muslim rights in Palestine. If these developments had not taken place we would not have dared to sign the accord nor embarked on such an experiment in the first place. The most important of these developments was the move from Beirut to Tunis following the Israeli invasion. Now that we were hundreds of miles away from the scene, we were able to see clearly the totality of both the external and internal issues. As a result, the leadership concentrated on rebuilding its inner structure in a way that would ensure its independence of stance and decision. At the same time, it succeeded in strengthening its links with the occupied territories in order to gain support for the nascent features of a political settlement.

The PLO won the battle for the preservation of its legal status with an absolute majority. Even so, the other factions did not give up and insisted on questioning this legitimacy and clinging to time-worn slogans. They got their chance when the Jordanian–Palestinian agreement, called the Amman Agreement, was signed on 10 December 1985. They portrayed it as a surrender of Palestinian independence of decision making to Jordan and a turning to America for a peaceful settlement. In the event, the Amman Agreement never saw the light of day, with the Americans contributing to its failure. Because America had kept on asking for more concessions, the agreement had been frozen, a fact that had damaged the Jordanian–Palestinian relationship. Later, this had almost disintegrated when the government of Jordan had announced the severing of links with the West Bank. However, by handling it with wisdom and extreme caution we had managed to defuse a potentially explosive situation.

The Beginning

At a meeting of the multilateral negotiations leadership committee, held in London on 3 December 1992, Faisal Husseini, Hanan Ashrawi and the PLO's London representative, Afif Safieh, asked Abu Ala, the PLO's finance chief, to meet Yair Hirschfeld, an Israeli Labour Party member and Professor at Haifa University who described himself as an adviser to Israeli Foreign Minister Shimon Peres and his deputy, Yossi Beilin. The meeting took place, but only Afif Safieh and Abu Ala attended, Husseini and Ashrawi being otherwise occupied. It was Abu Ala's first face-to-face meeting with an Israeli 'official'. Although he was leading the multilateral negotiations and the teams assigned to them, he did not attend meetings in a physical sense, as the agreement had stipulated that there should not be a PLO official at the negotiations. (This ban also applied to Nabil Shaath who supervised the Palestinian delegation to the Washington bilaterals but was not permitted to meet the Israeli delegation.) The Israeli Government had also forbade members of the Israeli delegation from meeting PLO representatives.

Abu Ala was a member of the negotiations follow-up committee by virtue of his position as supervisor of the multilateral negotiations that had a technical, specialist character. He was fully occupied with these negotiations, but was also aware of the proceedings of the bilaterals because of his membership of the follow-up committee, though it must be admitted that his knowledge of that committees' activities was not exhaustive. His activities within the PLO were concerned mainly with financial and economic matters which took up a great deal of time, organization and management.

The meeting with Hirschfeld did not deal with matters of an economic nature, nor with matters relating to the multilateral negotiations as might have been expected. The discussion centred directly on political issues that were of relevance to the Washington negotiations. Hirschfeld tried to give the impression that the meeting was unofficial, and that he was speaking as an academic who was not committed to anything and could not commit anyone else to anything either, and that, although he was close to Israeli officials, he had no authority to speak for them, and his words were not binding.

Abu Ala returned to Tunis and submitted a brief report to Arafat who referred it on to me for evaluation and a decision. When I read the report the thought flashed through my mind that a door for a secret dialogue was opening, that this man could not have acted on his own initiative, that he must have received authorization from his bosses, Peres and Beilin, that he had been sent to sound us out and that this faction in the Israeli cabinet wanted to open a channel other than the Washington channel. We were, of course, fully aware that according to the distribution of responsibilities in the Israeli Cabinet the supervision of the multilateral negotiations was assigned to Peres, while the supervision of the bilaterals fell to Rabin and his private advisers. I knew very well that entering into any form of dialogue or peripheral negotiations with an Israeli Government faction that had no official authorization was fraught with risks since, as well as not being binding on the cabinet, it could also lead to adverse reactions and be interpreted as manipulative. Worse still, it could cause a collision between the two cabinet factions which would put paid to future attempts. I asked Abu Ala to give me more time to study the report of his meeting with Hirschfeld so that I could make the appropriate decision and limit any damage.

On 7 December 1992 I met Abu Ala for a final discussion of the matter. We decided that we would agree to follow up the dialogue in Norway as Hirschfeld had suggested, but along certain agreed lines. The fact that Norway had been proposed indicated a serious desire to keep the dialogue away from the eyes and ears of the media. Furthermore, the Scandinavian countries (Norway, Sweden and Denmark) did not arouse American sensibilities, because of their minimal political ambitions and their limited political influence. Indeed, the Americans had chosen Sweden to pave the way for an American–Palestinian dialogue in 1988 when members of the PLO met a number of American Jews led by Rita Hauser. It will be remembered that that meeting had led to a meeting with Arafat at which it was revealed that the group had the authorization of the American Administration to engage in a dialogue with the PLO under the patronage of the Swedish Government.

That the Israeli side proposed Norway as a venue for a dialogue suggested that the contact was not fortuitous. It surely meant that Hirschfeld's initiative was not altogether spontaneous but had been planned and that the Norwegian Government had had a hand in it. We could not believe that Hirschfeld wanted to have meetings with the PLO as just a university academic seeking knowledge. We had complete information on him and, furthermore, we were used to the type of contact that began in this manner, the type that did not commit officials in any way, especially as the proposed dialogue was to be directly with the PLO. This fact alone could lead to the fall of Rabin's Government which was balanced on a knife's edge. So by claiming that he was just an academic, Hirschfeld was protecting himself as well as those who stood behind him.

There were no risks in it for us. If the dialogue proved fruitful we would have achieved something we were after, and if it turned out to be just small talk with an academic this could not hurt us. So we could lose nothing. Since the Israelis did not trust us to keep a secret, we had to make doubly sure that the lid was tightly screwed on this new channel. This meant that we had to tell those who knew about the first meeting that it had not turned out to be a serious proposition, one that we decided to end. If they did not ask then we would say nothing at all. At that stage, only three of us knew about it: Arafat, Abu Ala and myself. Abu Ala welcomed the secrecy because this would be his first experience of dealing with Israelis, because it was fraught with danger and because he is a naturally secretive person. We did not inform our Oslo office of Abu Ala's arrival there. If they happened to have found out we would have told them we were following up the multilaterals. We also had to avoid informing the PLO offices en route to Oslo such as Rome, Geneva, Paris and London. More importantly, we had to avoid contact with the PLO's travel office in Tunis which dealt with arrivals and departures and whose staff were in and out of Tunis airport day and night. We had to prearrange convincing stories in case of accidental encounters.

Abu Ala had expressed concern about facing Israelis on his own at the meetings and now suggested that Hasan Asfour should accompany him; Asfour was secretary to the negotiations committee, kept all the documents and had all the facts relating to these negotiations at his fingertips. Nor was Abu Ala's English all that good to cope with discussions on political and legal matters. It should be noted here that Asfour was a member of the People's Party (the Palestinian communist party)

and its central committee. However, I was certain he would be completely loyal to the task at hand and would not equate it with loyalty to his organization; I was quite sure that he would not say a word about this channel even if this would lead to his expulsion from the People's Party. We chose Maher al-Kurd, who knew English well, to be the third member of the delegation. He had worked as an economic adviser in Abu Ala's department before being transferred to work for Arafat.[1]

We then moved to the substance of the negotiations. 'Now,' wondered Abu Ala, 'what are we going to say? And what are the points we are going to raise and talk about? I am not completely in the picture as to the limits of the bilateral negotiations.' He was very conscious of the magnitude of the task, the weight of the responsibility he was shouldering for the first time and the possibility of failure. But at the same time he was confident he could succeed provided preparation was thorough and the material he was to take with him was convincing, accurate and realistic.

The Documents

I had studied the documents exchanged by the Palestinian and Israeli teams at the Washington negotiations, but I set them aside since they were dominated by political literalism and dealt more with formalities than with substance. Both sides had tried to show how brilliant their drafting technique was, and had done their utmost to outdo one another in refuting the other side's arguments as eloquently as possible in the face of the constraints imposed upon them. We had therefore to devise another style for the Oslo channel, a style that would deal directly with the substance and the framework of a declaration of principles. That would require abandoning the method of the 'joint action agenda' which our Washington delegation had clung to in the belief that agreement on it was a prerequisite for a well-ordered and correct beginning. Up until the ninth round no agreement had been reached concerning this matter.

I thought up some ideas that could be used as the basis for a declaration of principles and kept them out of sight until they had been discussed with the Egyptian Foreign Ministry. After we made a few amendments I asked Amr Moussa to put these ideas (which Moussa approved) to the Israelis to see how they reacted to them, but as this did not happen, I simply noted Egypt's view and put the ideas aside for

---

[1] Later, when a disagreement arose between him and Abu Ala during the negotiations in Oslo, he was replaced by Muhammad Abu Kush. Kurd proved totally trustworthy; not a word about the secret channel escaped his lips.

another time. The ideas were contained in ten points, the first of which related to reference to the UN Resolutions 242 and 338. On this point I quoted Djerejian who had met our delegation in Washington. The Israelis had severely criticized the position taken by our delegation on this point, and Djerejian had suggested a formula which I found suitable and acceptable. I had therefore asked our team in Oslo to adopt it and had made it the starting-block of my ideas on a declaration of principles.

I also tried to sound out a small Jewish American delegation composed of Steve Cohen, Dan Abraham and Owen Owen who had come to see us. They were Jews with whom we had had contacts going back some years. They were also close to the Israeli Foreign Minister Shimon Peres, and regularly visited the region. They would visit us in Tunis or meet us in Cairo and then visit Shimon Peres and his group in Tel Aviv. Steve Cohen often relayed ideas between us and Tel Aviv. So I put my ideas informally to the delegation who expressed great admiration, saying that they could be used as a starting point on which to build, especially the reference to the issues of security and confederation. The delegation wanted these ideas in writing and I promised to send them the text later when this had been finalized and translated into English.

Abu Ala, Asfour and I then met, 48 hours before the they were due to travel to Oslo, to discuss the outline of how we would present our ideas, views and proposals. I wrote down all our suggestions, and the delegation was also supplied with the minutes of the Washington delegation to read. The following points remained the basis of our position on a declaration of principles:

1. The objective is to achieve a just, lasting and comprehensive peace settlement through direct negotiations based on Security Council Resolutions 242 and 338. The negotiations between the Palestinians and Israel will be conducted in phases, which are, however, an integral whole.
2. The territory over which the Palestinian Interim Authority will exercise power includes the Palestinian territories occupied in 1967. Administrative exceptions are to be agreed during the negotiations, provided these exceptions do not violate Resolutions 242 and 338 and the principles of international law.
3. The Palestinian Interim Authority will exercise all the powers in the spheres that are agreed upon (a review of established laws will be taken into consideration).

4. The Palestinian Interim Authority will be chosen through direct, free and general political elections by all Palestinian residents who were registered in the West Bank, including Jerusalem, and the Gaza Strip on 4 June 1967.
5. International supervisors and observers, whose identity is to be agreed upon, will monitor the electoral process and the transfer of power.
6. A Joint Israeli–Palestinian Committee will be established to deal with common issues and disputes. (The Committee will be composed of members of the Palestinian Interim Authority and the Israeli Government.)
7. An Arbitration Committee is to be established to review all disputes that the Joint Committee submits to it if these cannot be settled by negotiations through the latter. The Arbitration Committee will be made up of the co-sponsors of the peace conference as well as Egypt, Jordan and the United Nations and will include two representatives from the Palestinian Interim Authority and the Government of Israel, or other parties to be agreed upon.
8. The issue of security, in its strategic future concept, and looked at from the point of view of peaceful coexistence, requires a study that will be based on the good intentions of all parties concerned. The study will stem from a true desire to seek common interests in a way that will give a positive meaning to security and would make everyone keen to maintain.
9. The permanent status negotiations will commence two years after the implementation of the interim period, or according to agreement, whichever comes first. In any event, they should commence not later than the beginning of the third year of the interim period.
10. Without prejudice to the permanent status negotiations, an informal study is to be carried out to examine the possibility of a confederation and the most suitable ways of promoting peace and stability in the area.

The First Meeting

The first meeting was held between 20 and 22 January 1993. The Norwegians had chosen Sarpsborg, 80 kilometres south of Oslo, as the venue for the launching of the Palestinian–Israeli meeting. The meeting was attended on the Israeli side by Yair Hirschfeld and Ron Pundak. Neither man explained the extent of his relationship to the Israeli

Foreign Ministry but both hinted to some sort of link with Deputy Foreign Minister Yossi Beilin, who had apparently encouraged them to hold such a meeting. In spite of this rather shaky start, I urged our delegation to express our interest since all beginnings tended to be like this.

It was the beginning of a new stage, and we were embarking on uncharted territory. Since it appeared that both the Palestinian and Israeli sides were new to such negotiations, and because of the huge responsibility that our team was shouldering by sitting face to face with the Israelis, Abu Ala had written down all he had to say even before he left Tunis. He therefore spoke in Arabic and left the translation to Maher Kurd. Abu Ala did well to speak in Arabic at the beginning since this left no chance for misunderstanding or ambiguity and enabled him to convey the message accurately, comprehensively and clearly.

But our team expanded on all the ideas at the start of the first round and then felt they had to observe the Israeli side's impressions and reactions. Abu Ala also brought up issues that related to the multilaterals because his job, of course, was to follow up the (official) multilateral negotiations. This meant that there was no focus on or any in-depth discussion of any of the points raised and that the first session had become more one of introduction than of negotiation. Thus at the end of the first round it was not the points raised that had to be analysed, but rather the atmosphere of the talks and the Israelis' opinions.

After careful study of the minutes we arrived at two important conclusions. The first was that Pundak and Hirschfeld were not far removed from the Foreign Ministry and not just academic researchers in Israeli institutions of learning. The second was that Knesset member and Deputy Foreign Minister Yossi Beilin was backing them and had given them his support and trust. Our sources in the occupied territories confirmed this after a quick telephone call. Even though Beilin's standing did not add a great deal of weight to the channel's importance this was an important indicator that Shimon Peres was on line. We were not entirely reassured, but, all the same, we proceeded enthusiastically with this channel. The minutes, translated from Arabic, were as follows:

Round One: 21 January 1993
(Minutes of Meeting, Sarpsborg)

Attending on the Israeli side:
  Yair Hirschfeld and Ron Pundak.
Attending on the Palestinian side:
  Abu Ala, Hassan Asfour and Maher al-Kurd

Abu Ala: We are going through a fateful and important stage that requires much courage and daring. Both our sides need to invest in this opportunity. You must be aware that if we miss it there will be further wars and suffering for both our peoples. We are serious and well-intentioned. The crucial decision to achieve peace has been taken on our part. The state of frustration that has resulted from the stalled Washington negotiations has helped the opposition in our camp to confirm its viewpoint. I shall not hide from you that the state of frustration is due to three reasons. First, the agitated and harsh Israeli policy which we believe must calm down now; second, none of the negotiations have achieved any positive results: on the contrary, we feel that they have had negative results; third, the deterioration of economic, social and financial conditions in the occupied territories.

It is up to you to eliminate these reasons provided the intentions are genuine. We witnessed a difficult period after the Gulf war. Our position was misinterpreted, although we overdid one point, we are not ashamed to admit. But in recent days we have begun little by little to regain our relations with the Arab countries. A delegation headed by Abu Mazen visited Qatar, Saudi Arabia and Oman. Needless to say, Abu Mazen's visit was supported by the leadership, as all the statements issued by its officials confirm. I can also say that our relations with Europe, the Scandinavian countries and Japan are improving. We have not recommenced relations with America after the suspension of the dialogue, although the outlook seems promising. I believe the resumption of dialogue with America will help us a great deal in our negotiations.

We proved the sincerity of our intentions when we agreed to attend Madrid under unfair conditions. We shall remain committed to the peace process as long as there is hope for success. And we shall continue to struggle from within the process to improve the conditions of our participation in it. But I believe you agree with us that we reached a crossroad in Washington after fifteen months of negotiations, even though the US letters of invitation and assurances set a year of negotiations to be followed by the implementation of interim autonomy in the occupied territories. We have done our best to offer many proposals and solutions to bridge the gap between us, but we did not succeed. We have come to believe that the opposition (within the Palestinian camp) and its arguments prove more or less that negotiations need to be suspended. Therefore I will put forward some proposals today.

Reference to the UN Resolutions

Edward Djerejian presented our delegation in Washington with a proposal that we find acceptable as a way of resolving the issue of the reference [to the UN Resolutions 242 and 338]. We also have another proposal we can read to you. [This was the proposal included in the ten points agreed with the Egyptians and taken by the delegation to Oslo.] Agreement on the reference will facilitate the conduct of the negotiations. I must also point out that the reference [to 242 and 338] also applies to the interim period.

Extent of the Palestinian authority

It must be clear that a Palestinian authority will extend to all the Palestinian territories occupied in 1967 and that any exceptions regarding administrative issues may be agreed upon through negotiations, provided that these exceptions do not conflict with the totality of the jurisdiction and the substance of Resolution 242.

Security

We have placed it today in its correct framework in a way that serves our interests and yours and our needs and yours according to a strategic future concept and all that this implies in terms of the presentation of ideas for peaceful coexistence in the region and the search for common interests. This means that security takes on a positive character, that makes everyone seek to preserve it and not be forced to adopt it. This is a security that begets interests and not the security that prevents fear.

Elections

We understand that a Palestinian interim council will be formed through direct, free and general elections by which all Palestinians in the West Bank and Gaza Strip will participate in accordance with the demographic statistics as at 4 June 1967. This council will legislate with all the powers transferred to it by mutual agreement, taking into account the need for a general review of the laws currently in force. International observers, who are to be agreed upon, will monitor these elections.

Israel must take certain steps and measures that will cost it nothing, including (1) as a first step: resolving the issue of the deportees. We believe that Israel's initiative to return persons deported since 1967 gives its stance significant credibility, especially the return of some personalities whose positions will consolidate the peace process; (2) as a second step: it is time to rehabilitate the part played by the PLO in the peace process by giving it a direct role that will push the process forward and facilitate decision making during the negotiations; (3) as a third step: the Government of Israel must declare the halting of settlement activities as an expression of goodwill and an indication that its policy is not expansionary. Also, the lifting of restrictions on economic activity and on human rights issues in general; (4) as a fourth step: Rabin and Peres spoke about withdrawing from Gaza. Why has there not been a withdrawal if Gaza gives you all these headaches? If that happens it will herald the beginning of cooperation with Israel, because Gaza needs a Marshall plan, and it could be made a free zone. If you show willingness to do so then the free zone can extend to Ashdod. This is an enormous and very important project of cooperation. Studies can be presented in absolute secrecy by you, by us and by international parties too. We have only just thought of this idea, which is why we have not discussed it in the past. Solving the problem of Gaza will resolve severe economic and social problems. I am not asking for a response from you now, but you should study this idea for the future because it represents an aspect of future cooperation. We have to consider the extent of its effect on the Arab region too, since we can establish various industries like a motor car industry and high-technology industries. Withdrawal from Gaza is not a deal at the expense of the West Bank, and I hope you do not see it in this context. But it is a plan that is important for the stimulation of the peace process and has a magical effect.

Abu Ala then touched upon the issues of the multilateral negotiations.

The development committee

There is a list of confidence-building measures in the economic sphere which can be presented to an economic development committee. We hope the Israeli delegation will not object to them. It will be beneficial for both of us if Israel grants permits for a development bank, a cement factory, Gaza commercial port and housing projects, including Jerusalem.

The water committee

I do not know what is at the root of Israeli thinking in refusing to discuss our water rights. Why do you reject the idea of forming a committee on water rights? The Palestinians only get a small share of their water rights. Why won't you allow the building of the Valley Canal along the lines of the Eastern Canal? It is now necessary to lift the ban on establishing, supplying and supporting a national Palestinian water authority. If I were in your place I would have put forward this proposal to the multilaterals.

The refugee committee

For many reasons, both political and humanitarian, a positive atmosphere should be created. This can be done by lifting the ban on reuniting families and allowing the deportees to return. We could then forge ahead with the discussion of other issues on this committee's agenda.

The environment committee

When we proposed the setting up of an environmental protection agency the Israeli delegation objected to it. We do not believe there is an excuse for such objection.

The security committee

We hope that no problems will be raised over the Palestinian representation in this committee.

The direction committee

We don't understand the reasons behind your objection to the formation of the Jerusalem committee because in our opinion it will help create a positive atmosphere for both sides. We also see a need to invite Iraq and Libya to become part of the political process.

Miscellaneous items

What about the canal linking the Mediterranean and the Red Sea? What about cooperation in investments in the Dead Sea; minerals, chemicals, tourism, and a free zone in the Jordan Valley?

Confederation

Rabin spoke of confederation as a future option. We are seriously considering this suggestion. We want you to tell us about it.

The following dialogue ensued:

Hirschfeld: I want to express my immediate reaction. What I am hearing now is extremely important. It expresses a determination to achieve peace and reflects a creative mind. If I want to talk about practical matters, I tell you: start with Gaza and develop many projects in it. I expect Labour to push in this direction so that Gaza will become a model for economic cooperation. I also consider that the majority in the Labour Party will understand that such action will reflect upon the West Bank.

As for your proposals which we have listened to, we will present a report to our side and we'll return to you with answers and ideas on all the matters you've raised. Your honesty and clarity will help us face many problems and will enable Rabin to convince the Labour Party to take quicker steps because our public opinion accepts the idea of withdrawal from the Gaza Strip. I would like to ask, do you have a suggestion on a timetable regarding the Gaza Strip?

Abu Ala: Gaza needs stability, security and development as soon as possible.

Hirshfeld: What will be the way? To whom do we have to give the key?

Abu Ala: That can be agreed upon. The United Nations, some international body, especially the co-sponsors.

Hirschfeld: We expect to give the key to you.

Abu Ala: It would be an important gesture of goodwill on your part if you give it to the co-sponsors. What is your position on the idea of turning one hundred to two hundred kilometres of the Gaza Strip and a similar area of Ashdod into a joint free zone?

Hirschfeld: We can conduct a serious study of this project within the framework of an economic cooperation plan. Can this be arranged in a proper way to benefit both sides? Would it be possible to arrange a meeting between Faisal Husseini and Rabin to discuss this issue and then follow it up here through this informal channel? Yossi Beilin and I conducted a study nearly two years ago on a unilateral withdrawal from Gaza and found strong support, not just from Labour but from Likud too, especially Moshe Arens. Public opinion is ready to respond to this idea of withdrawal.

Abu Ala: What about the [Jewish] settlements in the Gaza Strip?

Hirschfeld: This is a matter that needs studying because it has to be related to its effect on Jewish ownership. More importantly, whatever happens in the Gaza Strip the settlements will become a guiding model for the West Bank in the future. Why can the settlements not be used in joint projects?

We believe that if we move out of the Gaza Strip no one will be able to prevent the PLO from entering it. We might be able to find a way to merge the issue of Gaza with the preamble of the accord. Agreement on Gaza will determine the role of each party and will facilitate any amendment to the terms of the reference.

Abu Ala: This issue, that is withdrawal from Gaza, is to be dealt with as a separate issue that does not prejudice the final solution, and that it is not a deal at the expense of the West Bank.

Hirschfeld: We find it strange that there is a problem regarding the cement factory because we know the factory has been approved. We will confirm that.

Abu Ala: There are obstacles to the implementation measures, especially the question of testing the soil, geological activity and also the permit itself, which was only preliminary.

Hirschfeld: Regarding the Palestinian development bank there are problems relating to the nature of the currency. If you are going to use the Shekel there would be no problem.

Abu Ala: We want to deal in convertible currencies. We also want to be able to deal in the Palestinian pound in the future.

Hirschfeld: I believe that the construction of 7,500 housing units in Jerusalem will represent one of the most important confidence-building measures.

Abu Ala: Housing in general is a very important process and is the driving force for the Palestinian economy because of the job opportunities and the related industries that it creates. But in order for it to be practical, construction must take place in Jerusalem and on public lands.

Hirschfeld: Why do you insist on the water rights issue when it is actually one of the attributes of sovereignty and will be discussed in the final phase? We might be able to cooperate with you in increasing your share of water consumption. But to begin with we need to cooperate on a set of small projects before we get round to water, so that you can acquire the tools of a capable administration. That can be discussed to some extent in the multilaterals although it is mainly a matter for the bilateral talks.

Abu Ala: Water rights are to be discussed in the final phase of the multilaterals, but it is not a good idea to postpone discussion of them now. If we consider the peace process as a whole, the two of us can actually facilitate matters for each other in the bilateral as well as in the multilateral negotiations.

Hirschfeld: On the subject of the Western Valley Canal, the Syrians are using more than their share. The Jordanians have asked us to help them, which we have agreed to do. The remaining water resources will be insufficient for the Western Valley Canal. You could ask a country such as Switzerland or Canada to finance a study for you on how to handle the water issue by collecting the run-off water from the mountains above the valley.

Abu Ala: We cannot relinquish our right to water. If we have a surplus we would conclude an agreement with Jordan and with you so as to preserve everyone's interests. But we do not accept that our share be taken by either you or Jordan or Syria. We don't want anyone to have water at our expense.

Hirschfeld: We suggest another approach, which is that at the multilateral negotiations you propose a standard rate for water. This would mean that the Palestinian would pay the same price as the Israeli. This would contribute to improving conditions. You can also build a desalinization plant in Gaza. We would be prepared to purchase surplus quantities of water while you would reap extra benefit at the same time by generating electricity.

Abu Ala: Despite their importance, these are matters of detail. We consider the desalinization plant as unfeasible and too costly. More importantly, our water rights exist. If this can be agreed then discussion can proceed on the management and consolidation of the water resources. We can cooperate on them. A water problem could be a potential cause of war. If real peace is achieved then one or two nuclear-powered stations, financed by those countries that are concerned with the region's stability, can become the most important sources and resources of water. Of course the cost is high, some $10 billion.

Hirschfeld: Our position on the reuniting of [Palestinian] families is that this is a matter for discussion in the bilateral negotiations because raising such an issue with the multilateral working group on refugees will usher the problem of the right of return. You are aware of Israeli fears about the subject and what the return to Haifa and Jaffa means. This will lead to instability. After the final settlement and the Israeli withdrawal the issue of the right of return will become your problem. The question of the reuniting of families can be dealt with within the framework of the confidence-building measures at the bilaterals. In the meantime, the multilateral working group on the refugees will discuss the question of improving the condition of the refugees until the final settlement is reached.

Abu Ala: We view both tracks of the peace process as one process. Progress in one track permits progress in the other. Although the bilaterals are the focal point of the peace process, this issue is on the agenda of the multilaterals. There is a UN resolution on this subject, Security Council Resolution 237, while Resolution 194 refers to the right of return. If we were in the Israeli Government's shoes we would have launched a confidence-building initiative and begun reuniting families. We cannot see that there is any excuse for the Israeli Government's hesitation in this respect.

Hirschfeld: It would be possible to facilitate the reuniting of families by putting forward a set of projects that need specialists, and say that some of the applicants to be reunited are the ones who are able to help set up these projects.

Abu Ala: The total number of applications presented to the Red Cross exceeds fifty thousand. All these people have the right of return according the Resolution 237.

Hirschfeld: Regarding the formation of a national Palestinian environmental protection authority, we do not see any problem. I will see Environment Minister Yossi Sarid about it. As for the formation of a working group on Jerusalem, we honestly do not understand your position or know the reasons behind your wish. Some of the parties involved in this committee – if it is formed – will try to discuss whether we need the Syrians or the Saudis. We can hold various sorts of unofficial talks on Jerusalem. You notice that major steps have been taken but they are indirect. We appreciate the need for special status for Jerusalem. For example, the special status of Orient House [the official Palestinian delegation's headquarters], housing in Jerusalem, institutions and others. Therefore, let us discuss this matter in the bilaterals. There is no need to internationalize Jerusalem. For us, Jerusalem must remain united. At the same time, we understand that Jerusalem's Palestinians must not become part of Israel. We also understand Jerusalem's importance to you. To sum up, we are prepared to discuss Jerusalem but not in the multilaterals.

Abu Ala: Then let the discussion take place in the bilaterals and let us form an unofficial committee for it.

Hirschfeld: In this case the Israeli Government would fall immediately, especially because the Shas group would leave the coalition. We have a final comment on Palestinian representation in the security committee at the multilateral negotiations. We hope no changes will be made to the formula of this representation. I believe you understand our position.

We noticed that the first round of discussion dealt with many issues in a superficial way without concentration on specific topics. Our impression of the outcome was that we should continue with the discussions. We noted that Israeli 'red lines' had hardly been defined, a fact which would enable our team in the coming rounds to raise all the subjects we considered necessary for a framework of a declaration of principles. Analysis of the minutes also told us which issues it was possible to tackle successfully so that we could concentrate on them in the short run. In general, most of the main issues that were touched upon could potentially form a declaration of principles but needed further discussion to fix them and refine them. The problem we had on our minds was the extent to which these Israeli negotiators represented the Israeli political establishment, their ability to commit themselves to whatever was agreed and to subsequently promote these agreements in Israel.

This channel's main weakness was that it was secret, which meant the Israelis could either deny its existence or reveal it, thereby finishing it off. The second weakness was that Pundak and Hirschfeld denied that they were representing an official body, although they indicated more than once that there were links with one official or another. What was certain was that the two were Labour Party members and had an association with Deputy Foreign Minister Yossi Beilin. In spite of these encouraging signs our doubts hung over us throughout the ensuing three rounds, which on the Israeli side were only attended by the same men.

The dialogue was protracted and detailed and sometimes repetitious, elaborating points that had been raised sometime before. Meantime, trust and understanding was deepening between the two sides. Things started to become serious, and a determination to achieve positive results began to take hold. The following minutes are translated from Arabic.

Round Two: 11 February 1993
(Minutes of Meeting)

Hirschfeld: I would like to talk about the subject of the deportees. We have reached an understanding with the United States. Rabin has actually lost face in Israel. We have to seek an agreement in which no one loses. Is that possible? Such an agreement will improve the situation of both sides. At present, the repeated attacks against us by Boutros Ghali [Secretary-General of the United Nations] and the PLO make our situation harder. Rabin has spoken in special sessions of the danger of the Ikhwan movement [The Muslim Brothers] taking power in Jordan. Also, it seems that the Iranian position is gradually acquiring more legitimacy because of the interest of Western companies in the economic opportunities that are opening up in Iran as a result of Western cooperation with Iran.

As for America's current position we view it in this way:

President Clinton is concentrating on internal affairs. This means that America's foreign policy drive is waning; it is evident that the forces of the Western alliance which were mobilized by the United States during the Gulf crisis have begun to waver and disperse; we can however revive American activity in the peace process by establishing mutual understanding.

We have received a message of peace from you. This message is important in affecting our political thinking. For our part, we have come to this bilateral meeting with our own message of peace. We feel that we need to make great progress in the negotiations and to make tangible improvement in the economic and social conditions of the West Bank and the Gaza Strip. However, we need to have a quick look at the channels that are available to us; these are: Norway, Faisal and Hanan and Sari Nusseiba. We need a political channel that will affect the internal situation in Israel, but all these informal channels must feed into the official channel and make their results available to it.

Shimon Peres and Rubinstein will return from Washington to evaluate the negotiations with the Palestinians. This evaluation will be comprehensive, but it is evident that Yitzhak Rabin still favours continuing with the bilateral negotiations in Washington.

Here I must clarify some of the features of our new policy for you: it concentrates on the need to improve conditions in the West Bank and Gaza even if it leads to negative effects on the Israeli economy. Peres officially announced that Israel does not want to annex the West Bank and Gaza when he said, 'After achieving peace we can think about a confederation.' Another important aspect is Israel's readiness to assign more state land to the Palestinians for the purpose of development. We believe that the faster we can achieve common understanding the better it will be for us, for you and for the Americans. Therefore we want to discuss with you today the means of solving some problems and achieving understanding.

Pundak: The Israeli Government will introduce a fundamental change in the structure of support for the settlements. The Government has actually made a decision regarding a new policy whereby it will increase aid for the settlements and villages inside Israel at the expense of the settlements in the West Bank and Gaza. Another aspect of the new policy concentrates on giving a chance to the development of the economy there without considering the negative repercussions on our economy. To this end, the following steps have been taken:

1. Tax exemptions for three years for new industrial projects.
2. Encouraging Palestinians from abroad to invest in industry and housing by granting them two-year entry permits. To date, forty people from abroad have made use of this procedure. No restrictions or limits have been placed on the amount of money coming in or on the sources of the funds.
3. Encouraging direct exports.
4. Approval for establishing an independent office for the European Union representation in East Jerusalem.

5. Customs fees on bridges have been reduced with respect to exports to Jordan.
6. Approval for establishing eight industrial zones; five in Gaza and three in the West Bank. All will be created on state land.
7. Agreement for granting permits for new projects; 90 in Gaza and 108 in the West Bank.
8. The board of directors of the cement factory have now received an official letter of agreement and also permission to receive $150,000 to conduct studies.
9. Permits have been granted for the erection of a mill in Gaza or Ramallah.
10. Agreement has been given to approve the opening of seven new branches of the Cairo–Amman Bank and a new branch of the Bank of Palestine in Gaza. There are ongoing negotiations with Jordanian banks, specifically the Bank of Jordan.
11. Approval for the opening of two new insurance companies that will be officially accredited within two weeks.
12. Agreement in principle on the creation of housing projects on state land.

The head of the Israeli Chamber of Commerce put out a statement after he had met with Saudis and Qataris saying that he had stressed the need for promoting economic development in the West Bank and Gaza Strip in order to establish a unified Israeli–Palestinian economy with no customs barriers, permitting the full integration of the Palestinian and Israeli economies. A Knesset committee visited the Gaza Strip at the same time and afterwards called for a fundamental – and not simply a gradual – change in economic conditions. It suggested that finance for investments should come from abroad and from local Palestinian sources, money that is kept under the carpet.

I am bound to say that the thinking in Israel *vis-à-vis* the West Bank and the Gaza Strip is witnessing fundamental change.

Abu Ala: The Israeli practice of deportation has brought peace to the brink of collapse. It is regrettable that the international community is preoccupied with the deportation issue and is not following the negotiations. Sending Palestinian delegations to either the bilateral or the multilateral negotiations has become almost impossible, especially as the Madrid formulas regarding the composition of the delegations is giving rise to difficulties; on the one hand the members of these delegations are living under Israeli occupation and, on the other, they are exposed to the pressures of public opinion.

As for the American position we feel that America is neglecting its foreign policy and concentrating on its internal situation. This brings matters back into Israeli and Palestinian hands. America will not oppose the both of us but will support us because it will no longer have to deal with a complicated problem. Therefore, the question that poses itself is how serious are we in wanting to reach agreement?

Achieving an agreement on a declaration of principles would be a great breakthrough if we want to look to the future, to coexistence and to stability. We might not be able to attain that through the Washington negotiations, but we might succeed through the unofficial channels. Therefore this channel must be credible. We are both speaking with complete honesty. If our respective leaderships do not back us then hopes for success will diminish. In any case our dialogue must have no limits or 'red lines'. That is why I am worried that if the Israeli leadership is not fully informed of the proceedings of these meetings they would be a total waste of time. It is time that this channel is given the attention and the facilities for the success that it deserves. We can organize sub-branches for discussion of different issues. We have noted Rabin's remark that agreement with the Palestinians would require five to ten years. I hope you are aware that there will be no peace without the Palestinians because the Palestinian problem is the basis of the wider conflict in the Middle East.

Pundak: [Referring to the suspension or reduction of settlements construction] We believe the most important measure for confidence-building is to halt the settlement process. We do not ask that it be announced.

Hirschfeld: We reached an understanding here about achieving progress at the last meeting. We have noted two messages from you: first, that you want the peace process to continue with no Palestinian State being created in the meantime, but that this issue be left to later developments, and that the PLO's role be direct but made public years later. Second, that you understand the difficulties we are facing and that you are prepared to show some flexibility to ensure the success of the process, which means that you are ready to go underground and then emerge gradually at a later stage.

Abu Ala: I wish to confirm that a temporary Palestinian council will emerge from a Palestinian interim authority. It is understood that the interim arrangements are an integral part of the overall peace process leading to the implementation of Resolutions 242 and 338. We also believe that the election of a council must be direct, free and general and held under international supervision. All Palestinians from the West Bank and the Gaza Strip will participate in them according to the demographic record as at 4 June 1967. This includes East Jerusalem.

Hirschfeld: Regarding international supervision of the elections, Peres told Faisal Husseini that the elections held in 1976 had been fair and had resulted in the election of pro-PLO mayors. From another perspective, the presence of the international media is sufficient. For example, I believe that Barbara Walters is more important than Jimmy Carter in this respect. As for international supervision of the election it will be explained that our situation is similar to that of the Philippines. As for participation in the elections according to the demographic record as at 4 June 1967, do not expect us to accept your viewpoint on Jerusalem's participation in the elections. I hope you understand that the subject of Jerusalem is open for discussion, but I hope you will begin discussing it after the elections.

Abu Ala: The American letter of assurances confirmed the participation of the residents of Jerusalem.

Hirschfeld: Then take up the subject of Jerusalem's participation directly with the Americans and not with us. If we imagine a situation in which our Government agrees to the participation of Jerusalem's residents in the elections then it will definitely fall. We believe we must come to an arrangement enabling Palestinian leaders in Jerusalem to vote. We must arrange this in a manner that can be passed without arousing strong Israeli opposition to it.

Abu Ala: We cannot reach any agreement on a declaration of principles without mentioning Jerusalem.

Pundak: How can we get such an issue past the Shas Party? You must understand that Shas can cause the collapse of the Government if it withdraws. Therefore the participation of the Palestinian leaders in Jerusalem can be arranged through Ramallah or some other place. There is an electoral rule that states: 'Voting [may take place] from the nearest place possible.' If we were to accept your proposal that participation in the elections will be decided by the 4 June 1967 records, then the whole cabinet will erupt on the issue of Jerusalem.

Abu Ala: We wish to raise another matter, which is the scope of authority of a Palestinian self-government. This is a multidimensional and extremely important issue. Jurisdiction must cover all the Palestinian territories occupied in 1967, with administrative exceptions during the interim period.

Hirschfeld: Full jurisdiction over the territories is absolutely impossible during the interim period because the matter pertains to the final phase.

Abu Ala: We understand that the interim period is necessary to build trust between us in preparation for the achievement of peace in the final phase. But we do not accept that the Authority should lack jurisdiction over the territories during the interim period.

Hirschfeld: We have talked about creating an authority for the territories during the interim period. This authority will supervise the territories that are agreed upon. As for extending the authority's jurisdiction to all the territories, that is a most difficult subject because this would lead us to a discussion of the issue of the settlements and East Jerusalem. Let us begin with what is possible. As for the final status, our negotiations over it will focus on one subject. We say 'withdrawal from territories' and you say 'withdrawal from the territories'. This is a matter for the final status negotiations and therefore cannot be dealt with now. Your suggestion that the authority's jurisdiction should cover all the territories occupied in 1967 assumes that it would be possible to reach agreement now about an issue that is a matter for the final status negotiations.

As regards the [Israeli] withdrawal from Gaza we hope that it will start with the commencement of the final status negotiations. As regards arbitration, this issue is of utmost difficulty. If we allow arbitration to proceed, negotiations will stop each time you refer any issue we disagree over to arbitration. If accepted, arbitration must be clearly limited to one or two issues at the most.

The conversation then moved to the settlements.

Hirschfeld: We have prepared written pledges to be signed by the settlers, limiting their demands for compensation for their homes only in the event of their leaving. Compensation is calculated according to the actual cost that was borne by the Government in the construction of these settlement homes. This is to avoid repetition of the experience that we had with the settlers in Sinai who demanded compensation payments before moving out.

Round Three: 20 March 1993
(Notes and Minutes of Meeting)

The second round concentrated on basic issues of a declaration of principles such as reference to the UN Resolutions, the Palestinian council, Jerusalem, territorial jurisdiction, the withdrawal from Gaza and economic development. Thus the features of the main articles of the declaration of principles began to emerge, and the way was now open for the drafting of one or more drafts for the declaration. It took only two rounds to clarify matters as no time was wasted on formalities. Our team's concern was to ascertain for itself that this channel was backed by the Israeli Cabinet, first in order to satisfy itself that talking with these Israelis was not pointless, and second, if that were the case, then we would decline attempts by other Israelis to open up new channels with us.

In this round the Israelis said that the officials in Israel were pleased with the message of peace that our delegation had conveyed. They then talked about how close matters were to reaching a serious turning point that would transform us from a state of enmity to one of friendship and cooperation. They stressed that their priority was geared to the Palestinian track, followed by the Syrian track, so that peace would have two feet supporting it. They indicated that Syria's joining the peace process would finish off the Damascus-based Palestinian opposition. They spoke of the US role and of Warren Christopher's visit to Jerusalem and his negotiations with Faisal Husseini on the matter of the deportees. The minutes, translated from Arabic, ran as follows.

Hirschfeld: We feel you have not made use of some of the opportunities available to you. For example, the letter of invitation from the co-sponsors for participation in the bilateral talks at the impending ninth round contained a clear reference to Resolutions 242 and 338. You could have made better use of that. You made a mistake in not concluding the agreement with Warren Christopher when he came to Jerusalem. We stress that we briefed them in full about this channel, and the Norwegians also informed them but in less detail. As for Jerusalem, there are two sides to our position. One of them is negative. Our Government is very wary about it and finds it difficult to mention the word Jerusalem in any venue of negotiations with you. The second side is positive. We can work together to adopt measures favourable to you in Jerusalem because we are fully aware that we have to negotiate about it. Among the important indicators is Orient House.

The Israeli team went on to talk about attempts by Israeli officials to open channels with the PLO. It confirmed it had no objections to such contacts being made but that it wished to coordinate the talks through the Oslo channel. In fact it was a polite way of saying not to deal with them.

Yair Hirschfeld and Ron Pundak seemed keen to produce a mutually agreed document in order to achieve a breakthrough. This, they felt, would encourage the United States to participate. Our team, on the other hand, highlighted the necessity of Egyptian participation. The Egyptians were now beginning to examine the documents as they became available; these included Foreign Minister Amr Moussa and

President Mubarak's adviser on political affairs, Dr Usama al-Baz. Our delegation then said that it could not sign any agreement that did not include a text on Jerusalem. At this point in the proceedings the following dialogue ensued:

Hirschfeld: We have to find a way to get this [the question on Jerusalem] through, and we have to find a special language when talking about Jerusalem.

Abu Ala: Concerning the other [proposed] channels, we will concentrate our contacts in this channel. Also we can coordinate what takes place at meetings on security through this channel with a view to serving them.

Hirschfeld: About the elections, I want to concentrate on the role of the people outside because those outside are the partners of the future. Let the process of persons returning from abroad begin so that they may take part in the coming elections. The PLO leadership can nominate people from the outside to return and take part in the elections. The return of strong candidates on your part will help achieve our common interests. For example, you can choose to nominate five people for membership in the interim council, like Abu Mazen and Abu Ala.

Abu Ala: Concerning the mode and conditions of the elections, they must include the following points: the involvement of all citizens registered in the West Bank, the Gaza Strip and Jerusalem on 4 June 1967; the participation of the people of Jerusalem as candidates and voters. The elections can take place at al-Aqsa Mosque and the Church of the Holy Sepulchre; international supervision of the elections.

Hirschfeld: We cannot accept international supervision. We can guarantee free elections, as you know from the 1976 experience. We would prefer independent Palestinian supervision of the elections. As for your insistence on citizens registered on 4 June 1967, Abu Mazen, for example, might not be registered in the census.

Abu Ala: In discussing the article that is concerned with the extent of authority, what do you really want? Do you want an interim period to test good intentions? Or do you want to impose the de facto situation and annexation? If that is the case, this attitude will destroy the peace process, and there will be no settlement. No one can predict the kind of risks that the coming changes will pose, and there will not be real peace without a satisfactory solution for the Palestinians. If your security calculations are that only armies pose a threat, then we take on Israeli hearts and minds, and that is no less of a threat than that posed by military force.

Hirschfeld: The Israeli sovereignty borders are the 'green line' today.

This Government does not want annexation. Ultimately, negotiations will be needed to determine secure and recognized borders. These will include changes to some territories. This is Resolution 242, in other words. If we sign a declaration of principles in July 1993, for example, we will begin the permanent status negotiations in July 1995. In these negotiations a new order in the Middle East will be discussed, including the option of confederation and Israeli withdrawal from Gaza, which will give you what you want; then everyone in Tunis can move to Gaza. And by presenting plans for economic projects in the West Bank you will be able to bring more territories within Palestinian authority, such as the Mediterranean–Dead Sea channel project.

We are moving away from the situation where we are fully controlling the territories to a new state in which you can exercise control over parts of them and veto rights over others while leaving the third part [settlements] under Israeli control until negotiations have taken place over the permanent solution.

This round ended with a review of the document that had been prepared as a draft declaration of principles, after which Yair Hirschfeld confirmed that he would take the document back to Israel. He anticipated three possibilities: either they would say the document was not acceptable and so the channel will be suspended; or they would agree to the document in full; or they would say that the document needed some amendments and that the contacts with the PLO were leading to positive and encouraging results. Hirschfeld would then be asked to continue working on improving the document through this particular channel.

In the conclusion to the minutes of this session our team made a few brief comments on the positions of the Israelis, Norwegians and Americans. The comments were as follows:

The Israeli side

- The document that the Israeli team brought with them before any amendments were made is personally drafted by Mr Shimon Peres.
- Rabin is informed, but not fully aware of all the details.
- Only the specialized Foreign Ministry team concerned with the negotiations fully adopts and supports the results of this secret channel. The PLO has proved that it is a qualified partner.
- We expect and do not object to the return of the PLO leadership from Tunis to Gaza.
- Concerning the elections of the interim council, we will facilitate the return of a number of first-rank leaders from Tunis to run for the

election. There must be coordination with the Egyptians to have the boycott on the PLO lifted.

- Reduction of the time period previously mentioned for Israeli withdrawal from Gaza; the amended text is as follows: 'A period not exceeding two years from the date of signing of this agreement.'
- For the first time there is more discussion among the Israelis in their own language, and for the first time talks are being interrupted so that they can contact their officials.
- They expressed great interest in the 'messages of peace' from Arafat personally, whether in his press statements or in his meetings with some personalities from their side.
- At the next meeting they will present a document containing their plan for the early withdrawal from Gaza and their suggestions for the post-withdrawal period; these will consider security, the multinational forces, the immediate economic measures required for economic construction, transport for goods and individuals, as measures for creating stability and development to serve peace.
- Working groups will be set up to consider every article and paragraph and provide financial back-up for this channel. They expressed interest in the fact that Egypt is kept informed; their delegation head will travel to Cairo next week.
- This agreement will be presented at the next meeting of the reduced cabinet so that this channel may be given a full mandate and for the discussion of this project to proceed.

The American side

- Is aware of this channel at the level of the Secretary of State who expressed interest and encouragement.
- The document was studied in detail with Dan Kurtzer.
- On Tuesday the Deputy Secretary of State will speak via the telephone hot line from the American Embassy to the American Administration.
- At the written invitation of the American Department of State, a Norwegian Foreign Ministry envoy will go to Washington on Tuesday with the final document.

The Norwegian side

- The Foreign Minister, his deputy and two other people at the Ministry are exerting great efforts to provide all the appropriate facilities and support for this channel.
- They are in constant contact with the other side, with the American State Department and with us.

– Have expressed readiness to host and to finance all the requirements of the specialized teams for the preparation of the necessary reports, studies, research and plans that will be appended to this agreement.
– Has expressed tremendous optimism about the success of this channel this time round.
– Its view is that once both sides have adopted the document in its final form the Americans should put it forward. They see this as a valuable gift for the Clinton Administration.

There were contacts between us and the Norwegians in the period between the third and fourth rounds. The telephone message of 12 April 1993 from Terje Larsen ran as follows:

– The Norwegian envoy held meetings yesterday with Peres and Beilin.
– Rabin met Peres many times to discuss the agreement.
– Rabin said this channel is the most important and that the negotiations now have full authorization.
– The agreement can be considered as a completely acceptable framework.
– They will suggest a part of this agreement during the meeting on 20 April and you will see some sentences and texts quoted from it.
– We now have a very important paper.
– They want this channel to continue and suggest meeting on 25 April.
– Rabin and Peres admit that you are the most important partner.
– They discussed the channel with the Americans who now realize its importance and consider it the crucial channel.
– They want Oslo to continue to be the channel.

Our response was as follows:

– We are making efforts to attend the negotiations of 20 April despite the problems and difficulties.
– We hope this subject or any of its articles are not mentioned to our negotiating delegation.
– We suggest that the meeting be held on 15/16 April to initial.
– Afterwards we will agree on the presentation.

The Norwegians changed the venues of the meeting in every round. Rarely was more than one meeting held at the same place. For this round, the meetings moved from Sarpsborg to a small hotel, the Holmenkollen Park on the outskirts of Oslo where the two delegations would live in the same hotel. Surrounded by a forest, this small hotel was the ideal place for the two delegations to get to know each other for they had to spend both working and leisure hours together. It was very important for them to spend their free time in each other's company since this gave them time to speak freely, honestly and warmly.

Round Four: 30 April 1993
(Minutes of Meeting, Oslo)

Hirschfeld: We launched this channel after our London meeting; at the time it was a personal initiative built on an appreciation of the need to discuss what was possible to accomplish through direct contacts. I can say that a great deal has been achieved. The US gave the channel its blessing, you received Egyptian support and we obtained a fairly broad approval from Rabin to continue working through this channel.

What interests you most is the closure of the Gaza Strip. But this matter gives us a lot of help when we confront Likud because the closure creates the legality of separation. In this way we are achieving two things; the legality of separation and the legality of the dialogue with the PLO. But there has to be rapid progress in the talks because Rabin is under strong attack, and some people believe he has offered more concessions than is necessary. I hope you noticed his brave speech on Independence Day when he said, 'The Jews must be able to visit all of their holy places even if they are under the sovereignty of others.' Then he went on to say, 'I am talking about Sinai.'

Abu Ala: We firmly believe in this channel and we have enough support from behind the scenes. We are eager for it to succeed quickly even more than you imagine. We are also anxious to keep it secret, but we were surprised to find that Steve Cohen was aware of it and speaking about it in a way that embarrassed us, especially because he talked to people who have no relation whatsoever with matters of this sort. Therefore I wonder whether the channel that exists between Faisal Husseini and Ziad Abu Ziad[1] on the one hand and a prominent Labour deputy on the other has been sanctioned by you? We want clarity and honesty.

There's another point I want to make clear, that is our agreement not to raise any issue at the negotiating table in Washington before it has been agreed here beforehand. For this reason we directed our delegation there to discuss only general issues so as to give us time to complete our work here.

As for the withdrawal from Gaza, as confirmed by Rabin's statement as well as by our agreement reached here, and after studying this matter and

---

[1] Palestinian lawyer, publisher of a Hebrew newspaper.

carefully gauging the possible reactions in the West Bank and elsewhere, we consider that it is necessary to time the withdrawal from Gaza to coincide with the withdrawal from the West Bank so that the residents in the West Bank don't feel discriminated against. You know what a magic word 'withdrawal' is in the hearts of the citizens. We suggest then that there should be a simultaneous withdrawal from Jericho.

Hirschfeld: This channel of ours began without an agenda. In London I met Dan Kurtzer who told me: 'You have two options open to you. The PLO on the one hand, and Faisal and Hanan on the other, and it is absolutely necessary to create secret lines of communication everywhere with the PLO and with the various local leaderships.' Naturally, we speeded up moves with this channel, and are working to expand the circle of people convinced of it. But we have to understand that the strategy of Rabin and the US is to begin with great caution at the point where Likud left off, and then move gradually to effect conciliation. But they also see that it is necessary to continue the momentum of the Washington channel for another period so as to bring about a rapprochement between the two sides. Therefore we require your positive participation in Washington and a commitment from your delegation to attend the committees and demonstrate seriousness, even just by listening, for two weeks until much more has been accomplished here.

I would like to raise another matter, that we should begin talking to you about the ideas on the final status. At this point we can arrive at a document that will be signed at a later stage. Our discussion can centre on two possible concepts: (1) Jordanian–Palestinian confederation and (2) a tripartite model.

I would also like a straightforward discussion on our understanding of the gradual appearance of the PLO on the scene. We have to talk about ways and means for your participation in the elections, your nominating of people and the timing of the transfer of your institutions from Tunis to Gaza. The final status document, if it is agreed and signed, will form the basis of the formation of the Palestinian entity, and the Oslo agreement will become a part of a general agreement.

Abu Ala: I am hearing a new language that indicates a lack of will to complete the document we have in our hands now ready for signature, because this discussion of other topics is beginning to look like an escape into the future.

Hirschfeld: We have not yet agreed in full. We have developed the document here and it can be completed in Washington because we honestly need to think some more about it and we require wider participation on our side.

Abu Ala: How long will we have to wait?

Hirschfeld: During Usama al-Baz's meeting with Rabin, al-Baz said, 'The Palestinians cannot wait forever.' So Rabin asked him, 'What is the period you envisage?' Al-Baz replied, 'Six weeks.' Rabin said, 'We need more time to arrange our internal situation.' I believe a scenario for action can be drawn up for the coming six weeks comprising the following stages:

– The next two weeks we move in two directions: first, the delegation continues the talks in Washington without amplification, even if it only listens and smiles; and secondly, we need a week to ten days to discuss the situation on our side in Israel concerning some of the points of the agreement.

– During the following two weeks the final draft of the agreement will be presented to the Americans. This will create a situation in Washington that will call for active and direct American involvement.

– In the final two weeks the Americans will present the document in Washington as a compromise solution and it is then negotiated for another two weeks.

Abu Ala: It is difficult for us to wait all this time given the present Palestinian circumstances with the extremists gaining strength and the situation continuing to deteriorate in the occupied territories.

Round Five: 8 May 1993
(Notes and Minutes of the Meeting)

This round was held at the Norwegian Government's guest-house near the royal palace. Hirschfeld began the meeting by recapitulating the stages the present talks went through in Norway. He said that they had begun with information-gathering, then moved on to reaching consensus, then to getting official authorization. Now that the negotiating teams had received official authorization they must now go through the remaining steps, that is acquiring legitimacy and finally achieving a breakthrough. On the Israeli side, he added, there were ongoing discussions of the draft declaration of principles in order to complete it, but this did not mean that the delegation had achieved legal status. At this point Abu Ala asked about the Gaza–Jericho project and the following conversation, translated from Arabic, took place:

Hirschfeld: Mubarak presented this project to Rabin. When Rabin heard that proposal he returned home in a pessimistic state of mind having started his visit on an optimistic note. But I want it to be perfectly clear that if we agree to this project then we must have full control of the bridges. Perhaps we could first agree on the Gaza–Jericho project and then tackle the declaration of principles. We have to discuss the two points of disagreement: Jerusalem and arbitration. In light of this we will suggest either discussing the document here or leaving the points of disagreement to later stages, especially since Rabin now recognizes the need to agree with you first, whereas in the past he talked of priority to be accorded to an agreement with Syria. The reason is that when you were able to postpone the Washington round for a week, you proved the strength of your position, and that Syria cannot go along without you.

Abu Ala: Gaza is part of the agreement and once this is concluded we can talk about the other details.

Hirschfeld: The task of this channel is to support the bilateral and multilateral talks, and is not a substitute for them. Rabin wants to try out his negotiating style in Washington because he is convinced he will get better results there than he will here. Therefore, we must begin gradually.

9

The Document

The fifth round produced a draft Declaration of Principles based on the discussions sofar. But up to this point the language employed by the Israelis suggested that they still lacked confidence in this channel, had not yet endorsed it and was still under scrutiny. Though authorized, it was not considered a legitimate channel for negotiation since Rabin was hesitant and also still convinced that the Washington channel was the safer and surer route for him. Nor did he really believe that such meetings could result in an agreement, and even if the parties did reach agreement, he was afraid that the PLO would not honour its commitments and sign it. Probably, he was not completely certain that the Americans approved of it either. Besides the Oslo channel was Shimon Peres's channel with whom Rabin disagreed on many issues.

For our part we were entirely serious about the Oslo channel, since we had realized through our involvement in both the Oslo and Washington channels that the discussions in Oslo were realistic and dealt directly and in depth with the subject matter, avoiding the labyrinth of formalities. We were also ready to sign an agreement, although privately, we had doubts as to whether the Israeli negotiators really did have the support of their Government. While they were there to investigate, discuss and probe the intentions of the Palestinians they were not perhaps committed to any of the words they uttered, and would ultimately claim to be unauthorized.

The Draft Document

This is the draft document for the Declaration of Principles that effectively summarized the achievements of the first five rounds of discussions.[1]

---

[1] Translated from Arabic

Principles for Israeli–Palestinian understanding

The Principles for Israeli-Palestinian understanding include the following three documents:

(Declaration of Principles) DOP, Cooperation and Work Programs (CWP) and guidelines for the preparation of a 'Marshall Plan'.

Draft for the DOP

1. The aim of the Israeli–Palestinian negotiations is to reach an agreement to establish the Palestinian Interim Self-Government Authority, the elected Palestinian Interim Council, for a transitional period leading to a permanent settlement based on Security Council Resolutions 242 and 338. It is understood that the interim arrangements are an integral part of the whole process leading to the implementation of 242 and 338.

2. In order that the Palestinian people in the West Bank and the Gaza Strip may govern themselves according to democratic principles, direct, free and general political elections will be held for the Council under agreed supervision and international observation three months after the signing of this Declaration of Principles. An agreement will be concluded on the exact mode and conditions of the elections in accordance with the protocol attached as Annex I not later than one month before elections.

3. These elections will constitute a significant interim and preparatory step towards the realization of the legitimate rights of the Palestinian people and their requirements.

4. Jurisdiction of the Palestinian Interim Council will cover the territory of the West Bank and the Gaza Strip. The transitional period, which will not exceed five years, will commence directly after the signing of the Declaration of Principles. The permanent status negotiations will commence as soon as possible but not later than the beginning of the third year of the interim period between the Government of Israel and the Palestinian people's representatives. These negotiations will cover remaining issues, including: Jerusalem, refugees, settlements, security arrangements, sovereignty, borders and other issues of common interest.

5. Upon the signing of the Declaration of Principles a transfer of authority from the Israeli military government and its Civil Administration to the Palestinians and to the committees assigned by the Palestinian representatives, will commence. The transfer of authority to the Palestinian committees will be of a preparatory and

temporary nature and will include authority in the following spheres: education and culture, health, social welfare, taxation, tourism and other spheres as agreed upon.

6. In order to ensure economic growth, a Palestinian Land Authority Committee and a Palestinian Water Administration Committee will be established immediately upon the signing of the Declaration of Principles. The Palestinian Land Authority Committee and the Palestinian Water Administration Committee will be given immediate powers in accordance with what is agreed upon. Negotiations will be held on a coordinated land and water resources development plan between the Palestinian Land Authority Committee and the Palestinian Water Administration Committee, on the one hand, and the Government of Israel, on the other.

7. In order to guarantee public order and internal security for the Palestinians of the West Bank and the Gaza Strip, the Palestinian Interim Council will establish a strong police force. Preliminary arrangements for the establishment of the Palestinian police force will be made upon the signing of the Declaration of Principles in conjunction with the Palestinians, Israel, Egypt and Jordan.

8. In order to enable the Palestinian Interim Council to promote economic growth, upon its inauguration the Council will establish a number of institutions simultaneously. Examples of these institutions are: Palestinian Land Authority, Palestinian Water Administration Authority, Palestinian Electricity Authority, Gaza Port Authority, Palestinian Development Bank, Palestinian Export Promotion Board, Palestinian Environmental Authority. The Palestinian Committees will negotiate with the Government of Israel the necessary agreements for these Authorities.

9. The Palestinian Interim Council will be empowered to specify the powers and responsibilities of these Authorities as agreed upon. Both parties will review jointly laws and military orders presently in force.

10. A Joint Israeli–Palestinian Liaison Committee will be established in order to deal with issues requiring coordination, other issues of common interest, and disputes. Agreements on cooperation and liaison will be negotiated to provide mutual security and under-standing.

11. The two parties will negotiate an agreement to invite the Governments of Jordan and Egypt to participate in establishing further liaison and cooperation arrangements between the Government of Israel and the Palestinian Interim Authority, on the one hand, and the Governments of Jordan and Egypt, on the other,

to promote cooperation between them.

12. After the signing of the Declaration of Principles, negotiations will commence between the two sides to conclude an agreement on the redeployment of Israeli military forces in the West Bank and the Gaza Strip. Further redeployments to specified locations, to be agreed, will be gradually implemented commensurate with other security measures (an annex on security will be added). Complete withdrawal of Israeli military forces from the Gaza Strip will be implemented by not later than the end of the second year of the interim period in the spirit of a partial implementation of 242 and 338. The Israeli military withdrawal will be coordinated in full with the Palestinian Interim Council. Withdrawal from the Gaza strip does not in any way detract from the implementation of the principles agreed upon in the Declaration of Principles with regard to the West Bank. After the Israeli withdrawal from the Gaza Strip a trusteeship will be created according to an agreement to be concluded between the Government of Israel and the Palestinian Interim Authority. (The two sides will negotiate a future partial withdrawal from Jericho within three months of the signing of this Declaration of Principles.)

13. The Israeli and Palestinian delegations will negotiate an interim agreement to determine the arrangements for the transfer of authority as well as the structure, powers and responsibility of the Palestinian Authority.

14. An Arbitration Committee will be established to review all disputes that will be submitted to it. The Committee will only be established by agreement of the two sides as well as the co-sponsors of the Madrid conference. The disputes will be submitted to this Committee only if the two sides cannot settle them through negotiation. The two sides accept the need for a mechanism of conciliation and compromise, to be agreed upon by them, before resorting to arbitration.

   The co-sponsors will witness the signing of the Declaration of Principles and will follow up its implementation.

The Israeli side will consult with regard to the following three items:

I *Proposed annex on the mode and conditions of election:*

   1. Palestinians of Jerusalem have the right to participate in the election process as candidates and voters. Voters in Jerusalem will cast their ballots at the al-Aqsa Mosque and the Church of the

Holy Sepulchre.

2. All displaced Palestinians registered on 4 June 1967 have the right to participate in the election process. Their future status will not be prejudiced because they are unable to participate in the election process due to practical reasons.

3. Agreements covering the following issues are to be concluded between the two sides:

   (a) The system of election.

   (b) The number of members of the Palestinian Interim Council.

   (c) The mode of the international supervision and its personal composition.

   (d) Rules and regulations regarding election campaigns, including agreed arrangements for the organizing of media, and possibility of licensing a broadcasting and TV station.

   (e) Any other issues.

II *Paragraph on Jericho*

(To be added to paragraph 12)

III *The role of the co-sponsors*

(To be added to paragraph 14)

IV *Israeli–(CWP) Palestinian Cooperation and Work Programs*

The Israeli–Palestinian Declaration of Principles will be accompanied by a CWP, to be agreed upon, focusing, among other things, on the following:

1. Cooperation in the field of water, including a Water Development Program prepared by experts from both sides, which will also specify the mode of cooperation in the management of water resources in the Gaza Strip and the West Bank including the Jordan Valley, and will include proposals for studies and plans on water rights of each party, as well as on the equitable utilization of joint water resources for implementation in and beyond the interim period.

2. Cooperation in the field of electricity, including an Electricity Development Program, which will also specify the mode of cooperation for the production, maintenance, purchase and sale of electricity resources.

3. Cooperation in the field of energy, including an Energy Development Program, which will also provide for the exploitation of oil and gas for industrial purposes, particularly in the Gaza Strip, and will

encourage further joint exploitation of other energy resources. This Program may also provide for the construction of oil and gas pipelines.

4. Cooperation in the field of finance, including the establishment of a Palestinian Development Bank.

5. Cooperation in the fields of transport and communication, which will define guidelines for the establishment of a Gaza Sea Port Area and a free trade zone between Gaza and Ashdod, and will provide for the establishment of transport and communication lines to and from the West Bank and the Gaza Strip to Israel and other countries. Steps will be taken to carry out the necessary construction of roads, railways, communication lines etc.

6. The Industrial Development Programs will provide for the establishment of Joint Israeli–Palestinian Research and Development Centres, which will promote Palestinian–Israeli joint ventures, including a motor car industry in Gaza, and provide guidelines for cooperation in the textile industry, food, pharmaceutical, electronics, computer and science-based industries.

7. Cooperation in the field of trade and in Trade Promotion Programs, which will encourage local, regional and inter-regional trade.

8. A program of cooperation in, and regulation of, labour relations and cooperation in social welfare issues.

9. A Human Resources Cooperation Plan, providing for joint Israeli–Palestinian workshops and seminars, and for the establishment of joint vocational training centres, research institutes and data banks.

10. An Environmental Protection Plan, providing for joint and/or coordinated measures in this field.

11. An agreed security program and plan.

Guidelines for the preparation of a 'Marshall Plan' for the region including the West Bank and the Gaza Strip

The Israeli–Palestinian DOP and CWP will be accompanied by a Development Program for the region, including the West Bank and the Gaza Strip to be initiated by the G-7 and other OECD countries. The parties will request the G-7 and OECD countries to participate in the multilateral peace efforts by preparing a 'Marshall Plan' for the region, including the West Bank and the Gaza Strip, which will be put into effect after the inauguration of the elected Palestinian Interim Council. The Palestinians will also elicit significant additional aid from the regional Arab states and existing Arab institutions.

The 'Marshall Plan' will consist of two elements: (1) a Palestinian Economic Development Program (PEDP) and (2) a Regional Economic Development Program (REDP), the former taking priority.

(1) PEDP: Israel will support the PEDP in the multilateral negotiations. This will consist of three parts:
   (a) A Social Rehabilitation Program.
   (b) A Small and Medium Business Development Plan.
   (c) An Infrastructure Development Plan (water, electricity, transport and communications, human resources, financial institutions, etc.).
(2) REDP: Both sides will support a REDP proposing the implementation of a number of development projects:
   (a) The establishment of a Middle Eastern Development Fund and a Middle Eastern Development Bank.
   (b) The Mediterranean Sea (Gaza)–Dead Sea Canal.
   (c) The development of a joint Israeli–Palestinian–Jordanian Plan for coordinated exploitation of the Dead Sea area.
   (d) A regional desalinization and other water development projects including a power generating plant.
   (e) Interconnection of electricity grids.
   (f) Regional cooperation for the transfer, distribution and industrial exploitation of gas, oil and other energy resources
   (g) A Regional Tourism, Transportation and Telecommunication Development Plan.
   (h) Regional cooperation in other spheres.

Following the drawing up of these documents the talks continued.

A positive and surprising development took place in the sixth round with the addition of a third person beside Hirschfeld and Pundak. He presented himself as Uri Savir, Director-General of the Israeli Foreign Ministry. The information we gathered about him told us he was one of the bright young men of the Labour Party; his father had been a former Israeli ambassador and he himself had been consul-general in New York in charge of relations with the Zionist lobby. He had also been posted to the Israeli Embassy in Washington and had assumed his current post only two weeks previously. Savir was close to Rabin but more so to Peres and Yossi Beilin who is a close personal friend. He was a peace activist. I was generally pleased with this addition to the Israeli delegation because for the first time we would be dealing with an Israeli official, the other two having presented themselves rather as academics close to authority.

We did not rely on our own information about Uri Savir but contacted a number of other parties, including the Egyptian Foreign Ministry, to check the accuracy of our information. Everyone assured us that he was definitely Director-General of the Foreign Ministry and had been recently appointed in that position. Still, I did not feel completely confident about the standing of the Israeli delegation because of the persisting information, which Savir now confirmed, that Rabin was still not fully involved in the Oslo channel and might therefore disrupt it at any time. We could still remember the London agreement between King Hussein and Shimon Peres in 1987 which Shamir and the Americans had torpedoed when they got wind of it. But we had no option but to proceed with the Oslo channel and give it our full attention and support. We would have lost nothing if the unexpected should have happened or if the Israeli side had sprung any surprises.

Uri Savir arrived in Paris and went through the formality of performing his official duties for one day, before telling the Israeli Ambassador in Paris that he would be spending the next couple of days privately and that he would not need embassy escort or assistance. He then secretly travelled to Oslo via Copenhagen, leaving his luggage behind in his hotel room in order not to attract attention to his absence. Later, he reappeared in Paris, as if nothing had happened, and flew back to Tel Aviv. Savir's actions showed that he was anxious to keep the Oslo channel secret within its narrow confines, keeping the Israeli diplomatic corps in Europe at arm's length.

Round Six: 21 May 1993
(Notes from Minutes of Meeting, Holmenkollen Park, Oslo)

The following are notes, translated from Arabic, from the minutes recording what Savir said:

- Our [Israeli] leadership is following this channel and is eager to maintain its secrecy, but it is not considered a substitute for Washington.
- We [Israelis] did not imagine that we could start official talks, supported by both leaderships so quickly without intermediaries.
- He admired the way the Oslo channel focused on the overall picture of the issues while avoiding concentration on technical issues.
- He stressed the importance of the time factor because slow progress effectively meant going backwards. There was therefore a need for speed in reaching a comprehensive peace with the Palestinians.
- He criticized certain mediators who though sincere were basically pursuing their personal interests.

- He indicated that the Americans and some Arabs had warned them against the PLO and had advised them not to talk to the PLO because of its lack of credibility and its way of backing out of promises. He outlined various features of the policy of the new Labour Cabinet as follows:

  (1) Suspension of 90 per cent of settlement activities.
  (2) Suspension of hundreds of millions of dollars worth of aid earmarked for investment in the settlements.
  (3) Release of some prisoners and the return of some deportees.
  (4) Labour Government's desire to solve the Palestinian issue and its lack of desire to control another people's destiny.

- Savir commented: 'We have fears about the future, as you do, and this forces both of us into a defensive position. But a besieged Israel has the greater fears, especially because its map is unstable, and any conflict in the region harms it even if it is not a party to it, by which I mean Iraq and Iran.'
- Israel does not want to remain in a sealed fortress but wants security guarantees.
- Democracy in the region in general and among the Palestinians in particular is one of Israel's security guarantees.
- Neither of us have any need of American intervention. The proof is the papers they presented in the ninth and tenth rounds in Washington.
- He referred to the prevalent points of disagreement around the issues of Jerusalem, arbitration and Jericho.
- He wondered about the PLO's ability to implement the accord. They had fears about that, especially Prime Minister Rabin, who contrasts the PLO with President Asad of Syria who once committed he implements.

Round Seven: 13 June 1993
(Notes and Minutes of Meeting)

The negotiations entered a new phase in this round with the addition of a fourth Israeli negotiator, Joel Singer. Through his and his colleagues' remarks our delegation could tell that he was a personal representative of Rabin's, and he brought questions that had been prepared by Rabin. Singer had been a legal adviser to the Israeli delegation during the first and second disengagement talks with the Egyptians and the disengagement talks with the Syrians in the 1970s. He had worked with the Camp David team at Taba and had worked directly with Rabin as well as Peres.

He had left the Government four years previously and moved to America and carried out research on peace issues in association with academic institutions such as Harvard University.

We gathered that the Israeli delegation regarded Singer's involvement in the Oslo channel as representing full participation on the part of the Israeli decision-making centre. This meant Rabin had decided to move ahead constructively to evaluate it and ultimately to decide how to act. Thus Singer was a qualitative addition to the Israeli delegation while representing at the same time a new phase in the Oslo channel, adjusting the previous direction and returning almost to the beginning. The following are notes from the meeting with Singer translated from Arabic.

- Rabin's evaluation of the draft was that the construction was good and the structure excellent but its colours were not very distinct. Therefore the ideas for the implementation were unclear and required amendment.
- Referring to the attempts by some Israelis to open informal channels, Singer said: 'All of those trying to open secret channels are doing so on their personal initiative and are seeking a personal role for themselves. Similarly, the Palestinians contacting them [the Israelis] for the same purpose receive the same response. What is important is taking place here, and it is official between the Government and the PLO.
- All the documents that had been discussed in this and other channels up to the present had been studied and scrutinized by specialists in different fields and by various institutions starting with his office.
- He spoke in a positive language about the PLO and its positions in contrast with the way the PLO was usually referred to by Israelis in the past.
- He believed some of the leaks appearing in the press came from certain officials in the American Administration whose fruitless two-year-old efforts had been marginalized, meaning Edward Djerejian and some of those who would be leaving the Administration before the end of the year as well as others who had supported and espoused Likud's position.
- He criticized the manner of negotiating in Washington and considered everything he had read about them disappointing.

It then seemed that he had come with the aim of returning to point zero because of all the questions he was asking and demanding answers to. It seemed that he was waiting to decide whether to continue with this channel by the answers provided. Our delegation was frustrated by the questions which they were asked to respond to, thinking that Singer would try to cancel all previous efforts. When the delegation returned to Tunis they reported on the meeting, and we tried to evaluate it. Our opinion was that everything had now become critical and that we had reached an important and dangerous junction. Either the Oslo channel would succeed or it would be shut down, but as long as Singer, who was linked to Yitzhak Rabin, continued to head the Israeli delegation, then we had to assume that the Israelis would continue the process with us. These are the questions put to us by Singer:

1. Are the [Palestinian] government and the council one body or two ?
2. What form will the international supervision and observation of the election take? Has this been agreed yet?
3. What is the interval between declaration and the holding of elections? Is it six months or nine?
4. Will the annexes relating to Jerusalem and the displaced persons be discussed before or after the elections?
5. What is meant by the scope of authority? And what is its relationship with the [Jewish] settlements, Jerusalem, army camps and security?
6. Why is reference made to the refugees in the bilaterals while it is made in the multinationals?
7. How will the different aspects of the civil administration be organized? Will the person taking over be a politician, a technocrat or a professional? Will the administrative structure be altered?
8. What will Gaza's status be after the [Israeli] withdrawal from it?
9. What will the situation of the various spheres of activity be after the elections and the formation of the government?
10 Why have the land and water committees been singled out and placed in a special article? What is applicable to the committees will apply to them also? That is, will they be within the Interim Authority's jurisdiction?
11. What is the conception of internal security and overall security?
12. Who will handle external security during the interim period?
13. What are the limits of Palestinian security jurisdiction and the limits of Israeli security jurisdiction?
14. How will disputes be handled before the Palestinian Interim Authority is established?
15. Do you see the arrangement for the liaison of the quadripartite committee as [Egypt–Jordan–Israel–Palestine] continuous? And what are the subjects falling within the framework of the follow-up

arrangement with each of Egypt and Jordan? And do you see another role for Jordan?

16. If an agreement is reached here on the Declaration of Principles, who will sign in Washington? Will it be the Palestinian and Israeli delegations? Or the joint Jordanian–Palestinian and Israeli delegations?

17. Assuming a withdrawal from Jericho, what would its status be? And what is your understanding of it?

18. What will happen in the period between an Israeli withdrawal from Gaza and Jericho and the election of the council? Specifically, what will Gaza's status be? Who will be responsible for external security for it? What is the Egyptian role in security participation?

19. Do you see a need for an agreement to be signed between the PLO and Israel that includes arrangements for security in Gaza?

20. Is it possible for you to commit yourselves to collecting weapons in Gaza and the West Bank?

21. Is it possible for you to call for the halting of the intifada after the Declaration of Principles is signed?

22. Can you commit yourselves before us, as you have done before the Americans, to recognizing Israel and renouncing terrorism?

23. Can you commit yourselves to the amendment of the [Palestinian] Covenant?

24. Is it useful to have an agreement with us that refers to these amendments?

25. If there is agreement between the PLO and Israel, what leadership will return? Where will it reside? Will it return before the elections? Will the members participate as candidates, voters or both? Will they return to Jericho? Who will administer Gaza between Israeli withdrawal and the elections for the council? Can power be transferred in Gaza more quickly than in the West Bank? Can a security agreement be signed between the PLO and Israel on security in Gaza?

26. Where will the people who will be responsible for the various spheres of activity reside when these are transferred to the Palestinian Authority after the Declaration? In Jerusalem or Jericho? If your answer is Jerusalem this will create a problem.

27. If you decide that Arafat should return, then this will become a political issue. Are you prepared to conclude an agreement about this issue?

28. Do you want to agree on the system of election before the specified period elapses? Will they be held after withdrawal from Gaza? If you

are not ready by then will the council be created by appointment instead of election?

29. Do you insist on having multinational forces in Jericho or Gaza?
30. Do you insist on the need for international trusteeship?
31. How do you view Jericho's status in the event of withdrawal? For example, would it be different from Nablus?
32. By arbitration do you mean that it will be concerned with matters arising during the interim period?
33. Why do you not replace the word 'arbitration' with 'settlement of conflicts'?
34. What will happen if all the people who were displaced in 1967 ask to return to participate in the elections? Will you go to arbitration if they cannot return?
35. What is the mechanism you suggest by which to explain the content and terms of this Declaration of Principles to the Americans?
36. How will you reconcile the limited powers given to the Palestinian Authority in the West Bank with the greater powers given in Gaza? This also applies to the question of Israeli withdrawal.
37. Will the relationship between Gaza and the West Bank be a centralized one or decentralized one?
38. We might need an addition to the Declaration of Principles – an explanatory memorandum and an agreement with the PLO. Are you prepared for that?
39. If we do not arrive at clear agreements on all the issues, we might resort to secret texts – which was what happened with Egypt. Do you accept that we resort to secret agreements or exchanges of letters or letters to a third party? America for example?
40. Can you convince your delegation in Washington to issue a joint communiqué? [This foreshadowed the joint communiqué proposed by the American Administration in the ninth round.]

Our delegation tried hard to answer all these questions from the information that was available and what had been agreed previously. Singer wrote down all the replies and concluded the session by saying, 'We will go back to Rabin and Peres and we expect their reply to be along the following lines: either the previous position is accepted, or an amendment is required, or a compromise solution reached.'

The first session with Joel Singer ended, and our delegation tried to evaluate the situation but could reach no conclusion. However, we soon concluded that matters had got to a crucial stage and that we would therefore wait for the reaction of Rabin and the Israeli leadership now that they had begun to take the Oslo channel seriously.

The eighth round was held at the headquarters of the Norwegian Institute for Applied Social Sciences (FAFO) in Oslo, the venue for the meeting having once again been changed. We were anxious to find out the Israelis' reactions following the flood of questions that had been delivered by Singer in the previous round. What we heard gave us some confidence about the standing of the Oslo channel and about Israeli attitudes to attempts by others to open a similar channel and about the question of whether Oslo was regarded as a preparatory step to Washington or as a temporary channel supporting Washington. Following is a translation of the minutes.

Round Eight: 27 June 1993
(Extracts from Minutes of Meeting, Oslo)

Singer: We have authorization to put forward proposals to arrive at a final text. This text, if agreed, will then be passed on to Washington for announcement only, not as a proposal for negotiation or amendment. The proposals are:

– Preserving the suggested structure of the Declaration of Principles.
– Adding agreed minutes to the Declaration of Principles that form part of the agreement.
– Making some changes in light of the questions and answers.
– No additions of new concepts to the document.

Rabin has reviewed the minutes sentence by sentence, and he wants all the agreements to be written and specific. However, he still doubts the credibility of the PLO and whether it is manoeuvring or double-crossing.

Abu Ala: We frankly say that we too are keen and that we too have our doubts about your commitment to this channel whether you see it as a legitimate channel in its own right or a subsidiary channel. As for the texts, we see no need for alterations.

Singer: I do not think we will be able to discuss everything in two days, especially as the question of territorial jurisdiction will require a long time. Rabin has also demanded reassurance about the movement of Israeli citizens, their presence, freedoms and passage in the event of an Israeli withdrawal from Gaza and Jericho. We also want to discuss the question of the 'implementation' of Resolution 242 because the matter won't settle itself automatically. We understand that the final status negotiations will cover the final implementation. Also, there must be a review of such issues as the final status of the territories, the displaced, and whether people in Jerusalem may put themselves forward for election, as well as other subjects.

Abu Ala adopted a process of asking detailed questions in order to pinpoint the Israeli position on a number of specific issues. Regarding Gaza and Jericho he asked about crossing-points, security, the return of Palestinian leaders to Palestinian territory, international forces, the corridor linking the two areas (Gaza and the West Bank), Jewish settlements, liaison committees, the powers of the Palestinian Authority, the review of laws and military orders, the spheres to which power would be transferred to the Palestinian Authority, the elected Council and the elections and their timing.

In return, Singer raised many issues relating to the corridors, the movement of military forces and the settlements. He took a negative stand regarding the issue of international forces and explained his Government's position on the crossing-points and other issues such as Jerusalem and the settlements. He stressed that Jerusalem would not be mentioned other than in connection with the question of elections but that it would be discussed at the permanent status negotiations. As for the settlements, the Government would not announce a policy regarding their removal or their vacation. It would be left to the settlers to leave voluntarily; the Israeli Government would, however, withhold support for some politically motivated settlements as a matter of policy, though this would not be announced. The official view was that tackling the settlements issue had to be gradual in order to facilitate discussion of their future in the permanent status negotiations.

He then presented proposals on various points to be considered in relation to the issue of mutual recognition:

1. The PLO recognizes the right of the State of Israel to exist and commits itself to peaceful coexistence with it.
2. The PLO recognizes Resolutions 242 and 338.
3. The PLO renounces the use of terrorism and other acts of violence.
4. The PLO announces its total cessation of all forms of terrorism.
5. The PLO does not support any side that commits terrorist acts and does not incite such acts.
6. The PLO declares that in light of the commitment to the peace process it considers that those articles in the Palestinian Covenant which are inconsistent with this process are now inoperative and no longer valid.
7. The PLO is committed to the peace process and its goals in accordance with the letter of invitation.
8. The PLO will call on the Palestinian people to halt the intifada [uprising] once the Palestinian Interim Council assumes power.

9. The PLO will call on the Arab countries to suspend the Arab boycott of Israel.

The interval between this round, the eighth, and the previous one was quite short, the Israeli delegation having made a point of returning quickly to Oslo to confirm its interest in following up this channel. They did not intend to arrive at an agreement during the eighth round so much as to reassure the Palestinian side of their seriousness in dealing with it. Thus the dialogue was intended to enrich discussions, expand horizons and examine many details so that they could be accommodated in a new vision of the draft Declaration of Principles.

In addition to Rabin's accreditation of this channel, the other significant development on the Israeli side was its putting forward a proposal for the mutual recognition of Israel and the PLO. Previously, the understanding was that when agreement in Oslo was reached, the project would then be presented to the Palestinian delegation in Washington as an American-proposed document for signing, what was now happening was that the PLO would be recognized and publicly acknowledged as the partner in the negotiations, if both sides agreed on the terms for mutual recognition.

For our part, we wanted to make sure that we reached agreement on the Declaration of Principles first before discussing the issue of mutual recognition, which is what actually happened. When, however, the Israeli press revealed the first part of the process before the second part was completed, the scenario which we had envisaged was upset.

At the beginning of the eighth round, optimistic statements began to be made by Israeli officials, notably by Shimon Peres, who said that the Palestinian–Israeli accord was near completion, while all the news from Washington indicated utter failure. These starkly contrasting statements put us in a tight spot with the Palestinian and Arab leaderships who wondered what secret lay behind these contradictions. On the one hand, they were getting nothing but denials from us, while Peres sounded rather more optimistic than seemed necessary. But the matter was far more important than statements about a breakthrough and positive remarks about the PLO to the effect that it was the only party capable of carrying negotiations forward, making decisions and commitments.

The statements made by the Palestinian leadership were pessimistic. When asked about the outcome of the negotiations, Arafat would frequently reply that they were a 'big zero'. Others followed his lead, whereas my statements were inclined to be calmer and less pessimistic; I would think up various reasons for this attitude but of course avoiding all mention of the Oslo channel. At the same time, I was sending messages to Peres through that channel asking him to tone down his optimistic statements, which we could not go along with. The reply would come back that it was something he had to do in order to prepare Israeli public opinion for the next step. In general, a hopeful atmosphere prevailed in the Middle East with Israeli and Western media stepping up reports about secret channels and covert contacts between the Israelis and Palestinians. But most people ignored such reports on the grounds that they were simply rumours, and this helped us to proceed with our task without too much fear.

As the subsequent rounds would show, real progress had indeed been made at Oslo, as there were now firm indications that the matter had matured and that in fact, as Peres had said, the accord was nearing completion.

Round Nine: 6 July 1993
(Notes on Minutes of Meetings, Gressheim, Oslo)

In this round at Gressheim, near Oslo, the Israelis presented a new draft that was better constructed than the previous one and one in which the Israelis had left out many of their tough demands and conditions. They had obviously taken note of our delegation's comments and had abandoned manoeuvrings and tactics in the negotiations. They now expressed a desire to reach a final accord that would be signed in two stages according to the following formula: first, between the PLO and the representative of the Government of Israel in Oslo; and second, between Shimon Peres and Faisal Husseini at an official ceremony in Washington that would be attended by the co-sponsors, the Americans and Russians; it would then be possible to announce the activities of the Oslo channel officially.

A lengthy dialogue ensued on the content of a draft accord proposed by the Israelis. It was sent to us in Tunis for review and comment; in addition there were the points brought up by the Israeli delegation and recorded in the minutes. These were as follows:

1. The Americans

The Israelis were very worried that the Americans would wreck this achievement [in Oslo] as they had torpedoed the (Hussein–Peres) London agreement of 1987 for purely internal reasons, especially since negotiations were now being directly held with the PLO.

I was struck by the way that the Israelis had opened up to our delegation, speaking so critically of the Americans with such openness and daring. I also noticed how they distrusted the American position and how they named certain individuals in the American Administration whom they felt were trying to derail the Washington negotiations for personal reasons. Most significant was the Israeli rejection of the draft presented by the Americans in the tenth round of these negotiations. We too found it lacking but we had to discuss it so as not to offend the American Administration. It seemed that the Israelis shared our views. It may be worth mentioning, in this connection, that our own internal discussion over the American document was what had driven certain members of the Palestinian delegation in Washington to resign, a fact which caused a storm in the media. Again, speaking parenthetically, I recall that many Palestinian negotiators and members of the follow-up committee had found it strange that I had treated the American draft with indifference and inattention, and that I had accepted all the amendments suggested to me by my colleagues without much thought. This apathy had been due to two considerations: first, I had known the Israeli position on it, and secondly, I had regarded the events in Washington as irrelevant when we had been on the verge of a breakthrough in Oslo.

2. The PLO

Our delegation noticed that the Israelis were now regarding the PLO as the only side with which matters could be negotiated and agreed, although they still had some concerns. But the credibility that had pervaded the Oslo talks during seven months had contributed to confidence-building and to the belief that coexistence was possible.

3. Gaza and Jericho

The Israelis were finally convinced of the importance of the simultaneous withdrawal from Gaza and Jericho but they still considered that what was applicable to Gaza was not strictly applicable to Jericho.

4. Jerusalem

The Israelis refused even to mention Jerusalem, especially in relation to the elections, saying that this subject would lead to the fall of the Government.

5. The displaced Palestinians

The Israelis also refused to refer to them.

6. *Security*

They outlined their concept of security both in relation to external security and to its applicability to the practical aspects of internal security.

7. *Arbitration*

The Israelis were adamant in rejecting the idea of arbitration since they believed that we would seek arbitration on every minor and major issue, a fact which would thwart all progress.

After studying the Israeli draft and the comments of the Israeli delegation we, in Tunis, defined our position on the above points and gave the following instructions to the delegation in Norway:

1. The implementation of Resolutions 242 and 338 must be spelt out clearly. The two stages, namely the interim self-rule arrangement and the final status negotiations should be linked, the latter leading to the implementation of these Resolutions.
2. The issues governing the interim period must be clearly specified.
3. Withdrawal of the military government and the dissolution of the [Israeli] Civil Administration.
4. Palestinians from Jerusalem may participate in the elections though they may not necessarily vote.
5. The Palestinian Authority will be entitled to form the police force from the inside as well as from the outside.
6. The Gaza–Jericho accord will be part of the DOP and not a separate agreement.
7. Control of the Gaza Strip and Jericho will be handed over to the PLO when mutual recognition has taken place.

Round Ten: 21 July 1993
(Notes and Minutes of Meeting, Halvorsbole, Oslo)

In this round, which took place at a hotel in Halvorsbole, the draft agreement for the Declaration of Principles became crystallized as an acceptable framework in principle, but from our point of view it needed many amendments before it would become balanced, acceptable and capable of being promoted in the Palestinian camp and implemented in the future. This made us pay attention to every word, sentence and expression. It was even necessary to scrutinize every comma and full stop so that we could eliminate the likelihood of fatal pitfalls occurring in the future. We were of course negotiating with a seasoned and able delegation, long-practised in negotiations with other parties, especially the Egyptians. It could also fall back on many specialized teams that could provide it with data, analysis, ideas and alternatives. By contrast, our delegation had neither the experience nor the resources of the Israelis. Moreover, because the negotiations were shrouded in secrecy, our available resources could not be employed in full.

I remember that while we were discussing the matter of the displaced Palestinians, and after the Israelis had agreed in principle to make reference to them, we disagreed on the use of one word. The Israelis' wording was: 'The future status of displaced Palestinians . . . will not be prejudiced *because* they are unable to participate in the election process . . .', while we wanted it to read: 'The future status of displaced Palestinians . . . will not be prejudiced *if* they are unable to participate in the election process . . .'. A lengthy debate ensued about the use of the word 'because', but in the end we could not have our way.

There were many examples of such polemic. I must admit that throughout the Oslo negotiations we did not review the texts with a legal consultant for fear of leaks. We had therefore to depend on our own experience and knowledge of handling texts. I tried to make use of the remnants of the legal knowledge I had acquired while studying law at Damascus University, but I could not draw much comfort from them. I must mention, however, that the DOP documents were reviewed by our legal consultant, Taher Shash, whom we had sent to Oslo for this purpose just before they were initialled on 20 August 1993.

The Palestinian comments on the Israeli draft were presented during this round and the Israeli delegation requested an hour to review them and to express its opinion. When the session was resumed, the atmosphere became very tense. The Israelis seemed extremely disappointed, feeling that the Palestinian comments had not only altered their draft but had put an end to it. The following conversation ensued:

Savir: After hearing your comments we all feel very disappointed. You have completely misunderstood our position. The obstacle now is not of a linguistic nature but of disagreement on fundamental issues and notions. For example:
- It is unacceptable to link the institutions of Jerusalem to the elected Council.
- You spoke of controlling the corridors and we do not accept this.
- You mentioned those displaced in 1967. We cannot accept reference to this issue now, but this can be raised at the permanent status negotiations.

— To speak of executive, legislative and judicial powers [for the Palestinian Authority] is unacceptable for the interim period.

— Reference to national rights is a matter that pertains to the State and [these rights] are linked to it; this is unacceptable.

— You first asked for Jericho to be a symbol and now you talk about an area, the same with Gaza.

Abu Ala: We told you in the last round that we had important points to make and that we had not yet completed the discussion. You must realize that if we cannot promote the document with the public then it will not succeed. We can't put it forward in the form you suggest. Jerusalem cannot be ignored or left for the final stage without any mention of it now. Security does not concern you alone, and the matter of the displaced [Palestinians] must be discussed. Nor are the three powers: legislative, executive and judicial a novelty; they apply [to any governing body] even in an interim period.

Hirschfeld: We have transformed this channel from a special channel to an official channel in which our leadership is involved. This in itself is great progress. But the changes you have come up with have made this a black day.

Savir: We cannot discuss the ideas you have brought. If we do and return to Rabin and Peres, they will ask us to shut this channel down immediately. So, for the sake of this channel no minutes should be taken down.

Abu Ala: We will not force you into something you do not want, but we want to arrive at an agreement. A result can be achieved for everything through discussion. We are prepared to discuss the drafting of a new formula to be presented to each of our leaderships if you wish.

The session was adjourned amid much tension between the two sides and was resumed the next morning on 12 July 1993.

Savir: Reference to national rights is unacceptable now, because this would be talking about a State. Now is not the time for a State; this is to be discussed in the future. As for the issue of territorial jurisdiction, please understand that we are concerned about security because of our experience, the wars and the small size of our country. Security is not an obsession with us but a reality. We have seen a long struggle in our relations with you and these do not give us confidence. Also, the issue of the displaced [Palestinians] is to be discussed in the future. As for the issue of Jerusalem, this is a very sensitive subject. With regard to arbitration, we do not understand your insistence on it since we will be the best of partners; nor do we want other parties to come to the area where they will be looking after their own interests. We will seek a pragmatic solution for the participation of the Palestinians of Jerusalem as candidates and voters.

Singer: The DOP agreement must include articles that relate to Gaza–Jericho in the following way:

1. A symbolic Israeli withdrawal from Jericho and a full withdrawal from Gaza with the exception of [Jewish] settlements which will have full Israeli army protection.
2. As for Jericho there are no settlements there, so it is not a complicated problem.
3. Arrangements for the corridors require many details and will therefore not be included in the accord.
4. Gaza and Jericho are not isolated [entities] and are part of the [Palestinian] autonomy arrangements.
5. The powers of the Palestinian police force in Gaza are to be greater than its powers in the other territories. We accept that your police forces will take over upon [Israeli] withdrawal.
6. We agree to the presence of foreign observers, but not of military forces.
7. In principle there is no objection to the PLO leadership moving to the territories, but the matter hinges on a separate agreement that will clarify, among other things, its freedom of movement and use of the roads.

Abu Ala: Reference to the PLO in the DOP will require a dramatic gesture, for example a Rabin–Arafat meeting.

Singer: This will mean integrating both stages and will entail risk. Therefore the commitments must be clear and I think we need more time.

Savir: The following are just ideas and not an official proposal on our part. The idea is to change our standing from being a group for which a lute is playing to a group for which an orchestra is playing. Regarding Gaza and Jericho, it is true that the gap separating us is big, but even so the suggested ideas are acceptable. But the most important thing is the time factor which can harm the secrecy surrounding this channel. We and our leaders will try to overcome the obstacles. If we need to contact each other we can do so through Terje Larsen or meet for an hour or more in some European country. But it has to be clear that the documents must be ready for signing within two or three weeks.

Abu Ala: We will return to our leadership and you will do the same. We'll meet on the date proposed and I hope we will be ready to prepare the final joint document.

Although we did not arrive at an agreement with the Israelis at the end of the tenth round, we could say that we were at the gate of an agreement. We therefore had to inform others about the Oslo channel – to expand the existing base – and try to create the right climate for a wider acceptance of what we were about to do, especially since all the indications were that the Washington negotiations were failing, and that there was disagreement between the leadership and the negotiating delegation (despite the excellent reputation that this delegation enjoys at all levels). Thus there seemed little ground for optimism. But I had to resist the general gloom. When the first major opportunity presented itself at the meeting of the Fatah movement's Revolutionary Council on 17 July 1993 I spoke of the positive aspects of the ninth and tenth rounds in Washington but it felt like swimming against the current. I tried hard to present simple points by way of confirming that the negotiations in general had not failed and that many opportunities for success lay ahead. Then I delivered a purposeful speech in which I said:

> By the end of the year there will definitely be an agreement between us and the Israelis. This agreement might be imposed by the Americans. It might satisfy or displease you, it might satisfy the Israelis or displease them, but it will happen. I am talking from solid information, not by way of fortune-telling. This agreement will be concluded on the basis of two periods: interim and final. The first will run for two years and the second for up to five years. We will enjoy transitional self-rule during the first and there will be no sovereignty during that period. There might be [Israeli] withdrawal from Gaza and Jericho. Negotiations on the [Jewish] settlements, Jerusalem and the [Palestinian] refugees will take place during the second period.

In brief, I detailed the Oslo papers without mentioning the word 'Oslo' or hinting at any negotiations through a secret channel. During the next two days I did the same thing at the Central Committee. There was a lengthy discussion about my statements which some considered to be fanciful, and that the formula of the agreement I had described could not be carried out, let alone contemplated. This being so, some of those who professed toughness tried to embarrass me by putting down conditions which they knew could never be met. For example they said: 'Our securing a [Israeli] withdrawal from Gaza and Jericho and the PLO going there is quite sufficient. There's no need for an agreement. But I objected saying: 'Without a declaration of principles such a project would be unpatriotic, even if the PLO was to have full powers in Gaza and Jericho. Such a declaration must be drafted first and must include withdrawal from Gaza and Jericho. As for the presence of the PLO there, that is not on the table now.' I said this when I knew that we were still discussing mutual recognition, but I was afraid that we would not achieve agreement on this, and that the opposition would ignore all our achievements and cling to the issue of the presence of the PLO. Participation of the PLO had been hinted at by the Israelis, but had not been proposed for the interim period.

Some people thought that we were conducting secret contacts through Egypt and conjectured that such information was coming from this channel. However, I always denied this, suggesting that the information emanated from the American Administration and Israeli circles and said that the US Administration was preparing a project that would be imposed on both sides. PLO circles and the Fatah cadres accepted what I told them without question because they knew me not to exaggerate or understate. I always used to limit my words to describing events exactly as they were. Thus my supporters and the opposition accepted my words at face value.

Round Eleven: 25–26 July 1993
(Comment and Minutes of Meeting)

This round was full of nail-biting suspense. It felt like a countdown. The time factor pressured both sides to arrive at an agreement for fear that news of the channel would leak out and so come to fail. Therefore we plunged together into the basics of the draft we had originally prepared and in which many points of difference relating to substance, form and language had emerged.

We felt the Israelis were trying to use the pressures we were under in order to make us accept their proposals. We, in Tunis, told the delegation not to pay any attention to the pressures because this was in the nature of negotiations, and not to yield to extortion either, for our duty was to gain the necessary requirements for success. Furthermore, we were fully responsible to that part of the leadership which was not privy to these negotiations and could find a hundred reasons to reject the draft accord. It would look for the weaknesses in the document before seeing its positive aspects. Thus every word, sentence and expression had to be scrutinized so that ultimately we could defend the accord.

As zero-hour approached the mixed feelings about our enterprise deepened. On the one hand, we felt we were about to reach a historic accord, and on the other, we felt we were about to face the consequences of the heavy responsibility we had borne on behalf of the leadership, our people and the Arabs in general. None the less, we, the negotiators in Oslo and their supervisors in Tunis, felt privileged to shoulder the burden. The Israelis took every opportunity to question our position, our desire to reach agreement and our competence to sign when the time came. Whenever we raised an issue they suspected that we were looking for pretexts to avoid signing.

At this stage the Americans came up with the idea of an early handing over of power in exchange for economic aid. This formula was presented as a means of overcoming the impasse in the Washington negotiations. It was accepted by some of the Washington delegates because it would give some relief to our suffering people in the occupied territories, and also because of the dead end the Washington negotiations had reached. But acceptance of such a proposal would have posed a serious threat to the totality of the peace process because it would have signalled both the beginning and the end of the process.

The American delegation tried to promote and sweeten this idea, and the Israelis had no objections to it. Certainly, we had noticed during the ninth round of the Oslo negotiations that the Israelis were talking about the efforts of, a senior State Department official, Dennis Ross, and that he was making them for personal advantage. On the other hand, we could see the Norwegians subtly putting their weight behind the Oslo negotiations to ensure their success, not for any material advantage for themselves, but for a desire to bring about peace between Israel and the Palestinians.

The American proposal of an early transfer of power came after Faisal Husseini, Hanan Ashrawi and Saeb Oreiqat had tendered their resignation. But they withdrew it shortly afterwards and also turned their back on the American proposal when we explained to them the risks. We told them all the roads were closed in Washington, and that this climate of futility hanging over Washington did not encourage one to accept such ideas.

The eleventh round got under way in an atmosphere of considerable tension. The following (translated) exchange took place:

Savir: We did not get a good reception in Israel after we got back from the last round because we did not bring positive results. We took into consideration the comments conveyed by Terje Larsen while he was in Tunis. We are facing the time factor and the problem of leaks. Those who know about our activities deny any knowledge and those who do not know are making statements. We hope you will let us hear your new ideas.

Abu Ala: We came to this meeting hoping to arrive at the final formula that will take us from the stage of negotiating texts to the stage of implementation and understanding on the ground. We believe that time has become of the essence. Our work is no longer limited to the framework that we began with. Your press is jumping to conclusions and inventing new stories every day, and so is the Arab press, and international and Arab eyes are examining our every move. Furthermore, the American sponsor is starting to become active: we are about to be visited by Dennis Ross, Warren Christopher and the Russian Foreign Minister. There are many parties that will not like our reaching an agreement in this manner. Therefore, we have prepared our position in a comprehensive and objective draft that takes into consideration all factors and issues.

The Palestinian draft that our delegation had brought from Tunis was then distributed, and the session adjourned so that it could be read; the Israeli delegation also had handed our delegation a copy of their own draft.

Savir: We have tried to improve things with our leadership by blunting the sharpness of your previous position, pointing out that the new items in it were merely proposals. But we found twenty-six amendments in the document you handed us. Quite frankly, if we were to present your amendments to our leadership I believe this would be the end of this channel. However, let us review the document article by article so that you will at least recognize the big gap between us.

Abu Ala: I am extremely disturbed by the expression 'the end of this channel' which Uri Savir has repeated. The most important thing that we should both be doing is convincing our leaderships of the need to handle the issues of the interim period in a rational manner, and the need for agreement. I believe the first document prepared in Sarpsborg remains the basic groundwork. It was amended several times – you even brought amendments of a fundamental nature to the texts and annexes. Then there were joint amendments but some issues remained unresolved. If you look at this document in relation to previous versions you will probably find two hundred amendments not twenty-six. And if we read our own document again we will find many shortcomings in it as well. But I believe that if we read it jointly we will succeed in bridging the gap and find common ground.

Savir: Let us study your document and try to compare it with the positions on which we have already reached agreement so that we can mount a rescue operation.

At this point both sides started to review the draft, article by article and word by word, and then confirmed the points that had already been agreed while leaving aside points on which there was disagreement until all matters, whether agreed or not, had become clear. This took a very long time and eventually the session had to be adjourned for rest. In the next session the document as discussed was distributed, with the issues on which there was disagreement placed in parentheses. Reviewal of the material in parentheses showed that only secondary issues had been taken out.

Savir: I suggest that each side contact its leadership in the coming hour.

Abu Ala: I thought that there would be issues we could resolve, and others for which we could find common solutions, and also issues on which each side could consult with its respective leadership. But I see a completely different picture, where the main issues have not been dealt with and are still stuck in parentheses. We have accepted the harsh conditions for the interim period with courage because there was the hope that at the final stage we would deal with all the awkward and unresolved issues. But the texts that you are insisting on are disquieting because they greatly restrict powers in the interim period and transfer many issues to the permanent status negotiations. For example, as regards the extent of [Palestinian] authority and matters relating to security you have raised questions that cannot be dealt with. I personally cannot handle them or relay them to my leadership to deal with. Many other issues have been left indeterminate by the use of such expressions as 'according to agreement' or 'to be agreed upon'.

Today you are adding new exceptions and conditions that strip the draft of all meaning and substance. How can you object to the expression 'the political rights' when we are talking about and drawing up a reconciliation of historic dimensions? I thought, and it seems I was wrong, that we had not disagreed on the implementation of Resolution 242 in the final settlement. I had also imagined we were in agreement about specifying the issues that would be dealt with in the permanent status negotiations such as Jerusalem, refugees, settlements, security arrangements, borders and so on. I therefore wonder what is required? What do you want? I will leave here completely frustrated because the formulas which I have in front of me make the efforts of the past seven months meaningless.

Abu Ala then presented another collection of contentious issues, hinting that he might personally withdraw from this mission and request that the leadership appoint someone else. Here I digress to say that on the same day that Abu Ala was talking of leaving the Oslo mission, I informed Ahmad Tibi (who used to convey Haim Ramon's queries to me) that I too would relinquish my duties as head of the negotiations committee. It seems both these messages contributed to changing the Israeli leadership's position and disposition. But let us return to the discussions in Oslo.

Savir: If we terminate this channel then, regrettably, it will greatly harm credibility, and the PLO's viewpoint will no longer be explained to the Israelis. This will in turn rule out a high-level meeting. With these demands of yours you are seeking to gain the support of the opposition in your own ranks even though this is a hopeless case. This is what we have learnt from our experience with the Israeli right. Leadership requires courage, not to try to win over the opposition but to undermine it.

I am sorry to say that the Palestinians are the victims of this conflict. You must not persist in showing yourselves in a bad light, so that you 'waste the opportunity for the sake of wasting the opportunity'.[1] You are not alone in this respect because in 1971 we wasted an opportunity to make peace with Sadat which cost us dearly.[2]

The failure of our channel will lead to negative results. There is an alliance between the US and several parties in the region. Therefore, I prefer to reach agreement directly with the PLO. We hope that we will reconsider all the issues that for us cross the 'red line'. We will also recommend what should be recommended. I am not one of those who despair quickly. If you see any hope in salvaging this process I trust you will make the effort to understand what is being proposed to you and what is possible to attain. I hope you can imagine what it means to sign an accord whereby we will begin withdrawing, the Palestinians will live in freedom, and new realities will be created such as economic progress, the creation of a Palestinian police force and other things. At the end of 1993 you will rule Gaza and Jericho and the final phase will begin in 1995. What is the alternative to all of this? You know our feelings.

---

[1] A quip attributed to Abba Eban, the former Israeli Foreign Minister.

[2] In his memoirs Moshe Dayan, the late Israeli Defence Minister, relates how in 1971 the Israelis agreed with President Sadat to open the Suez Canal and move both the Israeli and Egyptian troops away from its banks. On hearing about this agreement President Nixon hastily sent a special envoy to inform Golda Meir that there should be no withdrawal whatsoever. Had this in fact been done, comments Dayan, the Yom Kippur War and all the losses resulting from it, would not have happened.

The most important points of disagreement on the draft document of 25–26 July 1993 were as follows:

1. Article I

Israeli proposal

It is understood that the interim arrangements are an integral part of the overall peace process and that the final status negotiations will lead to the implementation of Security Council Resolutions 242 and 338 as agreed upon by both parties at the permanent status negotiations.

Palestinian proposal

It is understood that the interim arrangements are an integral part of the overall peace process and that the final status negotiations will lead to the implementation of Security Council Resolutions 242 and 338 in all their aspects.

2. Article V, paragraph 3

Israeli proposal

It is understood that at these negotiations [for the permanent status] each party may raise any issues for negotiation.

Palestinian proposal

It is understood that these negotiations shall cover remaining issues including: Jerusalem, refugees, settlements, security arrangements, borders, relations and cooperation with other neighbours and any other issues of common interest.

3. Article VII, paragraph 5

Israeli proposal

After the inauguration of the Council, the [Israeli] Civil Administration will be dissolved.

Palestinian proposal

After the inauguration of the Council, the [Israeli] Civil Administration will be dissolved, and the Israeli military government will be withdrawn.

4. Article VIII, on public order and security

The basic text of the Article reads as follows: In order to guarantee public order and internal security for the Palestinians of the West Bank and the Gaza Strip, the Council will establish a strong police force, while Israel will continue to carry all responsibilities.

Israeli addition

. . . for defending against external threats or terrorist threats against the Israelis, as well as the responsibility for overall security of the Israelis.

Palestinian addition

. . . for defending against external threats.

5. Article XII, on liaison and cooperation with Jordan and Egypt

Israeli proposal

The two parties [the Government of Israel and the Palestinian Council] will invite the Governments of Jordan and Egypt to participate in establishing further liaison and cooperation arrangements between the Government of Israel and the Council, on the one hand, and the Governments of Jordan and Egypt, on the other.

Palestinian proposal

The two parties will invite the Governments of Jordan and Egypt to participate in establishing further liaison and cooperation arrangements between the Government of Israel, the Council, Jordan and Egypt to look into, among other things, the means of cooperation, problem solving and the modalities of the admission of persons displaced in 1967.

6. Article XIV, on Israeli withdrawal from the Gaza Strip and Jericho area

Israeli proposal

Israel will implement an accelerated and scheduled withdrawal of Israeli military forces from the Gaza Strip and Jericho area as will be agreed upon and as detailed in the protocol attached as Annex II. The offices of the Council will be located in Jericho.

Palestinian proposal

Israel will withdraw from the Gaza Strip and Jericho area, as detailed in the protocol attached as Annex II. The offices of the Council will be located in the Gaza Strip and in Jericho pending the inauguration of the Council.

7. Annex I, paragraph 3, on the mode and conditions of the elections

The future status of displaced Palestinians who were registered on 4 June 1967 will not be prejudiced (*Israeli proposal:* because they) (*Palestinian proposal:* if they) are unable to participate in the election process due to practical reasons.

Although the eleventh round ended with both sides expressing pessimism, this attitude was really a form of pressure exerted by each side upon the other. However, the points of difference had been determined and isolated, and the talks had begun to focus on them. This meant that there had been tremendous progress. But no one was bursting with optimism because there was still the possibility of failure at the last moment – over a word, expression or sentence. So contacts intensified, with the Norwegians playing an important role in arranging them and also in reconciling viewpoints.

After this draft had been drawn up and the points of agreement and disagreement determined, we raised another issue, namely the need to refer to the crossing-points (the Gaza–Egypt crossing-point and the Jericho–Jordan crossing-point) with a bid that the Palestinians should control them.

There was a consensus between the two sides that the moment the DOP was signed, we would enter into negotiations on mutual recognition which, if successful, would lead to an agreement enabling the PLO leadership to move to the Gaza Strip and Jericho. We also requested that the Israeli Foreign Minister delivers a letter addressed to his Norwegian counterpart about the preservation of Jerusalem's religious, social, cultural and other institutions. This way the whole picture would become clear. The gaps in the draft agreement would then be filled by exhaustive, last-minute negotiations.

Round Twelve: 14 August 1993
(Comment)

Both sides used this round solely to try to remove the parentheses surrounding the points of disagreement. This was followed by a competition in the use of expressions, words and sometimes commas and full stops, since all of these could affect the meaning.

Singer reviewed some of the points that the Israeli position made it necessary to concentrate on:

- Israeli withdrawal from Gaza and Jericho on the condition that the Council's headquarters would be located in Jericho.
- The word 'overall' regarding Israeli security powers would be required.
- Withdrawal from Jericho would not include the bridges.
- Withdrawal from Gaza would not be total; some troops would stay on.
- There was no objection to the use of the expression 'political rights'.
- The Israeli team wondered whether an early transfer of power was possible.

Uri Savir explained the Israeli view on the contentious issues such as the final status, the withdrawal of the Israeli military government, Israeli responsibilities regarding security control of bridges. After specifying the points of disagreement, the dialogue moved on to the question of mutual recognition.

This round too ended in clear differences on a set of points. The Israeli side again spoke of the possibility of the Oslo channel being shut down because of the differences and the difficulties it was experiencing.

10
The Crucial Moments

Seven hours in the lifetime and history of the Palestinian people were recorded; seven hours of dialogue by telephone ended a twentieth-century conflict, outlined the first steps along the road to liberty and freedom for the Palestinian people, outlined the features of the future of the region and accomplished what twenty months of fruitless negotiations in Washington had failed to do. These seven hours saw the conclusion of a total agreement on the arrangements for the interim autonomy period, including Israeli withdrawal from the Gaza Strip and Jericho area.

Both sides in Oslo had come unstuck on several points, some demanded by our team, some by the Israeli team. We thought that the matter would not be resolved, and that the agreement would never see the light of day.

Not long after, on 17 August 1993, Shimon Peres arrived in Stockholm and by an earlier arrangement met the Norwegian Foreign Minister, Johan Joergen Holst, architect and godfather of the Palestinian–Israeli secret negotiations, whose country had acted as host to them for nearly nine months. Now it would be Sweden's turn. The two ministers exchanged views, and Holst agreed to speak to Tunis on the telephone and be the Israeli Foreign Minister's mouthpiece. Peres was anxious to conclude the accord because he had staked his entire political reputation and his future in Rabin's cabinet on it.

Thus the negotiations began, between Stockholm and Tunis and Tel Aviv. Gathered in Arafat's room by the phone in Tunis were Arafat himself, Yasser Abd Rabbo, Abu Ala, Hassan Asfour and myself. On the other line in Stockholm were Shimon Peres, Johan Holst and Joel Singer, while Yitzhak Rabin was by the phone in Tel Aviv. Uri Savir stood by in Jerusalem. The talk began with the 'hot' points, the amendments required and each side's opinion regarding them. Several telephone calls later it was decided to iron out all differences and a meeting was arranged for Thursday, 19 August 1993, in Oslo where the agreement would be initialled.

It was after 5 a.m. the next morning when the last telephone call ended. We all stood looking at each other in amazement, unable to believe the finale had come. We did not exchange one word until one of us thought of summoning a photographer to immortalize this historic moment. But we soon remembered that it was only the minor struggle that had just ended, or nearly so, and that the greater struggle was yet to come. How would we manage? How would we succeed in the face of this supreme challenge? Could we succeed?

It was at about 10 p.m. the previous night, 17 August 1993, that we had gathered in Arafat's office to be told that Arafat had received a call from Sweden from Foreign Minister Holst saying that he and Israeli Foreign Minister Peres were waiting for us to talk to them to tackle the unresolved issues, this being an historic and perhaps unrepeatable opportunity to achieve a breakthrough. Holst thought that the issues could be decided on the telephone because Peres was beside him, and that if necessary, Rabin could be contacted in Tel Aviv where he was standing by. In this way a telephone conference could be held between the Israelis, the Palestinians and the Norwegian friends. We found ourselves facing a crucial moment. We could not let this opportunity slip by, especially as Shimon Peres had expressed a keen desire to overcome all the problems and to reach a solution before the media could get wind of the Oslo channel and wreck it. Johan Holst and his assistants saw this as a golden opportunity for their efforts to bear fruit and so carve for themselves a place in history.

Nine telephone calls were made between Tunis and Stockholm lasting for seven hours. In between, of course, a similar number of calls were made between Stockholm and Tel Aviv to consult with Yitzhak Rabin. Here is a summary of how the outstanding problems were solved.

1. Article I

Disagreement over this article concerned the implementation of Resolutions 242 and 338 with the Israelis stipulating that implementation was to be in accordance with what the two parties would agree upon at the permanent status negotiations and the Palestinians insisting that this should be clearly stated in the DOP from now. The Palestinian view was accepted and the accredited text of the article became: '. . . final status negotiations will lead to the implementation of Security Council Resolutions 242 and 338.'

2. Article V, paragraph 3

This paragraph related to issues that would be covered by the permanent status negotiations. The Israelis did not want to specify these issues in the DOP arguing that either side would be entitled to raise any issue at the permanent status negotiations, whereas the Palestinian side insisted that these should be specified in the DOP so that both parties would be committed to discussing them and finding solutions for them at the later negotiations. It was agreed on the telephone that these issues be specified in the DOP. Thus the clause became: 'It is understood that these negotiations shall cover remaining issues including: Jerusalem, refugees, settlements, security arrangements, borders, relations and cooperation with other neighbours, and other issues of common interest.'

3. Article VII, paragraph 5

In the beginning the Israeli Government agreed to dissolve the Civil Administration but insisted on maintaining the Israeli military government in the occupied territories on the grounds that there would be Israeli settlements and citizens in these territories. However, we insisted that both the Civil Administration and the military government be withdrawn, because it was not possible for two governments, an interim Palestinian government and an Israeli military government to exist side by side on the territories of the West Bank and the Gaza Strip. After a long discussion on the telephone the following formula was agreed: 'After the inauguration of the Council the Civil Administration will be dissolved, and the Israeli military government will be withdrawn.'

Abu Ala was the one speaking on the telephone while the rest of us followed the dialogue through the amplified extension that enabled us to hear whoever was on the line in Stockholm. Abu Ala would make his point, and silence would then ensue for about half an hour while, we presumed, consultations would take place between Stockholm and Tel Aviv.

It was past 1.30 a.m. and we had completed only three points with quite a few still needing clarification. The room we were sitting in was thick with cigarette smoke and the aroma of Arabic coffee; coffee cups were strewn all over the tables and the ashtrays overflowed. The telephone would ring, and we would carry on with the discussion of yet another point.

4. Annex II, paragraph 4

Ever since agreement had been reached on the withdrawal from the Gaza Strip and the Jericho area we tried to settle the problem of control of the crossing-points leading to them, respectively from Egypt and Jordan. The Israelis refused to even discuss the matter arguing that control of them was part of the external security which they would continue to be responsible for during the interim period. Moreover, as control of these crossing-points was an attribute of sovereignty it would not be proper that an interim authority, enjoying self-rule only, should assume such control. We, however, insisted on finding a compromise formula between the Israeli position and ours until finally we arrived at an ambiguous, though acceptable, formula: 'The above agreement will include arrangements for coordination between both parties regarding passages: a. Gaza–Egypt; and b. Jericho–Jordan.'

There was also a lengthy discussion on paragraph 5 of the same Annex, which dealt with the location of the offices from which the Palestinian authority would operate. We wanted to have offices not only in the Gaza Strip and Jericho but also in other locations in the rest of the West Bank, especially after the elections of the Council. Eventually, a compromise was struck, and the following formula was agreed: 'The offices responsible for carrying out the powers and responsibilities of the Palestinian Authority under this Annex II and Article VI of the Declaration of Principles will be located in the Gaza Strip and in the Jericho area pending the inauguration of the Council.'

Minor issues now remained. It was 3.30 a.m. and we were able within one hour to reach suitable arrangements regarding them. These were:

– The permanent status negotiations: We made the formula flexible by making the time frame for them to start, reducible. Thus we agreed that these negotiations could 'commence as soon as possible, but not later than the beginning of the third year of the interim period'. (Article V, paragraph 2).
– We also now agreed that there could be a 'temporary international or foreign presence' to oversee the Israeli withdrawal of military forces from Gaza and Jericho. This the Israelis had previously disallowed.

When the telephone calls with Holst and Peres were over, and when all the outstanding points of difference had been resolved and it had been agreed to meet in Oslo to initial the DOP, it was past 5 a.m. on 18

August 1993. I contacted our ambassador in Cairo, Saeed Kamal, and asked him to send our legal consultant, Taher Shash (who had been with the Palestinian delegation to Washington from the beginning of the negotiations), to Oslo as quickly as possible to review the texts and check that they were correct and accurate before signing. But Shash knew nothing of the Oslo channel and we could not reveal the nature of his mission to him beforehand. He was therefore asked to travel to Oslo and to stay at the Plaza Hotel where someone would meet him and explain to him what he had to do. He was asked to leave Cairo secretly and make his own travel arrangements as secrecy was of paramount importance.

Shash kept to what was asked of him. He arrived in Oslo at 5 p.m. on Thursday, 19 August 1993, and was met by Abu Ala who handed him the text of the DOP and asked him to review it and give his opinion. Shash studied it thoroughly, and a few hours later informed Abu Ala that it was a good text with no shortcomings. He then returned to Cairo.

The Final Session: 20 August 1993
(Minutes of Meetings)

Meanwhile our delegation had left Tunis for Oslo on 18 August 1993 to initial the agreement. This was done at 2.30 a.m. on 20 August 1993. Eleven hours later at 3.30 p.m. on the same day the final session was held between the two delegations to agree on the following steps. The session, translated from Arabic, went as follows:

Savir: It is necessary to preserve the secrecy of what has happened until this secret channel becomes an open channel because this is a very sensitive subject for us. In the meantime it is appropriate to maintain contacts, with Nabil Shaath for example, and we are prepared to continue to send people to meet him because such contacts are a good cover for this channel.
Abu Ala: We are aware of the sensitive nature of the subject and we share your views. We would even want to maintain the secrecy of this channel so as to be able to continue the activities of the committees.
Singer: Regarding the seven points, I know that the text is in Arabic; do you have a text in English?
Abu Ala: Well, we have an unofficial translation.
Singer: Can you hand us the translated text?
Abu Ala: It is better that I just read the translation [he then read it at dictation speed].
Singer: I understand from your discussion with Savir and Hirschfeld

that you reject our demand that you should stop the intifada, that you cannot confirm that it will be stopped.

Abu Ala: The intifada cannot be stopped by a decision. Look at what is happening in Egypt. The State makes decisions, but there are groups working against it. Therefore the matter is not one of decision. It is necessary for us to work together on the ground to bring our people round; but not to take a decision that puts us in confrontation with the people. This will not serve the peace we are seeking. And as you notice from the text I read there is a clear mention of security and peace. The intifada is a form of resistance to occupation and injustice. The reasons for which the intifada erupted must be removed.

Singer: We are not authorized now to discuss the text or drafts, so we can only reflect. Is there a particular date on which the intifada could stop?

Abu Ala: When there is practical and genuine progress on the ground consolidating the peace process, people themselves will change their behaviour, but it cannot be stopped by a decision. The intifada is not a holiday.

Singer: Can Tunis issue a proclamation calling for the end of the intifada?

Abu Ala: No, this is not possible. The intifada continues because its causes continue and unless there is tangible progress on the ground it will go on.

Savir: When the PLO becomes the representative of the Palestinian people in the eyes of the Israeli public, then its leadership must shoulder its responsibilities. We are not asking you for the impossible, like telling the people 'be happy', but the PLO has an influence on the people. The statements that are released in the West Bank and Gaza have the PLO behind them, and it is the PLO that issues the instructions. We now need to channel the people's energies towards peace. The PLO can contribute to that. We are aware that Hamas is there and we do not expect the PLO to control everything, but it is possible for it to issue a statement aimed at transforming the people's efforts from violence to productiveness and peace.

Abu Ala: We cannot ask our people to halt the intifada because, as I said, the causes are still there. We must make a future for their children and pull them out from the conditions of poverty and provide employment opportunities in the occupied territory. The continuing occupation and the deteriorating conditions are the causes of the intifada persisting.

Singer: Can the PLO not ask the people to be positive and so put an end to the intifada by other means? To tell them to go to work instead of carrying stones and to replace violence with cooperation?

Abu Ala: There is no place for this in the statement. The statement mentions terrorism which we are against and mentions security which we are for. Progress must be on the ground. Let me ask a question, do you want the PLO weak or strong?

Singer and Savir: We want it strong.

Abu Ala: Well, let us agree on the statement that contains your guarantees. When there is progress on the ground we will automatically ask our people to turn towards constructiveness.

Hirschfeld: We want to tell our people frankly that Israel is negotiating with the PLO as the leader of the Palestinian people. This means the PLO must shoulder its responsibilities.

Savir: We want to recognize the PLO. This requires that the PLO influences Israeli public opinion directly prior to recognition. In other words, the required statement must break the psychological barrier between Israeli public opinion and the PLO. We want to change the policy of Israel and we want you to help us do so. Peres said during the signing of the initials ceremony that no one wants to see the continuation of conflict, and that we must strive to ensure a better future for our children and the coming generations than our present.

Abu Ala: Concerning such a statement, you know the PLO well. There has been a dramatic change in the PLO policy and its serious orientation towards peace. You must not burden it with things that would weaken it. It is not possible to halt the intifada with a decision and you know that. The statement I read is entirely sufficient and meets your demands. The only way to halt the intifada is to eradicate the causes: occupation, domination and economic deterioration.

Singer: Can you say that the continuation of the intifada is incompatible with the DOP that we have agreed on?

Abu Ala: The intifada is not a building that can be demolished, but we can add to the statement that we are entering a new phase, for example.

Singer: I wonder. It is obvious that you have done your homework. We have not. But what can you add to the statement?

Abu Ala: An indication, for example, of our entering a period of reconstruction, economic development and cooperation, something along these lines. It is not in your interest or even ours to demand a halt to the intifada – let us not deceive ourselves.

Singer: I was very impressed with your opening speech. It contains words and expressions that can be mentioned in the statement. The DOP document is full of expressions that mean peace and cooperation. Why can the PLO not say: 'Stop the intifada.'

Abu Ala: The DOP document is a fundamental step towards peace and reflects the change in PLO policy. Thus the current statement and document are enough.

Singer: Please understand our demand. You have already mentioned terrorism in a statement made in Cairo and in another in Geneva. Can you not repeat this reference in the statement?

Abu Ala: Our position on terrorism has not changed, and the text in the suggested statement is clear and covers what you have mentioned.

Singer: You have mentioned to Uri Savir the draft of another statement that includes points on the issues and questions we have raised. Can I have a copy of that draft?

Abu Ala: I will read it [he read it at dictation speed]. These are the ideas from our side. I hope you will bear in mind that you do not want just a piece of paper, nor to put pressure on the PLO. You need a strong PLO. The real test is our cooperation and the implementation of the DOP. Each of us can make mistakes but we must coordinate. I suggest that Abu Mazen and Peres meet and agree on a text because there are things which I cannot answer. Afterwards a meeting can be held with Arafat.

Singer: Peres will not be involved in text drafting. This is a job for experts and anyway we are still exploring matters.

Savir: It is in our interest to strengthen and support the PLO. There are many other things we can do, like strengthening your relations with Europe, establishing relations with America and forming committees in the fields of economics and others. This requires Rabin's conviction that the PLO has changed and has become a real partner in the peace process. It is understood now that you are prepared to issue a statement, which is what I will tell Rabin and Peres. I will convey your views and the matter then needs to be followed up. There is no change expected in the composition of our delegation that is negotiating the question of the statement. We will inform you of developments.

Abu Ala: We understand each other and will await your response.

Savir: A Peres–Abu Mazen meeting will not be a meeting for negotiating. It will be a meeting for decision making. It is better to follow up the subject as we did with the DOP document and to continue using the Norway channel.

Singer: Let us suppose that the PLO leadership has returned to Gaza. Will Arafat, for example, be the head of the Authority or will he direct affairs without being the head of the Authority?

Abu Ala: I do not think he will head the Authority. He determines his own role and is the reference for all activities.

Singer: Will the PLO be the Government? Will you [Abu Ala], for instance, be responsible for finance?

Abu Ala: I have not even asked myself this question. The PLO will certainly direct affairs, but how I don't really know for sure. If you have ideas please tell us about them.

Singer: There could be a body responsible for the activities mentioned in the DOP document. But the PLO has greater responsibilities including external relations. This means that there would be two bodies. But these are just ideas.

Abu Ala: The PLO's responsibilities are much greater than those of the Authority referred to in the DOP document. We suggest, for example, and this is just an idea, convening a national council in Gaza in order to make the Authority's decisions consistent with the provisions of the DOP document.

Savir: We know that Arafat will be the activator and the Authority, but not all the state apparatus can be moved to Gaza. The PLO has the apparatus of a State. Maybe Arafat will have a centre in Gaza and a centre abroad so that we do not confuse the interim period with the permanent status. These are just my ideas.

Singer: We need to think together about these subjects.

Savir: I have not asked anyone about the subject of convening a meeting of the Palestine National Council; I believe this is no easy matter.

Abu Ala: If the PLO is in Gaza it will greatly facilitate the implementation of the DOP document.

Savir: There are many things which we must think about together.

11

Did the PLO Protect the Secrets of Oslo?

Protecting the secrecy of the negotiations in the Oslo channel was difficult, if not impossible, for entirely practical considerations. Because we
had to disclose the existence of this channel to some without compro-
mising its secrecy, whether at the Palestinian level or at the regional Arab
or international level, we found that choosing the individuals or countries
that had to be told about it was very difficult. There was the possibility
that by making a bad choice we would expose the secret and wreck the
talks. But it was necessary to strengthen the position of the negotiators
and the supervisors of the negotiations and also to build up advance
support for them from diverse sources. We were indeed caught between a
rock and a hard place, since we had to maintain secrecy and at the same
time gather the support that would be necessary to make these negotiations succeed.

When the negotiations began in Oslo, the Israeli delegation suggested
that the American Administration and the Egyptian Government should
be informed. When the Palestinian delegation conveyed this suggestion
to us in Tunis we agreed on condition that the Israelis would inform the
American Administration and that we would inform the Egyptian
Government. Shimon Peres duly told Warren Christopher and Dan
Kurtzer, but neither man took the matter seriously. They simply asked to
be kept in the picture, but without giving the matter much importance or
concern. As for us, our contacts continued with Amr Moussa and Usama
al-Baz to whom we passed on first-hand details of the negotiations. The
two made sure they kept the secret, and though, of course, they briefed
President Mubarak on developments, no one else in the Egyptian
Government had an inkling of this matter. The Egyptians often met
American officials such as Dennis Ross and others but they remained
tight-lipped because they knew that these people were not in the know.
They simply limited their discussions to the negotiations in Washington.

On our side, no one in Egypt knew of this matter except Saeed Kamal.
On one occasion I took Abu Ala with me to explain to the Egyptians the

details of what was happening in Oslo. Many members of the leadership found it strange that Abu Ala should go to Cairo since he had no role in political dealings with the Egyptians. We used the pretext that certain issues relating to the multilateral negotiations, in which he had a major role, had to be explained to the Egyptian officials responsible for this track. I was then able to take him on his own to the Egyptian Foreign Ministry for a meeting with Amr Moussa, without the Palestinian colleagues who normally travelled to Cairo on foreign relations business.

We were living and working on Tunisian soil without the slightest interference from the Tunisians in our affairs. They never tried to impose an opinion or a stance on us, but allowed us freedom of action on their territory, whether or not they approved. Moreover, we often used to ask them to convey a view or a request to the US or to individual European countries; so it was hardly reasonable that they should be left in the dark about Oslo. We knew how concerned they were with our cause and how ready they were to render any service or exert any effort for us. But how? It seemed that the best course was to have a private talk with the Foreign Minister or the Minister of State for Foreign Affairs outside the framework of the Foreign Ministry. I therefore arranged a private meeting with Saeed bin Mustapha in which I informed him of the Oslo channel, the gist of the Palestinian–Israeli exchanges, our eagerness to keep this channel secret knowing that the Tunisian reaction would be positive, and finally our wish to get their advice. I promised to inform him at first hand of all the developments as they occurred. The Tunisians protected the secret of Oslo throughout the negotiations, and even when the signing of the initials was announced in the Israeli press, they did not indicate that they knew anything about them so as not to embarrass us with others whom we had not taken into our confidence.

His Majesty King Hassan II of Morocco had suggested to us on more than one occasion that there should be direct contact with the Israelis. Our answer was always that the Israelis refused to talk to us and would have no truck with the mediators we sent them. On 20 March 1993 Faisal Husseini and I were visiting the King when he took me aside and said: 'Why do you not contact the Israelis? Is there no progress in their attitude?' Whereupon I said: 'Yes, there is something new, Your Majesty; we are meeting now.' He replied, 'This is excellent. I hope I can be kept directly informed of everything that goes on.' It was arranged then that the Moroccan Ambassador in Tunisia would contact me for information and convey this directly to His Majesty without any intermediation. The arrangement went according to plan until 17 August 1993 when the Ambassador was on holiday and the procedure interrupted. But on this

date I informed our own Ambassador in Morocco of the latest developments immediately we had completed the arrangements for the signing
of the initials. He then forwarded a secret report to His Majesty the King
through the Moroccan intelligence chief, General Qadri. On 20 August
1993 I telephoned the Ambassador and told him to inform the King that
the initialling of the accord had indeed been completed.

A few months after Oslo had got under way we began to feel very
embarrassed for not having informed Jordan and in particular His
Majesty King Hussein personally of this development. Jordan had been
our partner in the formal negotiations, had given us the legal cover to go
to Madrid, and had helped us during the 'corridor negotiations' in the
first Washington sessions to separate the Jordanian from the Palestinian
track. Furthermore, we had constantly spoken of a confederation with
Jordan because of the special relations binding the Jordanian and
Palestinian peoples. For these important reasons we shuddered even to
contemplate the consequences of King Hussein's anger if we were to reach
an agreement with the Israelis that took him completeley by surprise. We
therefore suggested to Arafat that he should disclose everything to the
King when they met in April and assure him that he would be put fully
in the picture once results were reached. When Arafat returned from
Amman he gave us to understand that he had briefed the King who had
approved of the Oslo track. But I know that when Arafat says something
he does not really want to disclose, the person listening to him will understand nothing; so I decided to go to Jordan to explain to the King what
was happening in some detail, but unfortunately he was not there, and I
had to return without informing anyone. On my second attempt I met the
King but he was not alone, neither was I, and I could not ask for a private
audience as this would have aroused the suspicion of those present and
provoked questions. So I went back to Tunisia, disappointed. A third
attempt was equally unsuccessful, because the King had left Amman
when I arrived. In the end I approached a mutual friend who was close to
King Hussein, Dr Ashraf al-Kurdi and told him: 'Please tell His Majesty
the King that I came to Amman three times to talk to him about a serious
matter relating to the negotiations. Unfortunately, I was not able to see
him but I hope to succeed on the fourth attempt.'

But there was no fourth time because it was too late; the signing of
initials took place in Oslo, the Israeli press published the news soon after,
and King Hussein was extremely angry because we had concealed the
matter from him. So I visited him on 17 October 1993 and explained the
matter from beginning to end. I do not know whether he accepted my
excuses or not, but I do say that he had every right to be reproachful.

On the fateful morning of 18 August 1993 when we had just finished
the telephonic negotiations with Peres and were preparing for the delegation's journey to Oslo for the signing of the accord, the Saudi Arabian
Ambassador in Tunisia, Ibrahim al-Saad, visited me. After discussing
various matters, I told him that we were on the verge of signing an
accord with the Israelis and asked him to convey the news to King Fahd
in person. I said that I hoped disclosure of the information would be
restricted since the matter was not yet finalized. As soon as he heard the
news, King Fahd expressed his pleasure and confirmed the Kingdom's
support for our decision, adding that he himself approved of this action
and he wished us luck. On 20 August 1993 I informed the Ambassador,
who had expressed his wish to be kept abreast of developments, that the
signing had taken place in Oslo and that we were in the process of
arranging for it to be announced.

These are the Arab parties who were informed about the Oslo
channel. None of them probed into the details but followed developments
with interest and treated the information we gave them with the utmost
seriousness. We attest that they did not leak the information, publish it or
even talk about it to anyone. We would have liked to inform all the Arab
countries which are concerned about our problem, but we feared that the
channel might fail, in which case we would be accused of frivolity.

On the international level the co-sponsors could not be kept in the
dark, and in any event we imagined that even if we did not tell them,
their intelligence services would find out. As the Israelis had officially
informed the Americans, we felt it incumbent on us to inform the
Russians, since we had long-standing, friendly relations with them as well
as a Joint Coordination Committee that met on a monthly basis in
Moscow and Tunis. This committee had been established five years
previously and had never failed to meet, which was proof of the Russians'
interest in our affairs and their desire to maintain policy coordination
with us as well as friendship. The Russians were no longer what they used
to be under the Marxist Soviet regime. The iron grip on staff and senior
officials had relaxed, and it was no longer possible to guarantee secrecy
as it used to be in the past. I therefore thought long and hard before
revealing any details to the Russian officials since I had to choose the
right person, someone tight-lipped whom I could trust not to let news
leak out to news agencies or intelligence services.

I had a friend whom I had known for twenty years, ever since he was
Minister Plenipotentiary at the Soviet Embassy in Damascus. From there
he had been transferred to the central administration and had then been
appointed Ambassador to Oman and to Iraq before finally becoming

Head of Middle East and Africa Department in Moscow, the department that dealt with us directly and on a daily basis. This man was Victor Pasavaliouk. I had complete confidence in him because he paid a great deal of attention to the Palestinian issue, was most eager to develop our bilateral relations and always tried to remove the many obstacles that beset such relations, especially during the Gulf war and at the time of the failed coup against Mikhail Gorbachev. Some members of the PLO leadership had supported the attempt, which prompted our opponents in Moscow to demand the closure of the Embassy of Palestine there. But this man had defended us and, by dealing effectively with our opponents, had succeeded not only in consolidating the Embassy's position but also in developing our relationship further.

I told Victor Pasavaliouk about the Oslo channel, especially as I had asked him in the past to approach the Israelis to establish a clandestine channel with us in Moscow, which the Israelis had refused. He took the news seriously, commenting, 'It is the right way and the only way if you want to achieve positive results, because the Washington channel is subject to the blackmail of the limelight, speeches, exchanges of words and posturing.'

As we were about to start the eleventh round in Washington which was due to be held at the end of August 1993, Victor asked me to come to Moscow and to introduce our ideas to the Coordination Committee for the benefit of the Russian envoy who would be liaising with our delegation in Washington. I arrived in Moscow on 23 August 1993, and we duly held an official working session that was attended by our Ambassador and our Chargé d'Affaires and by a number of the Middle East and Africa Department staff. The talks touched on the American paper that had been presented to our delegation in Washington by Djerejian before the end of the tenth round, and the discussions of that paper during the visits of Dennis Ross and Warren Christopher to the Middle East as well as US efforts at reconciling the Palestinian and Israeli positions generally. Then I spoke about our need to present positive and constructive ideas so that this round in Washington would not fail as its predecessors had done. The session ended with a business lunch with Deputy Foreign Minister Kolokolov. I then took Victor Pasavaliouk aside and said, 'Forget everything we said at the official sessions. We have already initialled an accord with the Israelis in Oslo. We will not need the eleventh round in Washington because everything is over. The Americans do not know yet because the Israelis have asked us to give them three days in which to inform the Americans. Therefore, please keep this information to yourself until Shimon Peres and the Norwegian Foreign

Minister visit Washington and personally inform Christopher.' I had barely finished speaking before Victor rushed up to me, embracing me and congratulating me on this great historic achievement. In his joy he quite forgot to ask me about the nature of the agreement, its scope and the issues it tackled. I saw exhilaration in his eyes, so much so that I thought he was shedding tears of joy.

Later, the Moscow correspondent of *al-Hayat* newspaper, Jalal al-Mashta, came to me to ask about the talks in Washington, so I said, 'I will give you a scoop. Within six months, or let us say just five months, there will be a settlement of the Palestine issue. I assure you that I am absolutely certain of every word I am saying.' But Jalal did not handle the news as a scoop. In contrast, our Embassy staff who were present at that encounter were dumbfounded by my words because they had never heard me speak in such specific terms with such certainty. When they pressed me for more details I said, 'Record today's date and as each day goes by strike it off the period that I have specified. What I am saying is not tentative, ambiguous or obscure. An agreement will definitely take place.'

Fortunately the news did not leak out, although Victor admonished the Israelis for keeping the news of Oslo from the Russians, saying, 'It is unfortunate that you ignored us, the co-sponsors of the peace conference, and told us nothing about the Oslo channel, whereas the Palestinians did. We are grateful for their trust in us.' The Russian admonition of the Israelis undoubtedly embarrassed them and it certainly embarrassed us with the Israelis because by not forewarning them of our admission to the Russians, they could not redress the matter with them in time.

On the home front, it was not possible or desirable to restrict the information to only three members of the Executive Committee – Yasser Arafat, Yasser Abd Rabbo and myself – for such a number could not have adequately maintained the cohesion of the Executive Committee. There was, for instance, a person like Bashir al-Barghouti, Secretary-General of the Palestinian People's Party, an intelligent man commanding considerable respect and admiration and residing in the occupied territories. He was also a main partner in the group involved in the conduct of negotiations for a peaceful settlement and a staunch defender of this policy. Such a man had to be informed right from the beginning so that he could share his views with us, give us advice and help us defend the accord once signed. Barghouti was kept informed of developments in Oslo, and he expressed his utmost satisfaction with them. I kept up contact with him throughout until the document was signed. When the matter became public he applauded the accord, and as all his party members respect his opinion they followed his example. This helped us attain a majority in the Executive Committee.

Abu Maher (Muhammad Ghuneim) is respected in Fatah circles, as well as among other Palestinian organizations because of his honesty and presence. He had participated in the follow-up committee for the Washington negotiations and had made his views known. After he had left the committee I continued supplying him with documents and news so that he could stay in touch with what was going on. When the Oslo channel was launched I told him about it straight away and kept him constantly informed of developments there. It goes without saying that Abu Maher gave no indication to any party whatsoever that he was aware of what was happening until the accord was signed. He then staunchly defended it. On 11 October 1993 he delivered a powerful speech in the PLO Central Council vigorously defending the Declaration of Principles and, in an objective way, attacking those who rejected it and vilified the leadership that signed it. Without a doubt he had a major influence on many members of the leadership and the Revolutionary Council.

Perhaps it is useful to note here the resignation of Mahmoud Darwish from the Executive Committee. His resignation came before the announcement of the Oslo agreement and was tendered in circumstances which had nothing to do with the agreement. The general atmosphere in Tunis was one of frustration and desperation. Darwish was a member of the Washington negotiations follow-up committee and was aware of the Oslo negotiations in a general way. He viewed the overall solution of the Palestine question with the heart of a poet and the mind of a politician. He was an experienced man who had suffered from the occupation when he was living in Israel, a man who understood the mentality of the Israelis with whom he had lived for over twenty years. He knew them and understood their lifestyle, their way of thinking, their ambitions, their contradictions and their circumstances from within. He was keen to follow developments in Oslo and, on occasion, he urged me to persevere, not to lose heart and walk away. But he felt he had to resign because from his standpoint, work on the Executive Committee was not compatible with the disposition of the artist, the emotion of the poet and the creativity of a man of letters.

Ever since Uri Savir, the Director-General of the Israeli Foreign Ministry, became involved in the secret negotiations (21 May 1993) I began to feel a bit secure about the Oslo channel and to place some hopes on it, hopes that were reflected in my optimistic attitude which did not escape the notice of my aides and co-workers whom I met in various places. Everyone found this optimistic note strange at a time when they could hear people in the leadership and members of the delegation in Washington say that the negotiations had reached a dead end and that they would not attend the coming round. From May onwards my statements to the press began to sound increasingly hopeful. In closed sessions I said firmly that the solution would materialize by the end of the year. I remember an amusing incident when I met my friend Haseeb Sabbagh in Tunis around that time. He asked me, 'Why do I hear you speak with such optimism?' I replied, 'There are many indicators that make me optimistic. I am aware of how internal matters are proceeding in Israel and America, and I am certain that we are very close to a solution.' Haseeb said, 'I trust what you say. Can I depend on that?' 'Rest assured,' I said, 'I can see the solution as close to me as you are; it is coming – inevitably.' Then I hinted that things were happening behind the scenes, identifying the kind of solution to be expected and giving him the constituent elements of such a solution together with all the relevant information.

Sabbagh began spreading the word without naming the source or giving details, but he used to say: 'The solution is coming by the end of the year, I am completely certain of that.' Another friend of mine, the very wealthy Palestinian, Mohsen al-Qattan, heard him. Mohsen had been a member of the PNC and the National Fund Council (NPC) (had headed the PNC in the late 1960s) before withdrawing from the PNC, NFC and other bodies during the Gulf war in protest at the PLO's pro-Iraqi stance. He said to Sabbagh: 'This is groundless rubbish. Whoever told you this is living a fantasy and is having false dreams. The PLO wants to promote this impression in order to assert its existence and distract attention from the deteriorating state of affairs that foreshadow its demise, a result of its foolish policy during the Gulf war.' Sabbagh stood his ground, repeating what he said to those present, including Abdel-Majeed Shuman, Chairman of the Arab Bank. At this point Qattan said, 'Will you make a bet? I will pay a million dollars if there is an agreement before the end of the year, and you will pay a million dollars if there is not. The money is to be donated to the cooperation fund.' Sabbagh accepted the wager, and Shuman officially witnessed it. Sabbagh then telephoned me asking: 'Are you sure of what you told me? I have bet a million dollars on it with Mohsen Qattan.' 'Rest assured, you will win,' I replied. Six weeks later the accord was announced and Sabbagh won the bet.

When we decided to initiate the dialogue with the Israelis in Oslo we faced the problem of finding the finance for the team's disbursements, air fares and living expenses, without attracting the attention of the NFC employees. I agreed with Abu Ala that he would offer me a personal loan of ten thousand dollars that would be recorded against me in Fatah's treasury and that I would repay in due course. Indeed, I received the cash and handed it over to the team to pay for their plane tickets and defray their living expenses. I insisted that they did not ask the PLO staff to book their tickets for them but that they should buy them themselves. As mentioned before, they did not travel directly to Oslo but varied their routes, each man following a different itinerary so that they would not meet anywhere in Europe. They also had to avoid contact with any Palestinian embassy staff in the course of their journeys, were never to use the telephone and were to return to Tunis at different times from different places. In Oslo they had to be careful not to run into our Ambassador there or any of his staff.

When the ten thousand dollars ran out I asked for another advance of ten thousand, and a third, a fourth and a fifth. When the treasury official handed me the fifth advance he said, 'Brother Abu Mazen, the advances have increased and you have not repaid them, nor have you informed us of how you have used them, and we want to close the accounts.' So I told him, 'I'm hoping to repay them as soon as possible, in not more than two weeks' time.' Barely two weeks later the Declaration of Principles was announced, and I told the treasury official, 'Your money was spent in Oslo and this is the account.' With these words I cleared my debt.

Meanwhile, in Israel was there anything that attracted attention to Oslo? Certainly we did not know the group that had access to the information on the Oslo channel because Rabin had restricted it to members of the reduced Cabinet comprising a few ministers and a number of senior consultants and staff who were close to him. But Shimon Peres was not conservative in his many statements, always implying that something covert was happening. He would say, for instance, 'We and the Palestinians are much closer to reaching a solution than some suspect.' Meanwhile, the politicians and journalists who could plainly see the discouraging accounts from Washington surmised from whatever they could glean from official statements that something was brewing behind the scenes. Peres repeated his statements to the press on an almost daily basis. He neither confirmed nor denied what was being said about clandestine meetings with him or meetings with others, but left it to the imagination of journalists and politicians to draw whatever conclusions they wished. As he explained via the Israeli team in Oslo, his motive was to prepare Israeli public opinion for what we were about to conclude using every opportunity to express his optimism about a settlement. On many occasions he seemed to be on the verge of revealing all.

It will be recalled that during a final stage of the Oslo negotiations the two delegations had agreed that the announcement of the Declaration of Principles would be made in the following manner: the text would be sent to the Americans who would then present it as a final American proposal to both parties at the Washington negotiations. This was not to happen, however. The Israelis soon leaked the text of the DOP with all its annexes which were published by the Israeli newspaper *Haaretz* on 29 August 1993. The plan thus spoilt, we had to deal with the procedure of an official announcement in some other manner. The American Administration was terribly embarrassed by the newspaper report because it had in fact known about the Oslo channel but had not taken it seriously enough to take the trouble of finding out more about its progress. As a result they did not know that the accord had already been signed. They were now in a quandary. If they were to announce that they knew all about it and were behind the accord, everyone would realize that they were lying, and if they were to say they did not know, this would mean that they, as the leading co-sponsor of the (official) negotiations, had actually been the last to find out. There had to be consultations on the method of the American announcement of the Oslo track. Later I found out that they had consulted Dr Usama al-Baz on the text of the American announcement which was released by the State Department following Warren Christopher's meeting with Peres and Holst. It stated that the Israelis and the Palestinians had reached an accord and referred to the important role that the US had played.

Thirteenth October 1993 was the final date for the ratification of the accord by the legislative bodies of both parties, after which the specialized committees immediately began to implement the terms of the Declaration of Principles. Agreement between Arafat and Rabin had been reached on 10 October 1993 in Cairo, to form a number of sub-committees that would report to a higher committee, called the Follow-up Committee, consisting of a Palestinian side, headed by myself, and an Israeli side, headed by Shimon Peres. It would meet in Cairo.

When the Follow-up Committee had completed its work I held a meeting with Peres, which was attended by the Israeli Environment Minister, Yossi Sarid, and by the Ambassador of the State of Palestine in Cairo, Saeed Kamal. We agreed on a number of issues relating to the nature of the activity of this and of other committees, and we also reviewed some side issues. We were invited to lunch at the Egyptian Foreign Ministry by the Egyptian Foreign Minister, Amr Moussa. Sarid sat beside me, and we talked about many things because we had known each other from way back we had not seen each for a long time. During the lunch we reviewed his political career ever since he had joined the Labour Party, his disagreements with Golda Meir, his withdrawal from the Party and his joining of the Citizen's Rights Movement headed by Shulamit Aloni, and then the tripartite coalition called the Meretz movement. When Rabin allied himself in government with Meretz, Sarid became a minister in the coalition government with Labour, even though he had disliked Rabin and had criticized him, preferring Peres because Peres was more open and flexible in his political positions; now he respected Rabin because he found that he was a man of his word.

The conversation then moved on to the Israeli–Palestinian accord, the importance of its implementation and the need for quick action in that respect. Sarid indicated that the Prime Minister (who trusted him), had been following the Oslo negotiations and had been very anxious to keep them secret as he had considered the matter of the utmost seriousness and importance. Sarid then said: 'The Prime Minister did not have complete confidence in the Oslo channel, perhaps because Shimon Peres was in charge of it. At the same time he still hoped for progress in the American-sponsored Washington channel. But Rabin's position was suddenly transformed when you sent him your letter with Ahmad Tibi through Health Minister Haim Ramon, the letter with the five questions and five answers.' I replied: 'But you already knew the questions and answers. We had already discussed them in Oslo and there was nothing new in them.' 'It was not the answers,' he explained, 'but your verbal message that caused him to change his position.'

At this point I remembered what happened. When Tibi arrived in Tunis carrying the questions, our delegation in Oslo had reached an impasse with its Israeli counterpart on a number of basic points, and it had decided to halt the negotiations and return to Tunis. I was in a state of considerable psychological stress and, venting my anger in front of Tibi, I gave him a tough message to deliver to Ramon and Rabin. I said that we would stop the (Washington) negotiations, and that I would resign my duties in the negotiations committee. Of course, I did not in any way hint at what was happening in Oslo to Tibi, but Tibi was astute enough to guess. He told Haim Ramon that Abu Mazen was on the verge of resigning and that this would naturally lead to the suspension of the negotiations and eventually to the fall of the coalition government in Israel. It seemed that it was this message, conveyed by Tibi, that led to the change in Rabin's attitude and so in the direction of the Oslo negotiations. After the accord was signed, I told Tibi the real purpose behind the message he had conveyed for me. He was extremely pleased to have done something that was so important for the peace process, albeit unwittingly.

Because of the small number of people involved from our side in the Oslo process – three negotiating in Oslo and three supervising them in Tunis – it was agreed that no telephone calls would be made from Tunis to Oslo. Therefore, no one knew the delegation's telephone numbers. Furthermore, their movements from one place to another in Norway made it difficult for us to communicate by telephone. However, we did allow the delegation to make brief, coded calls to us in Tunis. We gave each point under discussion a number, and we kept one copy of the list of numbers and the delegation kept another. Thus conversations referred to numbers and when details had to be discussed, this was done in the narrowest of contexts. Interception of telephone calls was later proved to have been fruitless, and none of the countries that liked to eavesdrop on international telephone lines discovered anything from those calls, even though they had gone on for nine full months. During each round, which lasted from 48 to 72 hours, only one or two calls were made at best. Hassan Asfour made most calls and spoke only to me. Abu Ala rarely called unless we had something urgent to discuss and then for only a short time. Arafat and Yasser Abd Rabbo did not speak to the team in Norway throughout the negotiations.

Nor did the negotiating and supervising teams ever meet at any of the PLO offices in Tunis. We always chose my house as a meeting place because there was no chance of a visitor dropping by there without a prior appointment. This gave us the reassurance that no one would knock at the door and embarrass those present, and start asking questions. In fact all our meetings were held at different times at night and were quite brief. All issues were discussed quickly, positions and decisions would be adopted, and those present would leave separately and at different times. Fortunately, none of the members of the delegation aroused any suspicion, and nobody could have imagined that they were engaged in any sort of negotiations.

Speaking on the telephone to each other in Tunis, we would not mention Oslo, but a code-name. Only one question was permitted, namely: 'What is the news of *al-mutaaded*?' Only one answer was allowed: either 'good' or 'bad'. No further discussion or questions were permitted, no matter what they were, and the inquirer had to wait for a meeting in order to talk about details.

If the question on the telephone concerned the whereabouts of the individuals in the team, this would be for example: 'Is the pilot back?' meaning Hassan Asfour. Abu Ala's code-name was 'Ahmad'. As for the

Norwegian mediators, we did not mention either the name of the country or any individual, except the code-name of Terje Larsen, 'Abu Ajqa'. Our delegation gave him this name, which in Arabic means 'Father of Rushing', because he was always rushing about. Sometimes this code-name was used to refer to the Norwegian delegation as a whole and also to Norway, depending on the context. As for me, the delegation never mentioned my name, but the Norwegians gave me the code-name 'The Holy Spirit'. The name spread among the three parties and was used as a matter of course when referring to me. I do not know why I was thus named. As mentioned before, when the Director-General of the Israeli Foreign Ministry, Uri Savir, joined the Israeli negotiating delegation in Oslo we felt it was a positive move by the Israeli Government as the first two, Yair Hirschfeld and Ron Pundak, had claimed they were speaking as academics only. His arrival fuelled our interest and enthusiasm for this channel and it was then that we gave the Israeli delegation the code-name 'Abu Jaafar'. Where did this come from? The Director-General of the PLO's Political Department, Abdel-Latif Abu Hijla, is also called Abu Jaafar because his eldest son's name is Jaafar ('Abu' in Arabic meaning father). As he was the PLO counterpart of Uri Savir the code-name seemed appropriate, and, before long, all the men in the three teams – Palestinian, Israeli and Norwegian – were using the name in ordinary conversation.

12

In Gaza and Jericho, Where Next?

For many years Israel's leaders from the parties on the left and on the right and during both the Likud and the Labour governments had spoken of the need to withdraw from the Gaza Strip. None of these statements had ever elicited a definitive reaction from the Palestinian side.

David Ben Gurion used to say 'Gaza is a cancer' and a number of figures – politicians, soldiers and journalists – often confirmed this fact in their own way and from their own different perspectives. General Chaim Bar-Lev, the Israeli Defence Forces Chief-of-Staff said: 'We occupy Gaza during the day, but the fedayeen occupy it at night.' Others in the Israeli army variously described it as 'the damned sector', 'the hornets' nest', 'the snake-pit'; many reiterated Ben Gurion's description, 'Gaza is a cancer that every healthy body must get rid of to prevent it from spreading.'

The majority of Israelis, whether members of parties, in power or out of power, the army and the population at large, were convinced that continued Israeli presence in this area was fruitless. Newspaper headlines and articles urged deliverance from this nightmare; so did many politicians. A poll taken in the summer of 1993 and published in *Maarev* daily showed that 77 per cent of Israeli respondents supported the idea of an Israeli withdrawal from Gaza as soon as possible. Half of them felt that such withdrawal should take place within the framework of a comprehensive agreement. Some wanted a quick withdrawal from the Gaza Strip by a unilateral decision. That opinion was shared by the doves in Labour and in the left-wing parties. Others preferred negotiations over withdrawal, an opinion expressed by Rabin and his group who represented the majority in the Labour Government.

On the Palestinian side, some said that Israel wanted to get rid of its heavy burdens in Gaza, whether these were economic and social or in matters of security. Others said that the intifada in the Gaza Strip was at its peak, so that if the Palestinians were to let Israel withdraw from it, the intifada would end, and since that was not in favour of the Palestinians, they should not help Israel out, but let it sink further into Gaza's quicksand. Still others felt that an Israeli withdrawal from Gaza might cost the Palestinians dearly for it might turn out to be the one and only withdrawal, with Israel free to swallow up the rest of the occupied territories leaving the Palestinians themselves to flounder in the quagmire of Gaza.

In one of his statements Yitzhak Rabin said: 'I wish the Gaza Strip would sink into the sea.' When some criticized this statement as violating human rights and bordering on racism, Rabin retorted: 'I did not mean what you think I meant. The Palestinians understand exactly what I mean.'

My attention was caught by the first statement ever made by an Israeli official about a withdrawal from the Gaza Strip, but I did not respond because I considered it merely a sop to the press and not a formal position or decision. Even when officials repeated such statements I did not try to bring up the subject in press interviews or at political meetings, although I was totally convinced that any Israeli withdrawal, even from one inch of Palestine land, let alone all of the Gaza Strip, would be a significant gain for us as long as there were no preconditions. When I later suggested that I saw no objection to an Israeli withdrawal from Gaza, provided there was no obligation on our part, many people criticized the idea.

When Yitzhak Rabin made an important statement in which he said he did not object to a withdrawal from the Gaza Strip if the Israelis and Palestinians were to agree on a declaration of principles, I immediately made a statement to a number of newspapers and press agencies that we were ready to accept an Israeli withdrawal from the Gaza Strip as long as this was done within the framework of a declaration of principles that was agreed by both parties. Some members of the Central Committee tried to criticize my statement without knowing any of its details. However, no one paid much attention to this subject as it was not considered attainable, and as the Israelis would not seriously contemplate it anyway.

On presenting the idea to Abu Ala, he rejected it out of hand saying: 'Not only do I have doubts about the idea, but I do not think it is possible that the Israelis would entertain it, so there is no point discussing it at all now.' After we had met several times Abu Ala became convinced that the idea of an Israeli withdrawal from Gaza would be a useful model, because withdrawal expressed a Palestinian demand that Resolution 242 be implemented, and also because it would be a test of Israeli willingness to implement the Resolution.

In Oslo when our delegation first brought up the idea of an Israeli withdrawal from Gaza the Israelis considered it a joke. But Abu Ala insisted on placing it on the negotiating table, and when the Israelis tried to reject it, he reminded them that Prime Minister Rabin had approved the idea provided a declaration of principles was agreed, and since a declaration of principles was now being discussed, there was no reason why the question of withdrawal should not also be discussed. The Israelis replied that what Rabin had said, was for press consumption and did not represent an official position. Abu Ala responded by saying, 'We do not believe that the Prime Minister was making a joke for the press. We do not know if he uses two languages, one for the negotiations and another for the press. We consider that when the Prime Minister says something then he is serious about what he says. Our leadership has taken his words seriously and we were instructed to put the matter to you. Frankly, this is a test of your seriousness in tackling serious issues.'

The Israeli side did not reply, but said it would go back to sound out the opinion of the leadership in Israel although it was doubtful that the leadership would agree. But Abu Ala implied that it was a very important matter for us and that the Declaration of Principles would not go through without it.

In the next round the Israelis agreed in principle to the withdrawal from the Gaza Strip without going into details. We hinted to them that Gaza should be taken over by a body capable of maintaining security and public order and able to provide answers to the main problems facing the population, such as economic, social and administrative problems. We noticed that the Israeli team accepted the idea of the PLO assuming control of the Gaza Strip after an Israeli withdrawal from it, but since such an issue would need much working out, we decided not to delve deeply into the subject until after the Declaration of Principles had been completed.

When Arafat heard the delegation's report giving details of Israel's initial agreement to the withdrawal, he began to make other demands such as that the Gaza Strip was not enough. The Israelis had to withdraw from a place in the West Bank so that it would not be claimed that the solution encompassed only Gaza to the exclusion of the West Bank. Therefore we had to demand a withdrawal from, say, Jericho. He then promoted the idea of 'Gaza–Jericho' as a complementary project. He talked about it to all the presidents and statesmen he met until we felt he had reduced the entire draft of the Declaration of Principles to this expression. He no longer paid any attention to the issues of the Declaration but confined himself to asking what had been done about the

'Gaza–Jericho' project, so that when the accord was finally concluded many people thought that it pertained to Gaza and Jericho only and that there were two phased solutions (instead of one phased solution), one known, the other unknown. Some even put out that the interim arrangement and the permanent solution applied to Gaza and Jericho only.

Before Rabin visited Ismailiyya in Egypt, Arafat met President Mubarak and asked him to sound out Rabin on the Gaza–Jericho project. President Mubarak did not know the background to this project because Arafat had not explained it to him, and so President Mubarak put the question straight to Rabin who became very annoyed, refusing to discuss it at all. It was said at the time that Rabin arrived in Egypt happy and left it angry.

Before Warren Christopher's visit to the Middle East we were in Cairo preparing for the discussion of the Palestinian response to the draft which the Americans had presented to the Washington delegation at the end of the tenth round of negotiations. After we had arrived at an appropriate formula (which the Egyptians would present to the Americans and the Palestinian delegation would present to Christopher in Jerusalem), Arafat spoke to us from Southeast Asia, where he was visiting, to tell us that he had received an offer from the US which Dan Kurtzer (one of Christopher's assistants) had presented to Hanan Ashrawi in the course of a conversation with her. He had informed her of America's approval of the Gaza–Jericho project and requested that we gave our thoughts on it.

Quite frankly, I did not believe that the Americans approved of this project and that the idea was no more than a peripheral subject of conversation between Hanan and Kurtzer. Kurtzer had merely said, 'No objections. Present what you have.' But Arafat insisted that these words indicated a serious American scheme and that it was a 'gift' from America that should not be turned down. When we told him that such a scheme had already been included in the Declaration of Principles which we had to secure agreement on he said: 'I want Gaza–Jericho. What would I do with the Declaration of Principles? Why do I need it? Do I frame it and hang it on the wall?'

The members of the Israeli delegation in Oslo were absolutely livid when they heard our demand for an Israeli withdrawal from Jericho too. At first they refused to even discuss the matter, but our delegation insisted on explaining the reasons behind this request: that Jericho was the gateway to the West Bank, that a withdrawal from there would be a symbolic gesture for the people of the West Bank, that anyway, withdrawal from Jericho would not be problematic seeing there were no

Israeli settlements in that area and other arguments of that nature. The Israelis then requested time to reflect and to refer back to Yitzhak Rabin in person as Peres could not decide on such an important and vital issue. The Israelis then came back and said: 'We have agreed to withdraw from the city of Jericho so that your leadership can assume control of it when the implementation of the accord begins.'

But thereafter our demands began to pile up in such a way that the Israelis became quite frantic. In the event, they accepted some, rejected others and left the door open for the permanent status negotiations.

When we asked that the withdrawal should be from the province of Jericho instead of the city of Jericho, they firmly rejected the request. We then changed it to the district of Jericho, but this was also refused. Finally we agreed that withdrawal should be from the 'Jericho area' which was to be defined later. This was followed by discussion on a special corridor which would link Gaza to Jericho and, which we hinted, would be a part of those two areas (Gaza and Jericho), but this was firmly turned down by the Israelis because such a corridor would effectively divide the State of Israel, a proposition they could hardly accept. Instead, they offered a safe corridor for VIPs, but we rejected the offer because it made a distinction between VIPs and ordinary persons, a suggestion which would be unacceptable to the VIPs themselves. Finally they agreed to provide 'a safe passage for persons and transportation betweeen the Gaza Strip and Jericho area'.

These points did not cover the whole question of Gaza–Jericho as there were other matters that had to be raised, the most important of which concerned the location of the crossing-points: Gaza–Egypt and Jericho–Jordan. We wanted both these crossing-points to be under our control, or to be jointly controlled by us and Interpol. Initially, the Israelis refused to even mention these crossing-points, then they rejected the notion that we would have sole control (or jointly with another party) over a function that was Israel's responsibility; control of the crossing-points would jeopardize external security which would remain Israel's responsibility during the interim period. At the end, it was agreed that reference would be made to the crossing-points in the document and that an arrangement for coordination between the two parties would be determined by agreement. This way the Israelis did not seem to be making concessions to us about the supervision of the passages.

Agreement on Israeli withdrawal from the Gaza Strip and Jericho opened the doors wide for a discussion about the relationship between the PLO and Israel, because withdrawal required some party to exercise authority in these two areas during the period between the entry into force of the Declaration of Principles and the inauguration of the Palestinian Council (for which elections were to be held not later than nine months from the date of the entry into force of the Declaration of Principles). It was therefore agreed that after the initialling of the accord, the necessary conditions for mutual recognition could be discussed.

Unfortunately, some people misunderstood the accord. Their statements portrayed the accord as embracing the Gaza Strip and Jericho only, whereas in fact there is only one article specifically about Gaza and Jericho out of many other articles; these included details of a firm linkage between the interim self-government arrangements and the permanent status of the occupied territories. The accord calls for the transfer of most powers in Gaza and Jericho to the Palestinian Interim Authority upon the withdrawal of the Israeli military government from these areas as well as a simultaneous transfer of certain powers in the rest of the West Bank. Pending the inauguration of the elected Council, the two parties would negotiate the transfer of additional powers and responsibilities. Thus there is no discrepancy between what occurs in Gaza and Jericho and what is to occur in the rest of the West Bank. The fact of the matter is that the accord simply enables the Palestinian leadership to establish itself on Palestinian territory – Gaza and Jericho – while in the other areas there would be a transfer of powers and the redeployment of Israeli military forces on the eve of the elections to specified locations outside the populated areas.

The inclusion of the Gaza–Jericho dimension in the negotiations was a crucial step forward and an acid test of Israel's intentions and sincerity for the future.

13

The Surprise

Following the initialling of the Declaration of Principles at 2.30 a.m. on Friday, 20 August 1993, and before the Israeli press published it in full on 29 August, I had to have a face-to-face session with the Palestinian leadership and official delegation members who were due to leave for Washington in a few days' time to resume the negotiations of the eleventh round. At this time, the PLO Executive Committee and the Palestinian leadership held a round of meetings. I hesitated to put the DOP documents on the Committee's agenda for fear of leaks, as some Committee members had become used to passing on information to the Arab press.

. So I had to resort to some guile to avoid speaking. I went to the Executive Committee's Secretary, Jamal al-Sourani, and asked him if he could guarantee the confidentiality of what I had to say, which was most important and secret. Sourani replied that he could not and helped me to remain silent on the first day and also the day after the Jordanian press had published the proceedings of the Executive Committee the previous night, including full details of what had actually transpired and what had not. Thus the Executive Committee's meetings continued without my saying one word about the accord, although I did approach some members, whose discretion I trusted, and informed them of the Declaration of Principles to secure their approval when the Declaration would be officially presented.

After the work of the PLO Executive Committee was over, I requested a meeting with members of the Fatah Central Committee who were in Tunis in order to put them in the picture with regard to the Declaration of Principles, hoping thereby to avoid complications that might lead to a confrontation with the two leading Committees. I knew that even if many members of the Palestinian leadership did not object to the accord itself, they would still take issue with us for having kept them in the dark, as they all considered themselves equal in responsibility and must therefore be equal in sharing knowledge. But human nature is such that no secret can be kept for long. Many people in politics tend to boast to their friends that they are privy to secrets and so confide in them, urging them not to say a word about what they have just heard. Inevitably, the friends tell other friends, and all say their mouths are sealed, but the ripple is bound to widen in ever-increasing circles. For this reason, maintaining secrecy over Oslo was unavoidable, but the potential consequences for those involved in its proceedings were bound to be disagreeable. There was a distinct possibility of their being attacked on a personal level as well.

With this background in mind, we approached both the Executive Committee and the Fatah Central Committee to explain the accord. We were immediately criticized for not having informed both Committees of the Oslo channel. It was with tremendous difficulty that we managed to shift the conversation away from the secrecy aspect to the subject of the accord. Eventually, the great majority of the members of both Committees approved the terms of the accord, having been convinced that what we had achieved could not have been possible except through this channel.

The main difficulty we faced was how to tell the members of the official Palestinian delegation. They had arrived from Washington to receive instructions regarding the eleventh round and the American proposal that had been put forward at the end of the tenth round. This document, for which Dennis Ross had visited the Middle East, followed by Warren Christopher, aimed at stimulating the peace process and putting pressure on the parties concerned to arrive at an acceptable formula that would form the basis for a declaration of principles. When the members of the Washington delegation arrived in Tunis we told them of the Oslo accord that had been initialled a few days before. They were amazed, poised between belief and disbelief, support for and opposition to the agreement. When they recovered from the shock and examined the details, they had to admit that such an agreement could not have been reached in Washington.

As mentioned before, when the Americans were originally informed of the Oslo negotiations they did not take the matter seriously and dealt with it with so much apathy that they completely forgot about it. When Warren Christopher visited Israel in late June 1993 and the Israelis repeated to him what they had already told him, he said that these meetings only expressed Peres's and Abu Mazen's optimism and would not result in anything concrete.

The nine months of negotiations in Oslo were sufficient to convince the Israelis that negotiating directly with the PLO leadership was much more productive than negotiating through a delegation that did not have enough authority to act. Furthermore, our delegation in Oslo proved their credibility by adhering to everything that was agreed and by maintaining the secrecy of the negotiations at a time when much news was leaked about them to the Israeli press. We continually denied these reports and asserted that they did not exist at all.

It was this correct conduct of our delegation that prompted the Israelis to revise their attitude towards the PLO, from regarding it as a terrorist organization to conferring with it and then recognizing it for what it was. If arriving at the Declaration of Principles was considered an important step, then even more important was the attainment of mutual recognition, because the historic enemies were ending their enmity, sitting together and acknowledging each other's existence.

From our political point of view, recognition of the State of Israel was not a difficult step because the Palestinian initiative adopted by the PNC in 1988 had clearly indicated the possibility of our agreeing to recognize Israel. But I must admit that the psychological and moral aspect was difficult for many. As for Israel, the matter was more complicated because the Israelis not only refused to recognize the PLO but also the existence of the Palestinian people. They had inherited this attitude ever since Theodore Herzl had arrived in Palestine at the turn of the century and proclaimed, 'A land without people for a people without a land.' This notion was the basis of every Israeli position thereafter. It was also the view of world powers. Britain's Balfour Declaration as well as the British Mandate for Palestine, approved by the League of Nations, made no mention of the Palestinian people, but referred to 'communities in Palestine'. So recognition of the PLO by the Israelis was difficult from the two aspects, the political as well as the psychological.

Joel Singer, the head of the Israeli delegation to the Oslo negotiations had said: 'For us, recognition of the PLO has its conditions and demands which you will have to meet if you want it.' Abu Ala replied: 'Our leadership has an open mind about this matter and wishes to explore with you this issue in a serious way. We now await your views on this question so that we can study them.' The Israeli delegation then brought us the following points:

1. Recognition of Israel's right to exist in peace and security.
2. Acceptance of Resolutions 242 and 338.
3. Commitment to conduct negotiations about terms for the interim period and the permanent status and that resolution of the conflict can only be achieved through negotiations.

4. Renunciation of terrorism.
5. Cessation of all acts of violence and terrorism.
6. Invalidation of all the articles in the Palestinian Covenant which deny Israel's right to exist or those which are inconsistent with it.
7. Assurance that Yasser Arafat, in his capacity as PLO chairman, is prepared to meet any Israeli official.

We studied these conditions carefully and thoughtfully because we genuinely wanted to achieve mutual recognition to enable direct negotiations to take place between the two sides. It was no secret that the Palestinian delegation in Washington was appointed, directed and supervised by the PLO, which scrutinized every detail in the negotiations, and that it therefore stood in for the PLO, yet the Israeli Government would still not recognize the PLO referring to it as a terrorist organization bent on the destruction of the State of Israel.

The Israelis at the Oslo negotiations vehemently emphasised that they were negotiating with the PLO, not with Yasser Arafat, ignoring the fact that he was the President of the State of Palestine – a State that was recognized by more than one hundred countries. In the talks they put much weight on the requirement that the articles in the Palestinian Covenant denying Israel's right to exist, be invalidated. Similarly, they demanded that the intifada be halted. As for the remainder of the seven conditions, the PLO had already committed itself to them on various occasions in the past without eliciting any similar commitment from Israel. We therefore considered that the reaffirmation of our commitment implied nothing new and was harmless. All the same, we were careful not to offer the Israelis the kind of recognition that would entail a firm commitment on our part to cancel the relevant articles in the Covenant because the authority to make such a commitment rested with the PNC. With respect to the intifada, it was difficult for us to make a statement about halting it since to demand from our people that they discontinue their resistance while the occupation remained, would have been unreasonable, especially prior to the signing of the accord. Instead, we agreed that a written pledge would be made to the Foreign Minister of Norway that upon the signing of the Declaration of Principles, Arafat would include in his public statements an invitation to the Palestinian people to take part in the steps leading to the normalization of life, rejecting violence and participating in shaping reconstruction, economic development and cooperation.

Talks on mutual recognition lasted for more than ten days because of disagreement about a number of expressions and words over which both sides pondered for a long time. Most of the dialogue on this matter was conducted through Johan Joergen Holst. The final meeting took place in Paris, where the final agreement on the wording of the three letters was reached: the PLO's letter of recognition, the Israeli Government's letter of recognition and a third letter from Yasser Arafat to the Norwegian Foreign Minister regarding the intifada. At 11.30 p.m. on Thursday, 9 September 1993, half an hour after the PLO Executive Committee had affirmed and endorsed the texts, Chairman Arafat signed the two letters on behalf of the PLO. Next day Prime Minister Rabin signed his letter on behalf of Israel.

Many members of the Central Committee and the Executive Committee had never imagined that the agreement we had reached was possible. At debates some said it was enough that explicit reference was made to the 'Palestinian people' in the Declaration of Principles and that anything else was relatively unimportant. Some found that Gaza and Jericho coming under the authority of the PLO was enough; others said, 'If this Declaration is accompanied by the signature of the PLO then this alone is a historic achievement,' while still others said, 'This is more than what we sought.' The strange thing is that when we finally did confirm that the accord was completely genuine, some backtracked and quite unjustifiably proclaimed their opposition to it. This was just opposition for its own sake, to preserve for themselves a long-standing image with the Palestinian people; these men could afford to do so because, in the final analysis, they had nothing to lose.

Some expressed opposition for purely personal reasons, for instance, for not having been invited to participate in the negotiations or having been kept in the dark. Because they had no hand in the agreement they stood against everything that others had achieved even if that was similar to, or better than, what they themselves had advocated. Some were quite amusing in their opposition. They reasoned that since it was impossible for us to put the accord into practice, because we lacked the administrative and technical know-how, then the accord should be rejected. But the people who appreciated this historic event far outnumbered those whose limited horizons and lack of responsibility made them see their homeland, their people and their future from the narrowest of perspectives.

Leadership is not just status, privileges and perks. It consists basically of a mixture of courage, an ability to sense the wishes of the masses, vision and self-denial in serving the cause. Leadership does not mean self-preservation, consolidation of personal position and basking in the comforts of a closed circle, but venturing out to do what is right.

The American Administration announced that the signing would take place on Monday, 13 September 1993, and that Foreign Minister

Shimon Peres would sign the accord for Israel. But, as usual, we, the Palestinians, did not decide who on our side would sign it. Our Foreign Minister, Farouq al-Qaddoumi, should have been the one to sign, but because he opposed the accord he refused to do so. Meanwhile, Arafat wanted to attend the ceremony, which of course required Rabin to be present too. As a result, intense contacts took place during the forty-eight hours that preceded the signing ceremony. The two men were eventually invited to attend, while I was asked to sign in the name of the PLO. I had some reservations about going, but many people made efforts to remove them. That was how some hours later I was on the royal Moroccan jet that carried our delegation to Washington on Sunday, 12 September 1993. The next forty-eight hours we spent in Washington were filled with much activity: meetings, contacts and official functions. Let us look at some of the events of the day.

When the Declaration of Principles was initialled in Oslo on 20 August 1993 there was no mutual recognition between the PLO and Israel, and as a result the preamble stated that the agreement was between the Government of the State of Israel and the Palestinian team in the Jordanian–Palestinian delegation to the Middle East Peace Conference representing the Palestinian people. This was natural since the negotiations in Washington had begun and had proceeded in this manner. But after the letters of mutual recognition had been signed the preamble was supposed to be changed so that the 'Palestine Liberation Organization' would be substituted for 'Palestinian' team. PLO was also to be substituted for 'Palestinian' in other parts of the document. We arrived in Washington thinking that the amendment would be made automatically without question or negotiation. The Palestinian delegation in Washington had not taken any steps to make the amendment on the grounds that we should tackle the matter ourselves with the Israelis, Americans and Norwegians. We then sensed that the Israelis were not prepared to make any change in the document on the pretext that time was short and that no amendments could now be made as it was now at the White House ready for signing.

Hayel al-Fahoum, a member of the Palestinian delegation in Washington and director of the West European Section at the PLO Political Department, recorded the final hours before the signing ceremony in these words:

At 6 a.m. on Monday, 13 September 1993, one of the members of the Israeli delegation called me and introduced himself as Shimon Peres's aide. He asked to speak to Abu Mazen to arrange a meeting between him and Peres at 6 p.m. on the same day. Meanwhile, from his suite at the hotel Arafat woke Ahmad Tibi and asked him to contact Peres in order to make the appropriate change in the preamble.

Ahmad Tibi came back with an answer that was half negative and half positive. Rabin had agreed to mention the PLO as a signatory to the accord at the end of the document. Tibi informed the PLO leadership of this, and Arafat said it was not enough and told him: 'We will not sign the accord because it does not mention the name of the Palestine Liberation Organization.' He then asked Tibi to contact Yitzhak Rabin, Shimon Peres and Haim Ramon who was in Tel Aviv.

At about 8 a.m. Hassan Asfour, Muhammad Abu Koush and Ahmad Tibi were sent to contact the Israeli delegation, but the three returned empty-handed. During the meeting Tibi threatened Shimon Peres that the Palestinian delegation and Yasser Arafat would not arrive at the White House, since Arafat had instructed all delegation members not to leave the hotel for the White House until the preamble was amended.

At 8.45 a.m. all the Palestinian delegation members met at Arafat's suite to discuss the matter. At 9 a.m. Arafat received James Baker [the former US Secretary of State] and informed him of the latest development. Baker then asked: 'When is the accord to be signed?' Abu Ammar [Arafat] replied: 'At eleven o'clock.' Baker then said: 'The Israelis will agree to the amendment at 10.58.'

It was nearly 9.35 when Hanan Ashrawi interjected: 'It is getting late. The Palestinian delegation members can barely make it to the White House to take their seats for the signing ceremony.' (Hanan Ashrawi and Nabil Shaath had earlier made intensive contact with Dennis Ross, Aaron Miller and Edward Djerejian [of the US State Department] to make the amendment, but the response had been negative.)

Arafat then told the delegation members to proceed to the White House. He stayed at the hotel with Abu Mazen, and I stayed with them. In a final attempt Arafat sent Ahmad Tibi to the Israeli delegation's headquarters to inform it that, if the preamble was not amended to incorporate the name of the Palestine Liberation Organization, there would be no signing. At 10 a.m. Abu Mazen asked: 'What will we do if the amendment is not made?' Arafat replied: 'We will not sign the accord.'

At 10.10 the telephone rang. Ahmad Tibi was on the line. He informed Arafat that Peres had agreed to substitute the words 'Palestine Liberation Organization' for the 'Palestinian team in the Jordanian–Palestinian delegation'. Arafat agreed the amendment.

At 10.15 we began moving to the White House. The procession arrived at 10.30, and Arafat and Abu Mazen were escorted into an inner hall in the White House. President Clinton, Rabin, Peres and their aides were there. Accompanied by the US chief of protocol, I went to the place where the signing ceremony was to take place and sat near the rostrum on which the table for signing was placed.

I asked to see the American legal adviser or the protocol official to take a last look at the texts of the document that was soon to be signed. The American adviser began describing the signing procedure, but I insisted on seeing the texts of the accord to ascertain that the agreed amendment had been made. When I examined the document I discovered that no amendment had been made to it. Rather, I discovered that the last line was as follows:

For the Government of Israel: For the Palestinian Delegation:

There was no mention of the Palestine Liberation Organization in the whole text.

I hastened to inform the American legal adviser that I had strict instructions not to present the accord to Abu Mazen if the required amendments had not been made. I asked him to go and see Peres, who was in the White House, and check with him.

The American legal adviser then rushed into the White House to consult with Peres. I proceeded to the first row of guests and asked Hanan Ashrawi to accompany me to solve the problem. The American adviser returned, and I told him to relate the response in the presence of Hanan Ashrawi. He said that Peres had confirmed his agreement to the amendment and that during the signing Abu Mazen could cross out the words Palestinian Delegation and replace them with Palestine Liberation Organization by hand. Hanan then said that Abu Mazen should sign the document before Peres so that the amendment would be seen to be agreed and legally fixed. But the American legal adviser said protocol required that Peres sign first. Hanan then told me to insist on the position and returned to her place.

I then asked the American adviser if the last page could be retyped in its new form. Indeed, he quickly had four copies of the amendment typed in the White House and returned with the Israeli legal adviser, Joel Singer. The new pages were added to the other pages of the accord but I asked that the final unamended lines be crossed out in all copies, which was done.

As for the first page, the preamble was amended by hand and the expression 'P.L.O.' was substituted for 'Palestinian'. The Israeli adviser, Joel Singer, and I initialled the amendment.

At 11.10 a.m., after a ten-minute delay, the signing ceremony began, after which everything went smoothly.

When we arrived at the White House, we were received by President Clinton and his wife Hilary, former presidents George Bush and Jimmy Carter and Mrs Carter, Vice-President Al Gore and others. Among those in attendance was the Foreign Minister of Norway who was considered the star of the ceremony because he had personally sponsored and shielded the accord until he had steered it to the White House lawn. Then Yitzhak Rabin and his wife entered the room with Shimon Peres, keeping away from us. President Clinton and the rest of the American officials moved to and fro between us and the Israelis to fill in the half-hour before the next function. Everyone praised the efforts of the partners who had reached this accord in complete secrecy without drawing the attention of the media or even the intelligence services of the great powers for nine full months. They also spoke about implementation, the need to honour the terms of the accord and to work for solving the economic and social problems that we would face when the time came. In this connection, President Clinton spoke in very clear terms about America's commitment to provide economic support. He then referred to the negotiations and said that if the negotiations had continued in Washington alone they would not have succeeded because they were taking place before the eyes and ears of the world, a fact which had inhibited the negotiators from speaking openly and freely round the negotiating table. They were in effect taking place in the street, whereas in Oslo the parties were able to air their ideas in complete freedom, and this helped them to achieve outstanding results in record time.

The Norwegian Foreign Minister Johan Holst who was listening to Clinton, appeared proud and jubilant because he and his country had nurtured these negotiations so carefully. I admired the president of the most powerful state in the world for speaking with such frankness, for giving credit where it was due, and for speaking without inhibition about negotiations whose principal sponsor he was supposed to be (although ultimately he was able to turn the outcome of these negotiations to his country's advantage).

Warren Christopher hosted a lunch held in honour of the Israeli and Palestinian delegations. It was attended by former American Secretaries of State, senior State Department officials and a number of foreign ministers from Arab and other countries who had attended the signing ceremony. Among those attending was Henry Kissinger the former Secretary of State during the Nixon and Ford presidencies and the proponent of the step-by-step doctrine. He spoke during lunch to his neighbours, Yasser Abd Rabbo of the Palestinian delegation and Yossi Beilin, the Deputy Foreign Minister of Israel, and said that he was still opposed to the creation of an independent Palestinian State, but that this accord, whose signing we were celebrating, had made the creation of this State inevitable. He then turned to Yossi Beilin and said words to this effect: 'If Golda was alive she would have erected the gallows for you and hanged you.' At the end of the lunch we ran into each other at the door of the State Department when he said: 'You did a good job.'

At 4.30 p.m. the entire Palestinian delegation was to meet with Secretary of State Warren Christopher again. But he wanted to meet Arafat and myself alone before the general meeting. When we entered his office Dennis Ross was there. Christopher said that he was full of enthusiasm for the day's achievement, that for the past three hours he had observed Arabs and Jews talking to each other in a spirit of reconciliation that had amazed him. He then addressed us as follows, though of course these were not his exact words, but my recollection of them:

> Your courage and that of the Prime Minister of Israel has opened the doors to everyone, and we have begun the journey. I believe that the commitment you have made is among the most important commitments that a leader in the world can undertake. I cannot say for sure how many people heard you today but they must be in excess of one hundred million people. I say therefore that there should be no equivocation and no delay in studying the issues. It is important that commitments be implemented with absolute clarity. I will say this to my friends in Israel too. This is a most important issue, and here I specify the issue of the renunciation of terrorism. Your commitment to renounce terrorism is the one thing that the whole world will monitor. Therefore I want to urge you, sirs, to proceed in a way that would end violence, and that your commitment should be unequivocal. There is not one way to achieve this. Sometimes it will be by taking a specific step when the source of violence is known to you, and at other times by speaking about it in public. You [Arafat] are not expected to be the man of steel capable of everything, but I believe it is important that you realize the need for carrying out this commitment. The success of the accord depends on that; I am speaking in the spirit of friendship that has arisen between us. There is another subject which I have spoken about over lunch with Mr Abbas [Abu Mazen], and that is the economy; I have suggested that you start with projects that will make the people feel the benefit of the accord.

Then Dennis Ross spoke words to this effect:

I would like to mention one point, which is the improvement of the atmosphere. Secretary Christopher spoke of direct contacts between you and the Israelis. The quicker you form the committees for different fields, like security and economics, the quicker the benefits. That will have a direct impact on the morale of the Israelis because they will feel that you are giving a big push to relations through these committees. These committees will also be an important part of the process of explaining the new developments and the new situation. A mechanism must be quickly drawn up whereby the committees' activities may be implemented.

To digress a little, I remember that from the beginning of the Oslo negotiations I always told the delegation not to confine their dealings with the Israelis to the lengthy and tiresome sessions, but that they should in their free time sit informally with the Israelis as individuals and talk about personal matters. Human relationships could thus be built up that would play a part in the process of persuasion, although I knew of course that such relationships had limited effect and could indeed have a negative effect if mishandled. Similarly, at the talks in Madrid and later in Washington we had asked the members of the Palestinian delegation to try and build personal relationships with their Israeli counterparts in order to lighten the heavy atmosphere that characterizes formal negotiations. But they had not complied for fear of being accused of illicit contacts with their adversaries; they had also feared that such behaviour might arouse the suspicion of their own colleagues in the team. Thus they had lost many opportunities for unofficial exchanges of ideas that might have led the two sides to come to an understanding over the issues under discussion.

In contrast, the experience of the Oslo delegation in this respect was successful. They established personal relationships with their opposite numbers, but kept a certain distance to allow them room for manoeuvre during the negotiations. This way, they could negotiate with firmness and tenacity when the issues were of fundamental significance. They quickly gained useful experience in the art of negotiation. For instance, they would raise the stakes when the Israeli delegation seemed implacable in meeting our demands. On many occasions I found this behaviour puzzling, but when they visited Tunis, and I had a chance to review the details with them, I supported their actions. Certainly this method often produced favourable and entirely unexpected results.

To come back to 13 September 1993, my encounter with Peres was warm even though it was the first. The presence of the two delegations who already knew each other well added to the warmth, and we thus began to talk about the practical aspects that could give the masses greater confidence in the accord. Peres made the following comment which I cite in my own words from memory:

> Contacts must be started, even unofficially, to discuss the formation and composition of the committees because of the need to continue with negotiations. Also, do not forget that forming the police force requires funds. Moreover, financial provisions must be made for the institutions, especially the universities. As for the question of financial support in general I propose the setting up of an American–European committee that includes the Palestinian and Israeli sides. There are urgent issues such as the water desalinization plant in the Gaza Strip and the establishment of a telephone network. This in particular can be contracted to a private company. The housing sector in Gaza must be addressed because of the population's dire need for housing and employment. I believe we will need Arab–Israeli investment corporations, and to adopt a common language when dealing internationally. I see no objection in providing training for people inside, bringing outside instructors into the Gaza Strip and Jericho. As for the issue of confidence-building from our side, whether in respect of the internees and deportees or in respect of the state of siege in Jerusalem, this will arise after the Knesset has discussed the accord. Discreet measures will then begin to lift the siege on Jerusalem. Finally, I propose the formation of a daily liaison committee composed of Abu Ala and Uri Savir.

The American trip ended with a visit to New York for a meeting with United Nations Secretary-General Boutros Ghali who expressed his great delight at the signing of the Israeli–Palestinian accord. Perhaps he was the most jubilant person in the Arab countries because he had been the first Arab statesman to show solidarity with the late President Anwar Sadat of Egypt and had not deserted him as others had done when Sadat signed the Camp David Accords with Israel.[1] Boutros Ghali offered the assistance of the UN and its specialized agencies in building the Palestinian infrastructure, and showed keen enthusiasm for the idea of sending fact-finding missions to the occupied territories to study what these UN agencies could do on the ground.

---

[1] Sadat's surprise visit to Israel in 1977 provoked the resignation of his Foreign Minister, Ismail Fahmi. In 1978, during the negotiations at Camp David, the new Foreign Minister, Muhammad Kamel, also resigned. The Minister of State for Foreign Affairs, Boutros Ghali, remained.

14

Thoughts for the Future

The long struggle of the Palestinian people was aimed at regaining their dignity, their rights and their place among the peoples of the world in an independent state. This struggle was a genuine expression of their refusal to submit to the 'reality' which had been imposed upon them. It was not vengeance but an expression of their collective will that drove them on. Though many were dispersed, they kept up the struggle under the leadership of the PLO. The intifada in the occupied territories was a natural extension of this struggle, and showed that the Palestinian people were a match for the Israelis who contested their existence and strove to crush them. But they were persuaded otherwise when the decisive hour came.

The secret meetings and contacts had clarified many issues that had been submerged by the bloody conflict that had gripped the region. The false dreams and theories that had dominated the mind came to an end; the Palestinians made their aim clear, and the Israelis understood it. There was no choice but that the protagonists should deal directly with one another, and this realization finally led to the negotiating table and to the signing of the Declaration of Principles and the recognition of the Palestine Liberation Organization.

In essence, Israel was created on the basis of Herzl's dictum, 'A land without people for a people without a land'. To this day, Herut's cry remains that Israeli territory should lie on both banks of the River Jordan, and some fundamentalist adherents of the Torah say the land of Israel should extend from the Euphrates to the Nile. Up to the sixth round of the Washington negotiations, Elyakim Rubinstein of the Israeli delegation, was using the expression 'Judaea and Samaria' when referring to the West Bank and when he was on his best behaviour he would refer to the occupied territories as 'the districts'. For a long time the word 'Palestine' was banned and taken out of usage because Israel had replaced Palestine, a name that now belonged to ancient history. The same fate befell the Palestinian people who were called the 'Arab population', implying that they had only civil and religious rights at best. They were often called the 'non-Jewish communities', the expression used in the Balfour Declaration and the British Mandate for Palestine. This expression continued to gain currency so much that after Israel had occupied the West Bank and Gaza, it created the so-called 'Civil Administration' in 1978 affirming this meaning. During the ten rounds of negotiations in Washington, the Israeli negotiators refused to use the expression 'the Palestinian people' but insisted on using the word 'Palestinians'. Even the American Administration had refused to use the term 'people' until the famous meeting of the PNC in 1988, and President Bush sent a letter to King Hassan II. This letter bore a gift to the PNC. It stated that from that date onwards the American Administration would use the expression 'the Palestinian people' instead of the expression 'Palestinians'. If further historical landmarks are wanted in this regard one has only to remember that in 1921 when Munif al-Husseini and Issa al-Issa arrived in Britain, the then Colonial Secretary Winston Churchill, refused to receive them as representatives of anything, but only as respectable men. In 1985 Margaret Thatcher refused to receive Archbishop Elia Khoury and Muhammad Milhem in their capacity as representatives of the PLO.

I mention these historical landmarks to say that if the matter had been left to Israel it would have recognized nothing and accepted no solution. At one point in the Palestinian struggle Israel created the so-called village leagues in an attempt to dampen resistance in the villages, but soon had to abandon them after they had failed to establish a presence and had been rejected by the people.

We do not claim that we signed an agreement that created an independent Palestinian State; none of the provisions in the Declaration of Principles make such a claim. We agreed that the Palestinian interim self-government should apply to the West Bank and the Gaza Strip, not, as is sometimes supposed, to Gaza and Jericho only. To interpret the Declaration of Principles thus is to deny the truth, for if we consider Article IV, for example, we find that the two signatories 'view the West Bank and the Gaza Strip as a single territorial unit, whose integrity will be preserved during the interim period'. Furthermore, Article V, paragraph 4, states 'The two parties agree that the outcome of the permanent status negotiations should not be prejudiced or preempted by agreements reached for the interim period.' In addition, Article VI shows that even during the interim period, the authority of the Palestinians is not limited to Gaza and Jericho, but extends to the West Bank in many spheres at the same time. A glance at paragraph 4 of Article VII shows that the accord requires the Palestinian Council to establish corporations (Authorities) for electricity, environment, land, water, export promotion and for a Gaza sea port, the kind of corporations that bear the hallmark of sovereignty which we would seek to formalize at the permanent status negotiations in the future. The allegation that the Palestinian Council will be established merely to undertake the duties on behalf of Israel is plainly refuted by many of the articles of the accord. Moreover, the fact that the priorities of the Interim Authority differ from those of the Israeli Civil Administration shows conclusively that the Palestinian Council will not merely do Israel's work. Thus the basic needs of the people will be catered for as a matter of priority, especially since the Interim Authority was assuming control of a devastated land on which a decent life was effectively to begin from zero.

It is known that the Palestinian people and the Israeli people are not separated by a wide cultural gap, nor is there a great disparity in their intellectual levels. The presumption of Israeli superiority is unfounded. On the economic level, the Palestinian energies that are poised to pour into the schemes which the Palestinian authority will be undertaking will make this homeland a beacon of prosperity.

When discussing the issue of sovereignty we must not forget to take into consideration the nature of the negotiations and the Palestinian–Israeli conflict, for this is a special conflict and sovereignty has a special meaning. Sovereignty for the Palestinians should not be seen as a text-book principle of national rights but more as a reflection of a national existence that was not originally recognized. However, the mechanism by which the terms of the accord will be implemented will eventually give rise to the emergence and crystallization of many features of sovereignty, and this process will go on until complete national sovereignty is realized. In this connection, it is well to remember the preamble of the Declaration which calls for mutual recognition of the two parties' 'legitimate and political rights' and also Article III, paragraph 3, which stipulates that the election of the Palestinian Council 'will constitute a significant interim preparatory step towards the realization of the legitimate rights of the Palestinian people and their just requirements'.

The establishment of a new entity in the Middle East for the first time in its history requires a comprehensive view of this entity's future development, not only *vis-à-vis* Israel but also in relation, first, to its immediate neighbours and, second, to the other Arabs. These various relationships are so complicated that great care must be taken in properly determining them so that the new entity does not become easy prey to the Israelis and also that it does not lose its Arab identity.

If we look at the Declaration of Principles we can identify the issues that require constant effort so that they can be completed within the next two years. If implementation of the accord proceeds smoothly, we would then tackle the other issues of the permanent status, such as finding a just solution to the refugee problem in accordance with international legality. At the final status negotiations we would proceed further in the attainment of our independence. And when I speak of independence I assume the resolution of all outstanding issues: Jerusalem, settlements, security arrangements, borders and relations with neighbours.

Israel seeks to annex parts of the West Bank and of the Gaza Strip, and will try to control the water resources and will strive to annex Jerusalem, whether the final status of the Palestinian entity will be an independent state or a confederation. In this connection, I must say that many people are confounded by the expression 'confederation'. Confederation has a single definition in international law, which is that a confederation is a contractual agreement between two or more independent entities. This means that a confederation and an independent State are not different alternatives, but rather that confederation emanates from a decision of an independent State. We must not therefore link Israel's desire for annexation and hegemony with the choice that will be made at the end. Thus, whatever the choice of our permanent status will be, it is our duty to continue the struggle until Resolution 242 is fully implemented and Israel withdraws completely from all the territories occupied in 1967. In this way, the Palestinian entity will be in full control of its own wealth, including its water resources.

In speaking of the problem of the refugees we must distinguish between two aspects; first, the kind of solution we might reach as a result of the negotiations that will start not later than the beginning of the third year of the interim period; and second, the duties of the Palestinian State towards the refugees. This is related to the question of how the Palestinian side can alleviate the suffering of the refugee population until the problem is solved. The duties of a Palestinian State towards the refugees may be encapsulated in the proposition that every Palestinian, wherever he may be, has the right to citizenship, social welfare, education, health and retirement benefit. Moreover, it will be the function of the Palestinian entity to regulate the relationship between the Palestinian communities abroad and their host countries and to safeguard their interest there, pending the resolution of the problem through negotiations with Israel.

At first the Israelis refused to specify the issues for the permanent status negotiations and suggested that each side would present whatever issue it considered appropriate at the negotiating table without advance commitment that these would in fact be discussed. However, these issues as they are specified in the accord (together with an Israeli commitment to discuss them), provide an idea of how the permanent status will shape up especially if we consider the questions of borders, relations with neighbours, security arrangements and other issues of common interest, not to mention the three important issues of the refugees, settlements and Jerusalem.

It is known that a Knesset resolution annexed Jerusalem to Israel, but by placing the issue on the agenda for the permanent status negotiations, the Israelis admit that the issue is subject to debate; in other words, the annexation of Jerusalem has now become null and void. But we must be aware that such issues require a great deal of effort, patience and a long time to resolve. There will be a struggle ahead and there will be risks, but has there been agreements reached without risk?

Western countries led by the United States pledged to grant the Palestinian Authority economic support to enable it to stand on its own two feet. After the Declaration of Principles was signed America called a conference of wealthy nations in Washington where it was agreed that $2.6 billion would be given to the Palestinian entity over five years on certain conditions. All financing from donor countries and the World Bank must go directly to Palestinian/PLO projects through a strict cash control system, as a way of reassuring all donors that their money has been properly used. Individual experts and institutions will be asked to advise on the setting up of projects for the economic development of the liberated territories. They will be chosen for their excellence and will have total freedom of action. The transfer of powers and responsibilities from the Israelis to the Palestinians assumes that we have the qualified personnel with technical, scientific, technological and administrative knowledge to replace the Israelis who have managed the departments and establishments for 26 years. It is hoped that the foreign experts will help fill the gap. As in the case of these experts, the leaders of the new Palestinian Authority must be carefully chosen from among prominent figures who are known for their patriotism and honesty.

I do not believe that the Palestinian people wish to choose a life other than the free, democratic life based on freedom of thought, expression and belief, or an economy other than a liberal economy. This requires a multi-party system with different outlooks and beliefs because it has been proved without a shadow of doubt that the idea of a single party or the idea of a state-run command economy is outdated. Such systems have been rejected by millions of people at this end of the century and have collapsed. The Palestinian people who fought occupation for decades in order to gain their freedom cannot allow a ruler, whoever he might be, to deprive them of this freedom. Most, if not all, of the leaders and cadres of the Palestinian Authority should come from among the residents of the West Bank and the Gaza Strip. This is necessary for practical reasons that are related to the tasks they will be performing and for their success as well as for reasons of psychology and morale. The political reasons are no less important. Political considerations require that there should be organic coherence of functions so that the leadership conducting international affairs is firmly and organically linked with that dealing with internal matters. High on the agenda of the former will be the conduct of affairs arising during the final period, especially with respect to the refugee problem – which is expected to take long to resolve. These are difficult ideas to accept by those who are preparing to assume senior positions in the Palestinian Authority and for those who expect an elevated status as a reward for their long years of struggle. But these ideas are merely my own personal vision of the future of a homeland that will need the best talents to serve the people after the long years of pain and suffering.

One major question remains about how the Palestinian economy will avoid falling permanently into the trap of absolute subservience to the Israeli economy, and how it can be linked with the Arab market and the Arab economy. This must be dealt with very carefully since, even if the Israelis have good intentions to want to raise our people's standard of living, we should not assume that such intentions will permit independence from the economic grip of Israel. Israel sees a ready market for its goods in the Palestinian homeland as well as a source of labour. Both these factors combined with the eventual opening up of the wider Arab market will offer a potentially enormous opportunity for the Israeli economy to flourish and develop. It is not only a Palestinian duty to overcome subservience to the Israeli economy but an Arab duty as well. We, the Palestinians, not only have the responsibility of establishing the specialized corporations (Authorities) and attracting capital but also of forging close links with the Arab world, links that will call for economic integration on the basis of common interest. Before this can happen we will have to pass through three stages. First, there will be gradual disengagement from the Israeli economy; second, there will be economic cooperation with Israel, though still on unequal terms; and finally, cooperation on equal terms. We know that the task is difficult and complicated, but if each side acknowledges its responsibility and shoulders it, then no doubt the end of the twentieth century will see the economies in the region in a sound condition. This requires serious study of the Arab economic market.

This leads us to a major question: how can this Palestinian political achievement be transformed into actual independence. There is no similarity between us and any people who have gained autonomy and thereafter attained independence. There is also no similarity between us and any people whose land was colonized by others and thereafter attained independence.

The nascent Palestinian entity is striving to break away from the dominance of Israel and build for itself an independent existence protected by a strong shield. The provisions in the accord that might be considered the seeds of independence are not enough to bring about full independence, because what really determines the final outcome is might, for might is more compelling than law, despite what the world says about sovereignty and respect of the law. 'Reality' imposes itself, but we have the right to change it. Meanwhile, there are certain conditions that must be fulfilled:

– The new Palestinian entity must represent all the Palestinian people, wherever they may be, and their interests. The sacred right of citizenship for Palestinians wherever they may be must be upheld. This is not the State of the West Bank and the Gaza Strip, it is the State of Palestine.

– Until the permanent status negotiations are concluded, the Interim Authority should strive to make the Palestinian refugees feel that they have a direct interest in being associated with this State through a sense of identity and through the protection of their interests.

– We must, before all else, respect human rights in our new entity, and establish this entity on the bases of modern democratic principles, total freedom, a multi-party political system and a free economy. This does not mean that there should not be a public sector in some vital fields. We must move from the mentality of revolution to the mentality of state-building so that we could successfully establish the various corporations (Authorities) and other projects as well as an effective administration run by individuals whose honesty, abilities and industry are beyond doubt. (Some regions have governed by the motto 'loyalty before merit', meaning that persons who are most loyal to the regime get the best jobs, regardless of merit. This had proved calamitous to the countries concerned.)

– Relations with neighbouring Arab countries should not be underestimated. Rather, there must be close links with them on the political, social, intellectual and cultural levels so that we may secure their firm support in our quest for development and independence. All the sources of rivalry and alienation between them and us, no matter what they are, must be stemmed, for this new Palestinian entity needs strong relations with all the Arab States which will make a significant contribution to the establishment and development of this entity.

— Building firm relations with countries worldwide will consolidate the Palestinian entity and will induce these countries to offer the means of development and survival. It will therefore be necessary for this entity to establish a strong international network of relations that will facilitate economic and cultural interaction as well as technical cooperation.

— Finally, it is vital to build relations with the State of Israel on mutual trust so that the Israelis could feel confident about their new neighbour and old enemy and about this neighbour's ability to transform enmity to normality in step with the Arab countries.

APPENDIX 1

DECLARATION OF PRINCIPLES ON INTERIM
SELF-GOVERNMENT ARRANGEMENTS

N.B.: *In the preamble, the letters P.L.O. were substituted for 'Palestinian' minutes before the document was signed. P.L.O. was also substituted for 'Palestinian' in other parts of the document.*

The Government of the State of Israel and the PLO team (in the Jordanian–Palestinian delegation to the Middle East Peace Conference) (the 'Palestinian Delegation'), representing the Palestinian people, agree that it is time to put an end to decades of confrontation and conflict, recognize their mutual legitimate and political rights, and strive to live in peaceful coexistence and mutual dignity and security and achieve a just, lasting and comprehensive peace settlement and historic reconciliation through the agreed political process.

Accordingly, the two sides agree to the following principles:

Article I *Aim of the negotiations*
The aim of the Israeli–Palestinian negotiations within the current Middle East peace process is, among other things, to establish a Palestinian Interim Self-Government Authority, the elected Council (the 'Council) for the Palestinian people in the West Bank and the Gaza Strip, for a transitional period not exceeding five years, leading to a permanent settlement based on Security Council Resolutions 242 and 338.
It is understood that the interim arrangements are an integral part of the overall peace process and that final status negotiations will lead to the implementation of Security Council Resolutions 242 and 338.

Article II *Framework for the interim period*
The agreed framework for the interim period is set forth in the Declaration of Principles.

Article III *Elections*
1. In order that the Palestinian people in the West Bank and Gaza Strip may govern themselves according to democratic principles,

direct, free and general political elections will be held for the Council under agreed supervision and international observation, while the Palestinian police will ensure public order.

2. An agreement will be concluded on the exact mode and conditions of the elections in accordance with the protocol attached as Annex I, with the goal of holding the elections not later than nine months after the entry into force of this Declaration of Principles.

3. These elections will constitute a significant interim preparatory step toward the realization of the legitimate rights of the Palestinian people and their just requirements.

Article IV

Jurisdiction of the Council will cover West Bank and Gaza Strip territory, except for issues that will be negotiated in the permanent status negotiations. The two sides view the West Bank and the Gaza Strip as a single territorial unit, whose integrity will be preserved during the interim period.

Article V *Transitional period and permanent status negotiations*

1. The five-year transitional period will begin upon the withdrawal from the Gaza Strip and Jericho area.

2. Permanent status negotiations will commence as soon as possible, but not later than the beginning of the third year of the interim period, between the Government of Israel and the Palestinian people representatives.

3. It is understood that these negotiations shall cover remaining issues, including: Jerusalem, refugees, settlements, security arrangements, borders, relations and cooperation with other neighbors, and other issues of common interest.

4. The two parties agree that the outcome of the permanent status negotiations should not be prejudiced or preempted by agreements reached for the interim period.

Article VI *Preparatory transfer of powers and responsibilities*

1. Upon the entry into force of this Declaration of Principles and the withdrawal from the Gaza Strip and Jericho area, a transfer of authority from the Israeli military government and its Civil Administration to the authorized Palestinians for this task, as detailed herein, will commence. This transfer of authority will be of preparatory nature until the inauguration of the Council.

2. Immediately after the entry into force of this Declaration of Principles

and the withdrawal from the Gaza Strip and Jericho area, with the view to promoting economic development in the West Bank and Gaza Strip, authority will be transferred to the Palestinians in the following spheres: education and culture, health, social welfare, direct taxation, and tourism. The Palestinian side will commence in building the Palestinian police force, as agreed upon. Pending the inauguration of the Council, the two parties may negotiate the transfer of additional powers and responsibilities, as agreed upon.

Article VII *Interim agreement*

1. The Israeli and Palestinian delegations will negotiate an agreement on the interim period (the 'Interim Agreement').
2. The Interim Agreement shall specify, among other things, the structure of the Council, the number of its members, and the transfer of powers and responsibilities from the Israeli military government and its Civil Administration to the Council. The Interim Agreement shall also specify the Council's executive authority, legislative authority in accordance with Article IX below, and the independent Palestinian judicial organs.
3. The Interim Agreement shall include arrangements, to be implemented upon the inauguration of the Council, for the assumption by the Council of all of the powers and responsibilities transferred previously in accordance with Article VI above.
4. In order to enable the Council to promote economic growth, upon its inauguration, the Council will establish, among other things, a Palestinian Electricity Authority, a Gaza Sea Port Authority, a Palestinian Development Bank, a Palestinian Export Promotion Board, a Palestinian Environmental Authority, a Palestinian Land Authority and a Palestinian Water Administration Authority, and any other authorities agreed upon, in accordance with the Interim Agreement that will specify their powers and responsibilities.
5. After the inauguration of the Council, the Civil Administration will be dissolved, and the Israeli military government will be withdrawn.

Article VIII *Public order and security*

In order to guarantee public order and internal security for the Palestinians of the West Bank and the Gaza Strip, the Council will establish a strong police force, while Israel will continue to carry the responsibility for defending against external threats, as well as the responsibility for overall security of the Israelis to protect their internal security and public order.

Article IX *Laws and military orders*
1. The Council will be empowered to legislate, in accordance with the Interim Agreement, within all authorities transferred to it.
2. Both parties will review jointly laws and military orders presently in force in remaining spheres.

Article X *Joint Israeli–Palestinian liaison committee*
In order to provide for a smooth implementation of this Declaration of Principles and any subsequent agreements pertaining to the interim period, upon the entry into force of this Declaration of Principles, a Joint Israeli–Palestinian Liaison Committee will be established in order to deal with issues requiring coordination, other issues of common interest, and disputes.

Article XI *Israeli–Palestinian cooperation in economic fields*
Recognizing the mutual benefit of cooperation in promoting the development of the West Bank, the Gaza Strip and Israel, upon the entry into force of this Declaration of Principles, an Israeli–Palestinian Economic Cooperation Committee will be established in order to develop and implement in a cooperative manner the programs identified in the protocols attached as Annex III and Annex IV.

Article XII *Liaison and cooperation with Jordan and Egypt*
The two parties will invite the Governments of Jordan and Egypt to participate in establishing further liaison and cooperation arrangements between the Government of Israel and the Palestinian representatives, on one hand, and the Governments of Jordan and Egypt, on the other hand, to promote cooperation between them. These arrangements will include the constitution of a Continuing Committee that will decide by agreement on the modalities of the admission of persons displaced from the West Bank and Gaza Strip in 1967, together with necessary measures to prevent disruption and disorder. Other matters of common concern will be dealt with by this Committee.

Article XIII *Redeployment of Israeli forces*
1. After the entry into force of this Declaration of Principles, and not later than the eve of elections for the Council, a redeployment of Israeli military forces in the West Bank and the Gaza Strip will take place, in addition to withdrawal of Israeli forces carried out in accordance with Article XIV.
2. In redeploying its military forces, Israel will be guided by the principle that its military forces should be redeployed outside the populated areas.

3. Further redeployments to specified locations will be gradually implemented commensurate with the assumption of responsibility for public order and internal security by the Palestinian police force pursuant to Article VIII above.

Article XIV *Israeli withdrawal from the Gaza Strip and Jericho area*
Israel will withdraw from the Gaza Strip and Jericho area, as detailed in the protocol attached as Annex II.

Article XV *Resolution of disputes*
1. Disputes arising out of the application or interpretation of this Declaration of Principles, or any subsequent agreements pertaining to the interim period, shall be resolved by negotiations through the Joint Liaison Committee to be established pursuant to Article X above.
2. Disputes which cannot be settled by negotiations may be resolved by a mechanism of conciliation to be agreed upon by the parties.
3. The parties may agree to submit to arbitration disputes relating to the interim period, which cannot be settled through conciliation. To this end, upon the agreement of both parties, the parties will establish an Arbitration Committee.

Article XVI *Israeli–Palestinian cooperation concerning regional programs*
Both parties view the multilateral working groups as an appropriate instrument for promoting a 'Marshall Plan', the regional programs and other programs, including special programs for the West Bank and Gaza Strip, as indicated in the protocol attached as Annex IV.

Article XVII *Miscellaneous provisions*
1. This Declaration of Principles will enter into force one month after its signing.
2. All protocols annexed to this Declaration of Principles and Agreed Minutes pertaining thereto shall be regarded as an integral part hereof.

DONE at Washington, D.C., this thirteenth day of September 1993.

For the Governement of Israel   For the P.L.O.

_____   _____

witnessed by:

_____   _____
The United States of America   The Russian Federation

Annex I *Protocol on the Mode and Conditions of Elections*

1. Palestinians of Jerusalem who live there will have the right to participate in the election process, according to an agreement between the
two sides.

2. In addition, the election agreement should cover, among other things,
the following issues:

   a. the system of elections;

   b. the mode of the agreed supervision and international observation
   and their personal composition; and

   c. rules and regulations regarding election campaign, including
   agreed arrangements for the organizing of mass media, and the possibility of licensing a broadcasting and TV station.

3. The future status of displaced Palestinians who were registered on 4th
June 1967 will not be prejudiced because they are unable to participate in the election process due to practical reasons.

Annex II *Protocol on Withdrawal of Israeli Forces from the Gaza Strip and Jericho
Area*

1. The two sides will conclude and sign within two months from the date
of entry into force of this Declaration of Principles, an agreement on
the withdrawal of Israeli military forces from the Gaza Strip and
Jericho area. This agreement will include comprehensive arrangements to apply in the Gaza Strip and the Jericho area subsequent to
the Israeli withdrawal.

2. Israel will implement an accelerated and scheduled withdrawal of
Israeli military forces from the Gaza Strip and Jericho area, beginning
immediately with the signing of the agreement on the Gaza Strip and
Jericho area and to be completed within a period not exceeding four
months after the signing of this agreement.

3. The above agreement will include, among other things:

   a. Arrangements for a smooth and peaceful transfer of authority from
   the Israeli military government and its Civil Administration to the
   Palestinian representatives.

   b. Structure, powers and responsibilities of the Palestinian authority
   in these areas, except: external security, settlements, Israelis, foreign
   relations, and other subjects mutually agreed upon.

   c. Arrangements for assumption of internal security and public order
   by the Palestinian police force consisting of police officers recruited
   locally and from abroad (holding Jordanian passports and Palestinian
   documents issued by Egypt). Those who will participate in the
   Palestinian police force coming from abroad should be trained as
   police and police officers.

d. A temporary international or foreign presence, as agreed upon.

e. Establishment of a joint Palestinian–Israeli coordination and co operation committee for mutual security purposes.

f. An economic development and stabilization program, including the establishment of an Emergency Fund, to encourage foreign invest-ment, and financial and economic support. Both sides will coordinate and cooperate jointly and unilaterally with regional and international parties to support these aims.

g. Arrangements for a safe passage for persons and transportation between the Gaza Strip and Jericho area.

4. The above agreement will include arrangements for coordination between both parties regarding passages:

   a. Gaza–Egypt; and

   b. Jericho–Jordan.

5. The offices responsible for carrying out the powers and responsibilities of the Palestinian authority under this Annex II and Article VI of the Declaration of Principles will be located in the Gaza Strip and in the Jericho area pending the inauguration of the Council.

6. Other than these agreed arrangements, the status of the Gaza Strip and Jericho area will continue to be an integral part of the West Bank and Gaza Strip, and will not be changed in the interim period.

PROTOCOL ON ISRAELI–PALESTINIAN COOPERATION IN ECONOMIC AND DEVELOPMENT PROGRAMS

The two sides agree to establish an Israeli–Palestinian Continuing Committee for Economic Cooperation, focusing, among other things, on the following:

1. Cooperation in the field of water, including a Water Development Program prepared by experts from both sides, which will also specify the mode of cooperation in the management of water resources in the West Bank and Gaza Strip, and will include proposals for studies and plans on water rights of each party, as well as on the equitable utilization of joint water resources for implementation in and beyond the interim period.

2. Cooperation in the field of electricity, including an Electricity Development Program, which will also specify the mode of coopera-tion for the production, maintenance, purchase and sale of electricity resources.

3. Cooperation in the field of energy, including an Energy Development Program, which will provide for the exploitation of oil

and gas for industrial purposes, particularly in the Gaza Strip and in the Negev, and will encourage further joint exploitation of other energy resources. This Program may also provide for the construction of a Petrochemical industrial complex in the Gaza Strip and the construction of oil and gas pipelines.

4. Cooperation in the field of finance, including a Financial Development and Action Program for the encouragement of international investment in the West Bank and the Gaza Strip, and in Israel, as well as the establishment of a Palestinian Development Bank.

5. Cooperation in the fields of transport and communications, including a Program, which will define guidelines for the establishment of a Gaza Sea Port Area, and will provide for the establishing of transport and communications lines to and from the West Bank and the Gaza Strip to Israel and to other countries. In addition, this Program will provide for carrying out the necessary construction of roads, railways, communications lines, etc.

6. Cooperation in the field of trade, including studies, and Trade Promotion Programs, which will encourage local, regional and inter-regional trade, as well as a feasibility study of creating free trade zones in the Gaza Strip and in Israel, mutual access to these zones, and cooperation in other areas related to trade and commerce.

7. Cooperation in the field of industry, including Industrial Development Programs, which will provide for the establishment of joint Israeli–Palestinian Research and Development Centers, will promote Palestinian–Israeli joint ventures, and provide guidelines for cooperation in the textile, food, pharmaceutical, electronics, diamonds, computer and science-based industries.

8. A program for cooperation in, and regulation of, labor relations and cooperation in social welfare issues.

9. A Human Resources Development and Cooperation Plan, providing for joint Israeli–Palestinian workshops and seminars, and for the establishment of joint vocational training centers, research institutes and data banks.

10. An Environmental Protection Plan, providing for joint and/or coordinated measures in this sphere.

11. A program for developing coordination and cooperation in the field of communication and media.

12. Any other programs of mutual interest.

PROTOCOL ON ISRAELI–PALESTINIAN COOPERATION CONCERNING REGIONAL DEVELOPMENT PROGRAMS

1. The two sides will cooperate in the context of the multilateral peace efforts in promoting a Development Program for the region, including the West Bank and the Gaza Strip, to be initiated by the G-7. The parties will request the G-7 to seek the participation in this program of other interested states, such as members of the Organization for Economic Cooperation and Development, regional Arab states and institutions, as well as members of the private sector.

2. The Development Program will consist of two elements:
   a) an Economic Development Program for the West Bank and the Gaza Strip:
   b) a Regional Economic Development Program.

A. *The Economic Development Program for the West Bank and the Gaza Strip* will consist of the following elements:
   (1) A Social Rehabilitation Program, including a Housing and Construction Program.
   (2) A Small and Medium Business Development Plan.
   (3) An Infrastructure Development Program (water, electricity, transportation and communications, etc.).
   (4) A Human Resources Plan.
   (5) Other programs.

B. *The Regional Economic Development Program* may consist of the following elements:
   (1) The establishment of a Middle East Development Fund, as a first step, and a Middle East Development Bank, as a second step.
   (2) The development of a joint Israeli–Palestinian–Jordanian Plan for coordinated exploitation of the Dead Sea area.
   (3) The Mediterranean Sea (Gaza)–Dead Sea Canal.
   (4) Regional Desalinization and other water development projects.
   (5) A regional plan for agricultural development, including a coordinated regional effort for the prevention of desertification.
   (6) Interconnection of electricity grids.
   (7) Regional cooperation for the transfer, distribution and industrial exploitation of gas, oil and other energy resources.
   (8) A Regional Tourism, Transportation and Telecommunications Development Plan.
   (9) Regional cooperation in other spheres.

3 The two sides will encourage the multilateral working groups, and will coordinate towards its success. The two parties will encourage inter-

national activities, as well as pre-feasibility and feasibility studies, within the various multilateral working groups.

AGREED MINUTES TO THE DECLARATION OF PRINCIPLES ON INTERIM SELF-GOVERNMENT ARRANGEMENTS

A. *General Understandings and Agreements*
Any powers and responsibilities transferred to the Palestinians pursuant to the Declaration of Principles prior to the inauguration of the Council will be subject to the same principles pertaining to Article IV, as set out in these Agreed Minutes below.

B. *Specific Understandings and Agreements*

Article IV
It is understood that:
1 Jurisdiction of the Council will cover West Bank and Gaza Strip territory, except for issues that will be negotiated in the permanent status negotiations: Jerusalem, settlements, military locations and Israelis.
2 The Council's jurisdiction will apply with regard to the agreed powers, responsibilities, spheres and authorities transferred to it.

Article VI(2)
It is agreed that the transfer of authority will be as follows:
(1) The Palestinian side will inform the Israeli side of the names of the authorized Palestinians who will assume the powers, authorities and responsibilities that will be transferred to the Palestinians according to the Declaration of Principles in the following fields: education and culture, health, social welfare, direct taxation, tourism, and any other authorities agreed upon.
(2) It is understood that the rights and obligations of these offices will not be affected.
(3) Each of the spheres described above will continue to enjoy existing budgetary allocations in accordance with arrangements to be mutually agreed upon. These arrangements also will provide for the necessary adjustments required in order to take into account the taxes collected by the direct taxation office.
(4) Upon the execution of the Declaration of Principles, the Israeli and Palestinian delegations will immediately commence negotiations on a detailed plan for the transfer of authority on the above offices in accordance with the above understandings.

Article VII(2)
The Interim Agreement will also include arrangements for coordination and cooperation.

Article VII(5)
The withdrawal of the military government will not prevent Israel from exercising the powers and responsibilities not transferred to the Council.

Article VIII
It is understood that the Interim Agreement will include arrangements for cooperation and coordination between the two parties in this regard. It is also agreed that the transfer of powers and responsibilities to the Palestinian police will be accomplished in a phased manner, as agreed in the Interim Agreement.

Article X
It is agreed that, upon the entry into force of the Declaration of Principles, the Israeli and Palestinian delegations will exchange the names of the individuals designated by them as members of the Joint Israeli–Palestinian Liaison Committee.
It is further agreed that each side will have an equal number of members in the Joint Committee. The Joint Committee will reach decisions by agreement. The Joint Committee may add other technicians and experts, as necessary. The Joint Committee will decide on the frequency and place or places of its meetings.

Annex II
It is understood that, subsequent to the Israeli withdrawal, Israel will continue to be responsible for external security, and for internal security and public order of settlements and Israelis. Israeli military forces and civilians may continue to use roads freely within the Gaza Strip and the Jericho area.

Article XVI
Israeli–Palestinian Cooperation Concerning Regional Programs
Both parties view the multilateral working groups as an appropriate instrument for promoting a 'Marshall Plan', the regional programs and other programs, including special programs for the West Bank and Gaza Strip, as indicated in the protocol attached as Annex IV.

Article XVII

Miscellaneous Provisions

1. This Declaration of Principles will enter into force one month after its signing.
2. All protocols annexed to this Declaration of Principles and Agreed Minutes pertaining thereto shall be regarded as an integral part hereof.

DONE at Washington, D.C., this thirteenth day of September 1993.

For the Governement of Israel   For the P.L.O.

_____   _____

witnessed by:

_____   _____

The United States of America   The Russian Federation

DECLARATION OF PRINCIPLES ON
INTERIM SELF-GOVERNMENT ARRANGEMENTS

P. L. O.

The Government of the State of Israel and the ~~Palestinian~~ team
(in the Jordanian-Palestinian delegation to the Middle East
Peace Conference) (the "Palestinian Delegation"), representing
the Palestinian people, agree that it is time to put an end to
decades of confrontation and conflict, recognize their mutual
legitimate and political rights, and strive to live in peaceful
coexistence and mutual dignity and security and achieve a just,
lasting and comprehensive peace settlement and historic
reconciliation through the agreed political process.
Accordingly, the two sides agree to the following principles:

Copy of the preamble of the Declaration of Principles showing the substitution of the letters P.L.O. for Palestinian by hand and the initials of Hayel al-Fayoum for the P.L.O. and those of Joel Singer for Israel.

2. All protocols annexed to this Declaration of Principles and
    Agreed Minutes pertaining thereto shall be regarded as an
    integral part hereof.

DONE at Washington, D.C., this thirteenth day of September,
1993.

For the Government of Israel: For the P.L.O.:

_____   _____

_____   _____

                     Witnessed By:

_____   _____
The United States of America   The Russian Federation

Copy of the last page of the DOP showing the signatures of (clockwise) Shimon
Peres, the author Mahmoud Abbas (Abu Mazen), Andrei Kozyrev and Warren
Christopher.

APPENDIX 2

THE LETTERS OF RECOGNITION

FROM ARAFAT TO RABIN
9 · 9 · 1993

Mr Prime Minister,

The signing of the Declaration of Principles marks a new era in the history of the Middle East. In firm conviction thereof, I would like to confirm the following PLO commitments:

The PLO recognises the right of the State of Israel to exist in peace and security. The PLO accepts United Nations Security Council Resolutions 242 and 338.

The PLO commits itself to the Middle East peace process, and to a peaceful resolution of the conflict between the two sides and declares that all outstanding issues relating to permanent status will be resolved through negotiations.

The PLO considers that the signing of the Declaration of Principles constitutes a historic event, inaugurating a new epoch of peaceful coexistence, free from violence and all other acts which endanger peace and stability.

Accordingly, the PLO renounces the use of terrorism and other acts of violence and will assume responsibility over all PLO elements and personnel in order to assure their compliance, prevent violations and discipline violators.

In view of the promise of a new era and the signing of the Declaration of Principles and based on Palestinian acceptance of Security Council Resolutions 242 and 338, the PLO affirms that those articles of the Palestinian Covenant which deny Israel's right to exist, and the provisions of the Covenant which are inconsistent with the commitments of this letter, are now inoperative and no longer valid.

Consequently, the PLO undertakes to submit to the Palestinian National Council for formal approval the necessary changes in regard to the Palestinian Covenant.

Sincerely,
Yasser Arafat,
Chairman, The Palestine Liberation Organization

FROM RABIN TO ARAFAT

10 · 9 · 1993

Mr Chairman,

In response to your letter of September 9, 1993, I wish to confirm to you that, in light of the PLO commitments included in your letter, the Government of Israel has decided to recognise the PLO as the representative of the Palestinian people and commence negotiations with the PLO within the Middle East peace process.

Yitzhak Rabin

Prime Minister of Israel

APPENDIX 3

LETTERS FROM ARAFAT AND PERES TO THE NORWEGIAN FOREIGN MINISTER, JOHAN JOERGEN HOLST

FROM ARAFAT (*Translated from Arabic*)
9 . 9 . 1993

Dear Minister Holst,

I would like to confirm to you that, upon the signing of the Declaration of Principles, I will include the following positions in my public statements:

In light of the new era marked by the signing of the Declaration of Principles, the PLO encourages and calls upon the Palestinian people in the West Bank and Gaza Strip to take part in the steps leading to the normalisation of life, rejecting violence and terrorism, contributing to peace and stability and participating actively in shaping reconstruction, economic development and cooperation.

Sincerely,

Yasser Arafat,

Chairman, The Palestine Liberation Organization

MINISTER OF FOREIGN AFFAIRS   ש ר ה ח ו ץ

749503

Jerusalem, October 11 1993

Dear Minister Holst,

I wish to confirm that the palestinian institutions of East Jerusalem and the interests and well-being of the palestinians of East Jerusalem are of great importance and will be preserved.

Therefore, all the palestinian institutions of East Jerusalem, including the economic, social, educational and cultural, and the holy Christian and Moslem places, are performing an essential task for the palestinian population.

Needless to say, we will not hamper their activity; on the contrary, the fulfilment of this important mission is to be encouraged.

Sincerely,

Shimon Peres
Foreign Minister of Israel

His Excellency
Johan Jorgen Holst
Foreign Minister of Norway

APPENDIX 4

THE WASHINGTON SPEECHES
13 September 1993

RABIN'S SPEECH
The following is a partial text of Yitzhak Rabin's speech:

This signing of the Israeli–Palestinian declaration of principles here today, it's not so easy, neither for myself as a soldier in Israel's war, nor for the people of Israel, nor for the Jewish people in the diaspora who are watching us now with great hope mixed with apprehension.

It is certainly not easy for the families of the victims of the wars, violence, terror, whose pain will never heal; for the many thousands who defended our lives in their own and have even sacrificed their lives for our own. For them, this ceremony has come too late.

Today, on the eve of an opportunity . . . for peace, and perhaps end of violence and wars, we remember each and every one of them with everlasting love.

We have come from Jerusalem, the ancient and eternal capital of the Jewish people. We have come from an anguished land. We have come from a people, a home, a family that has not known a single year, not a single month, in which mothers have not wept for their sons.

We have come to try and put an end to the hostilities so that our children, our children's children, will no longer experience the painful cost of war, violence and terror. Let me say to you, the Palestinians, we are destined to live together on the same soil in the same land.

We, the soldiers who have returned from battles stained with blood; we who have seen our relatives and friends killed before our eyes; we who have attended their funerals and cannot look into the eyes of their parents; we who have come from a land where parents bury their children; we who have fought against you, the Palestinians, we say to you today in a loud and a clear voice enough of blood and tears.

Enough! We have no desire for revenge, we have – we harbour no hatred towards you. We, like you, are people – people who want to build a home, to plant a tree, to love, live side by side with you in dignity, in affinity, as human beings, as free men. We wish to open a new chapter in the sad book of our lives together. Today here in Washington we will begin a new wakening in the relations between peoples, between parents tired of war, between children who will not know war.

Our inner strength, our higher moral values have been derived for thousands of years from the Book of the Books, in one of which, Koheleth [Ecclesiastes], we read: 'To every thing there is a season and a time to every purpose under heaven.

'A time to be born and a time to die, a time to kill and a time to heal, a time to weep and a time to laugh, a time to love and a time to hate, a time of war and a time of peace.' Ladies and gentlemen, the time for peace has come.

In the Jewish tradition, it is customary to conclude our prayers with the word 'amen' . . . with your permission, men of peace, I shall conclude with words taken from the prayer recited by Jews daily, and I would ask you to join me in saying 'amen'. Amen.

ARAFAT'S SPEECH
The following is a partial text of Yasser Arafat's speech:

In the name of God, the most merciful, the passionate, I would like to express our tremendous appreciation to President Clinton and to his administration for sponsoring this historic event which the entire world has been waiting for. Mr President, I am taking this opportunity to assure you and to assure the great American people that we share your values for freedom, justice and human rights – values for which my people have been striving.

My people are hoping that this agreement which we are signing today marks the beginning of the end of a chapter of pain and suffering which has lasted throughout this century.

My people are hoping that this agreement which we are signing today will usher in an age of peace, coexistence and equal rights. We are relying on your role, Mr President, and on the role of all the countries which believe that without peace in the Middle East, peace in the world will not be complete.

Enforcing the agreement and moving toward the final settlement, after two years, to implement all aspects of UN Resolutions 242 and 338 in all of their aspects, and resolve all the issues of Jerusalem, the settlements, the refugees and the boundaries will be a Palestinian and an Israeli responsibility.

It is also the responsibility of the international community to help the parties overcome the tremendous difficulties which are still standing in the way of reaching a final and comprehensive settlement.

Now as we stand on the threshold of this new historic era, let me address the people of Israel and their leaders, and let me assure them that the difficult decision we reached together was one that required great and exceptional courage.

We will need more courage and determination to continue the course of building coexistence and peace between us. This is possible, and it will happen with mutual determination and with the effort that will be made with all parties on all the tracks to establish the foundations of a just and comprehensive peace.

Our people do not consider that exercising the right to self-determination could violate the rights of their neighbours or that it might infringe on their security.

Rather, putting an end to their feelings of being wronged and of having suffered an historic injustice is the strongest guarantee to achieve coexistence and openness between our two peoples and for future generations.

Our two peoples are awaiting today this historic hope, and they want to give peace a real chance. Such a shift will give us an opportunity to embark upon the process of economic, social and cultural growth and development, and we hope that international participation in that process will be extensive as it can be. This shift will also provide an opportunity for all forms of cooperation on a broad scale and in all fields.

APPENDIX 5

UNITED NATIONS SECURITY COUNCIL
RESOLUTIONS 242 AND 338

TEXT OF UN SECURITY COUNCIL RESOLUTION 242

22 November 1967

The Security Council,

Expressing its continued concern with the grave situation in the Middle East,

Emphasizing the inadmissibility of the acquisition of territory by war and the need to work for a just and lasting peace in which every State in the area can live in security,

Emphasizing further that all Member States in their acceptance of the Charter of the United Nations have undertaken a commitment to act in accordance with Article 2 of the Charter

1. *Affirms* that the fulfilment of Charter principles requires the establishment of a just and lasting peace in the Middle East which should include the application of both the following principles:

(i) Withdrawal of Israel's armed forces from territories occupied in the recent conflict;

(ii) Termination of all claims or states of belligerency and respect for the acknowledgement of the sovereignty, territorial integrity and political independence of every State in the area and their right to live in peace within secure and recognized boundaries free from threats or acts of force;

2. *Affirms further* the necessity

(a) For guaranteeing freedom of navigation through international waterways in the area;

(b) For achieving a just settlement of the refugee problem;

(c) For guaranteeing the territorial inviolability and political independence of every State in the area, through measures including the establishment of demilitarized zones;

3. *Requests* the Secretary-General to designate a Special Representative to proceed to the Middle East to establish and maintain contacts with the States concerned in order to promote agreement and assist efforts to achieve a peaceful and accepted settlement in accordance with the provisions and principles in this resolution;

4. *Requests* the Secretary-General to report to the Security Council on the progress of the efforts of the Special Representative as soon as possible.

UN SECURITY COUNCIL RESOLUTION 338
22 October 1973

UN Resolutions between 1967 and October 1973 reaffirmed Security Council Resolution 242 (see above). In an attempt to end the fourth Middle East war, which had broken out between the Arabs and Israel on 6 October 1973, the UN Security Council passed the following Resolution:

The Security Council,

1. *Calls upon* all parties to the present fighting to cease all firing and terminate all military activity immediately, not later than 12 hours after the moment of the adoption of the decision, in the positions they now occupy;

2. *Calls upon* the parties concerned to start immediately after the ceasefire the implementation of Security Council Resolution 242 (1967) in all of its parts;

3. *Decides that,* immediately and concurrently with the ceasefire negotiations start between the parties concerned under appropriate auspices aimed at establishing a just and durable peace in the Middle East.

INDEX

DOP   Declaration of Principles
PLO   Palestine Liberation Organization
PNC   Palestine National Council
passim   indicates that the subject matter of the heading is scattered throughout the pages mentioned.